BAD BOYS

Jeremy Reed is the author of over fifty books of award-winning poetry, fiction and biography, and also a celebrated performer of his work with Itchy Ear as The Ginger Light. Concerned with writing from the visionary present into the near future, J.G. Ballard described Reed's talent as "almost extraterrestrial in its brilliance." Controversial, edge-walking and propelled by luminous imagination, he has for both his work and looks been described as "British poetry's glam, spangly, shape-shifting answer to David Bowie." Amongst his recent books are the poetry collections *Sooner or Later Frank*, *Candy4Cannibals* and *When a Girl Loves a Girl*, and two non-fiction books, *The Dilly: A Secret History of Piccadilly Rent Boys*, and a biography of Lou Reed titled *Waiting for the Man*. He lives in London.

JEREMY REED

BAD BOYS

THIS IS A SNUGGLY BOOK

Copyright © 2021
by Jeremy Reed.
All rights reserved.

ISBN: 978-1-64525-073-9

CONTENTS

Starman / 9
Oscar Wilde as Dilly Punter / 28
Waiting on a Friend / 74
An Apple with Orange Signature / 80
Robert Duncan: The H.D. Book / 86
"Johnny, Remember Me": Hart Crane's suicide / 94
As Your Eyes Are Blue: Lee Harwood's Collected Poems / 105
Wasn't It a Strange Way Down:
    Peter Perrett and The Only Ones / 119
Sister Ray and Cecil's New Piece / 135
Biker Boys, Elizabethans and Thom Gunn's Cool Line / 141
And the Stars Were Shining:
    The Glitter and Menthol Cool of John Ashbery's Poetry / 163
Pink Cadillacs and Suburban Psychopaths:
    Elvis Presley and J.G. Ballard / 181
Orange Sunshine in Robert Duncan's Poetry / 192
Kit Marlowe, Brawling and the Parish of St Giles / 212
All or Nothing / 230
William Blake's *Vala* and Bob Dylan's *Desire* / 248

BAD BOYS

STARMAN

*Temenos Academy Talk, 30ᵗʰ January 2017
Royal Asiatic Society, Euston*

At 4 p.m. in January, the Soho sky, smeared by pollution as an additive, turns optimal cobalt, or on my favourite Farrow & Ball colours chart, Black Blue, underlit by drizzled haze. I'm writing 'Starman' at Patisserie Valerie on Old Compton Street, a residual bohemian café that David Bowie would use for intermittent tea breaks when recording round the corner at Trident Studios in St. Anne's Court, a pre-gentrification red-light alley cluster of brothels and hip coffee bars.

There's an undervalued song of Bowie's, 'London Boys', written in his late teens, and first released on 2ⁿᵈ December 1966, as the B-side of 'Rubber Band', that not only unalterably fingerprints Bowie as indigenous Londoner, but is seminal to his own lifetime identification with an alienated subspecies, a variant type belonging to a different reality, an alternative demographic fusing the droog delinquent sociopaths of *A Clockwork Orange* to roaming messianic starmen. At the time of writing 'London Boys', Bowie was a self-identified Mod, fascinated by the movement's immersive culture of fashion, pills and trending music. He was also living with his friend and manager, Ken Pitt, at 39 Manchester Street, Marylebone, back of Fitzrovia. Bowie's close relationship with Ken Pitt immediately sharpened pointers to his bi-sexuality, his older guardian and mentor being openly gay, and the latter's protégé, androgynously beautiful. In his account of the five years (1966–1970) they spent together, *David Bowie: The Pitt Report*, Ken Pitt writes of the first time he saw Bowie onstage at the Marquee on Sunday, April 17th, 1966. 'From my favourite position, leaning against the wall at the back of the club, I could see that he was wearing a biscuit-coloured, hand-knitted sweater, round-necked and buttoned at one shoulder, its skin-tightness accentuating his slim frame . . . I was particularly struck by the artistry with which he used his body, as if it were an accompanying instrument, essential to the singer and the song.'

The distinctly homoerotic focus of Pitt's on detailing Bowie's jumper, its sexiness on his size-zero torso, and what was the three-button fastening on the left shoulder, displays the hawkish male-on-male design central to Pitt's interest in London's pretty boys. But more importantly to the formative teen Bowie, Pitt was a highly literate reader and book collector, his apartment furnished with a personal library, and it was there, and encouraged to do so, that Bowie picked up on Wilde's *Dorian Gray*, Jean Genet's *Our Lady Of The Flowers,* Edward Bulmer-Lytton's 19th-century novel *The Coming Race,* James Baldwin's *Giovanni's Room,* as well as the dystopian futurology of Orwell's *1984,* Anthony Burgess' *A Clockwork Orange,* and the New Wave SF of J.G. Ballard and Michael Moorcock as urbane pioneers of ecological crashes, and the arrival of altered tourists from the future into our neural pathways. So too, the cut-up, chemically driven, non-linear verbal clips of William Burroughs' novels, like *The Naked Lunch* and *The Wild Boys,* also fed into the young Bowie's ambition to compose musicals and write theatrical adaptations for the stage. But for Bowie this was more an unrealised theatre of imagination, given eventual form through rock configurations like Ziggy Stardust and *Diamond Dogs,* rather than through concretization as a writer, not performer, for the stage. Steeped in apocalyptic dramaturgy, the young Bowie's sci-fi themed vignettes were managed in pop songs, a frustrating medium in that lyrics are usually secondary to the music, a regulation Bowie would happily have reversed. And on Ken Pitt's eclectic bookshelves he discovered, through reading, the building-blocks of his future personality swaps, Ziggy Stardust, Aladdin Sane, the Thin White Duke etc., clones or humanoids through which to project mini pop-operettas.

Back to 'London Boys', with Bowie masking his identity as a seventeen-year-old runaway, pilled-up, sexually ambiguous as Mods were, hanging out on Wardour Street and learning how to act cool in his chosen milieu. Sung in a flat, slovenly London voice, expressing a downbeat, fragile vulnerability, the damped, morose sensibility only takes life as the song builds with attitude into defiance.

> Oh, the first time that you tried a pill
> You feel a little queasy, decidedly ill,
> You're gonna be sick, but you mustn't lose face
> To let yourself down would be a big disgrace
> With the London boys, with the London boys

Bowie flattens the vowel in London from an 'o' to a 'u' as part of the song's disaffected raw digestion of streetlife. It's probably in sync with how he felt at the time, impatient to succeed, but invariably failing. What Pitt neglects to tell us, is how tiny Bowie's audience was at the time of first seeing him perform, with one fan commenting on 'six girls in the front row, and half a dozen of us queens at the back, hanging on his every move.' At nineteen, this isn't a deterrent, as self-absorption overwrites it, and the future seems an indefinitely extensible platform. Bowie's extraordinary look was noted before his music, and was to be integrally built into its increasing gradient of success. Its gay referentials were to attract both Ken Pitt and the mime shuffler Lindsay Kemp, each drawn singularly to Bowie's disarming, gender-bending sexuality, and the potential shapes it could throw at an emergent youth audience.

I isolate 'London Boys' with its reference to 'Bright lights, Soho, Wardour Street,' as a song precognitively anticipating Soho as Bowie's future workspace, with Trident Studios in a cut off Wardour Street, the modality where he would record the albums *Space Oddity* (1969), *The Man Who Sold The World* (1970), *Hunky Dory* (1971), *The Rise and Fall of Ziggy Stardust and the Spiders from Mars* (1972), *Aladdin Sane* (1973) and *Pin-Ups* (1973). This specific W1 grid was to be the hub for his explosive creative energies at a time when his ascendant celebrity as rock's gender supremacist was at its stardust apogee.

At 39 Manchester Square, Bowie adapted to Ken Pitt's decadent fin-de-siècle leanings, the stripped pine floors and Victorian furnishings, the holly-green chaise-longue finished in rosewood, and of course the first edition books by Wilde, Beardsley, Huysmans, (and particularly mentioned by Pitt, James Baldwin's *Nobody Knows My Name)* that helped flavour Bowie's idea that he wasn't like anybody else and so would create his own version of reality, and his later assumption, 'I must be only one in a million' on *Station to Station,* was another affirmation of the intellectually cold dissociation that so often defeated Ken Pitt's understanding. In later life, Bowie was to comment on his overt emotional freeze as: 'I always had a repulsive need to be something more than human. I felt very puny as a human. I thought, fuck that, I want to be a superman.' *Rolling Stone, 12/2/76.

And of course that alien cold is in the depersonalised voice, flat or theatricalised into ambivalent gender, as the narrator of cut-up that keeps him at a remove from involvement in the lyric. In fact, after the end of the sixties, Bowie filters all subjective content in his songs through either a persona, or a sort of cosmonaut alluding to brain-chatter in the universe. The methodology originating from Brion Gysin and William Burroughs of atomising the self into quantum potentialities fitted well with Bowie's notion of multiple identities and not wishing to be fixed by the limitations, as he saw it, of rock. And while Bowie grew into a rock supremacist and inimitably androgynous icon, he always appeared marginally displaced in rock as an art form that didn't collect him integrally, while at the same time not willing to renounce the celebrity, fame and wealth it provided. It's an arguable fact that most rock stars, including a luminary like Bowie, exhaust their creative resources by forty, and don't get better, but simply different. Something in Bowie intuited this right from the start, that rock was only a partial expression of a bigger arts infrastructure latent within him. It was also in some weird way a platform to starmen, or the beginnings of Bowie's identification with the alien, an empathetic association endorsed by his first and only hit single of the sixties, 'Space Oddity'.

I'm stopped in my writing by a skinny guy in a black zippered leather jacket and deconstructed jeans with knee-holes, who tentatively tells me he saw me perform at the Horse Hospital with the Ginger Light, and the shift in time and place travelled mentally puts me in a bilocated window, as I thank him for his appreciative comments. I notice, too, the Thai girl sitting at the table next to me has nude makeup, and two-tone blended eye shadow, burnt-orange dusted into gold, and with earbuds in she's in a split dimension. Her makeup's how I imagine Mars.

I get back to Major Tom, Bowie's fictional astronaut launched through 'Space Oddity', as an instantly durable counterculture anti-hero, in the way of J.G. Ballard's subversive protagonist Robert Vaughan in the novel *Crash,* with Bowie/Tom getting off on the exhaust plume of the Apollo 11 mission, as the first manned moon landing, five days after the release of 'Space Oddity' on 11th July 1969. Recorded at Trident Studios on 20th June 1969, Major Tom's virtual space tourism seemed real-object travel and Bowie's voice pitched suitably off-world. So who is this Brixton interloper, wired-up on space travel, UFOs, aliens, time-slip futurology, and still without a hit record after three years of mutant pop experimentation? Bowie's opportune purchase on the international space programme got him the Top Ten hit he so desperately needed after an agonisingly slow long haul to No. 5. The lyric gets off modern – *Ground control to Major Tom / Take your protein pills and put your helmet on* – only Tom is a rogue astronaut, who is off-mission – *For here/Am I sitting in a tin can/Far above the world/Planet Earth is blue/And there's nothing I can do* – or anyone, about Tom's evident, dissociated self-destruct. Bowie got the blue right, as for an observer in space, the water bodies reflect the colour of the sky, that appears blue because of the way sunlight is selectively scattered as it goes through our atmosphere. The chart success and realist sci-fi incorporated into 'Space Oddity' – the word *oddity* being equally applicable to Bowie in his creative quest – pushed pop's boundaries forward into tech, at a time when psychedelia's saturated colour wavelengths promoted hallucinated journeys out of the body and into neural, rather than physical space. Bowie was largely out there, alienated and alone within the remit of pop's acid pioneers, reporting back from the future. Bowie was Tom and Tom Bowie as empathy swap, something perfectly consistent with Bowie's psychological need to put a character between him and the song. 'As an adolescent, I was painfully shy, withdrawn. I didn't really have the nerve to sing my songs on stage, and nobody else was doing them. I decided to do them in disguise so that I didn't have to actually go through the humiliation of going on stage and being myself.' It was this artificially layered disguise of first-person Bowie that built the impenetrable mystique integrated into his myth as interspecies or replicant, but also basically glacial, cold climate English, the formal reserve of Bowie's British generation of the 40s/50s, as a generational characteristic. There's a photo of Bowie extending a handshake to David Hockney on the occasion of their first meeting backstage at the Los Angeles Forum in 1976 that says it all in refrigerated formality. The divisive is psychological miles, charm in this instance preceding gesture, as the distance he establishes between himself and Hockney, with Christopher Isherwood amenably looking on, is the maximum attainable with personal physical contact. It's quite literally alien contact, appearing to exude little physical warmth between two contemporary artists, drawn to, but perhaps suspicious of each other's magnitude.

Bowie's Soho, where I'm writing this, extended along Wardour Street to the Marquee Club at No. 90 and almost next door, The Ship, at 116, an Edwardian pub with chocolate-coloured tiles, dark wood panelling and stained glass, where he conducted early interviews with music journalists through hung scrolls of cigarette smoke. There was also the Moka Bar on Frith Street and, tucked into Soho's niche yards, Peter Burton's Le Duce in lugubrious D'Arblay Mews, a gay Mod disco, where clubbers threw their recreational pills into the aquarium tank when raided by the police. Bowie's Soho topology that was his geographic locus for the first formative decade of his career, also included practice sessions at Charlie Chester's Casino on Archer Street, or in a warren of rooms and brothels on Windmill Street, when Soho was essentially red light, as well as socialising at the Regency Club, a hangout for the notorious Kray Twins and their extortionist racket. Bowie and his mid-sixties band parked a military green Bedford van in potholed Ham Yard, its panels scrawled on with pink lipstick by early fans.

Soho fame was right on the moment of what was happening. It was the epicentre of emergent British rock and youth culture, and Bowie was local, but still relatively unknown outside its trending bohemian milieu. Photos taken on the rooftop of the Manchester Street apartment by Ken Pitt show Bowie with fashionable, long Mod-styled hair and deep-collar button-down shirts, before his transitioning morph into wearing dresses and full makeup after meeting Angela Barnett in 1969, and going trans for the withdrawn album sleeve cover of *The Man Who Sold The World*.

As vibrant colouring to the often edgy, potentially violent Soho the nascent starman inhabited, I quote from Chris Moore who worked at Charlie Chester's casino during this period for aspects of Soho's B-side gambling thuggery. 'There was a slightly dangerous side to working in Soho in those days. Heated arguments would often ensue as immediate entry was refused. The staff breakroom and canteen was above the Horseshoe casino. I can remember standing in the reception at Charlie Chester's for twenty minutes smoking cigarettes and watching the violence in the street unfold, rather than run the gauntlet and try and cross the street. Chester's doormen were definitely of a different breed in those days. I vividly remember one of the crew being a small, overweight, red-faced man in his early forties. He was known as Mick the Hammer, a nickname reputedly acquired from his earlier days as a member of the Kray gang. However, whilst the pedigree of the Chester's doormen was undoubtedly dubious, they teamed together perfectly to create a hermetic seal from the violent undercurrent that ran through Soho in those days.'

But sixties Soho also had a place for pretty boys in makeup, like David Bowie and endemic Mods who competitively swanked transitioning Carnaby Street fashion into gossipy coffee bars like Moka, Bar Italia, and where I'm writing at Patisserie Valerie surrounded by mixed fruit tart cognoscenti. It rains outside, and I'm reminded by reading *New Scientist* it hasn't rained on the moon for four billion years.

Bowie simply couldn't find a follow-up hit single to endorse the chart success of the NASA-tinted 'Space Oddity', but in 1969 wrote his next interplanetary excursion with 'Life on Mars', as another attempt at pulling pop into the helium-torched high-tech plume of rocket science. Bowie described how he wrote the song. 'Workplace was a big empty room with a chaise longue; a bargain price art nouveau screen (William Morris, so I told anyone who asked); a huge overflowing freestanding ashtray and a grand piano. Little else. I started working it out on the piano and had the whole lyric and melody finished by late afternoon.'

Life On Mars was held back from the album *The Man Who Sold The World* (1970), to be released as a piano-led, cinematic mélange, sci-fi track on his breakthrough fourth studio album *Hunky Dory* (1971). While the track is not specifically about Mars, but more a blend of ludic surrealism with kitsch cults substituting for politics, the plot suggests in Bowie's imagination not only America's unrest over Vietnam, but recognisable strains of universal psychoses that point to Mars as an alternative planet for migrant astronauts. That there is only a small symbiotic relationship between the red planet's rocky desert landscapes and thin carbon dioxide atmosphere, and Earth's provision of water to transport reactive molecules like hydrogen, carbon monoxide and ammonia, our collective consciousness has always targeted Mars as Earth 2. And Bowie's song does that, almost fifty years before the initialisation of Mars One, a private spaceflight project proposing to land the first humans on Mars by 2024, as a one-way destination only, the selection discussions also introducing how willing the stringently chosen astronauts would be to become cannibals in order to survive.

'Life On Mars', which arguably would have been Bowie's ideal follow-up to 'Space Oddity', lyrically maps out something of his *Clockwork Orange*/J.G. Ballard-inspired overview on dystopian chaos.

> It's on Amerika's tortured brow
> That Mickey Mouse has grown up a cow
> Now the workers have struck for fame
> Cause Lennon's on sale again
> See the mice in their million hoards
> From Ibiza to the Norfolk Broads
> Rule Britannia is out of bounds

To my mother, my dog and clowns

Like all fragmented, lyric cut-ups, we know the meaning without the need for explanation. Having scorched Vietnam with the defoliant Agent Orange, America faced civil riot from its youth, and this violent turbulence was taken up in London too; but for Bowie writing a song, the process is morphed into an anarchic imaginative documentation of potential futures that revisit us as wars. If the song got little attention on its initial release, then its re-issue as a single in 1973, on the back of Bowie's Ziggy Stardust fame, took it to No.3 in the charts. Mick Rock filmed and directed a promotional video backstage at Earls Court on 12th May 1973 to accompany the record's release, in which a heavily made-up Bowie, wearing a turquoise suit designed by Freddi Buretti, personifies sexual alien, or the characterisation of a new subculture species to which Bowie imagined himself integrated into the emergent zeitgeist. It was this belief in being set apart that led to Bowie throwing political gestures like a Nazi salute at Victoria Station in 1976, as a self-designed instrument of gender-bending elitism. Of the dichotomy in his own personality, he remarked, 'Offstage I'm a robot. Onstage I achieve emotion. It's probably why I prefer dressing up as Ziggy to being David.' And it was the elevation of his impossibly high cheekbones as facial scaffolding that gave Bowie a Greta Garbo look, something accentuated by his mismatched eyes, that weren't, as often assumed, two different colours, but the result of anisocoria, a condition characterised by an unequal size in a person's pupils. In Bowie's case his left pupil was permanently dilated. This can create the illusion of having different coloured eyes, because the fixed pupil does not respond to changes in light, while the right pupil does.

It was the disconcerted look this accident created that gave Bowie the association with aliens or visitors from the future; a connotation enhanced, of course, by his playing the role of extraterrestrial mutant in the Nicholas Roeg movie *The Man Who Fell To Earth* (1976). Bowie characteristically plays the part of an extraterrestrial humanoid alien, Thomas Jerome Newton, who crash-lands on Earth to take water back to his home planet, which is experiencing a catastrophic drought. Bowie's role in a film based on Walter Trevis' 1963 novel of the same name helped consolidate the myth that his origins were off-world, and that he was in some way an interplanetary plenipotentiary, something first explicitly enforced by his supernova arrival with *Ziggy Stardust and the Spiders From Mars*. The name suggested an immersion not only in H.P. Lovecraft and J.G. Ballard, but a generation of sci-fi writers like Ray Bradbury, James Blish, Thomas Disch, Brian Aldiss etc., and the lurid technicolor covers of their mass-market paperbacks, with dusty planetary sunsets like the high-res shock tactics of Bowie's nasturtium-red coloured hair. Sci-fi in the mix of drenched psychedelics was in the air – a generation mining Middle Earth, acid, sexual ambiguity, ufology, smoked botanicals, was awaiting its rock messiah, its liberated avatar in the form of Ziggy, patron saint of deviated glamour, urban apocalypse, SETI, and pushing personal boundaries to rock 'n' roll suicide.

New wave science fiction produced in the sixties and seventies, with its focus on soft as opposed to hard science, had turned inwards psychologically, and like Bowie looked to encounter the alien on Earth. In a remarkable 1962 essay called 'Inner Space', as the compass for creative orientation, J.G. Ballard as pioneering futurist wrote: 'The biggest developments of the immediate future will take place, not on the moon or Mars, but on Earth, and it is inner space, not outer, that needs to be explored. The only true alien planet is Earth. In the past the scientific basis of SF has been towards the physical sciences – rocketry, electronics, cybernetics, and the emphasis should switch to the biological sciences. It is that inner spacesuit which is still needed, and it is up to science fiction to build it.'

Whether Bowie was aware, or not, of Ballard's essay pointing the stars into our neural pathways rather than making them the subject of object travel, he was certainly influenced by Ballard's fiction in which urban landscapes, rather than space colonisation, are the domain of the aberrant psychopath, rather than the re-anatomised tribes of biomorphs native to real or invented planets. Ballard, leading into Bowie's creations in the early seventies, clearly saw that the alien was apparent in the human, and that sci-fi was now a reality programmed into our electronic networks, rather than the resource of higher intelligence theoretically located, say, in the hydrocarbon lakes of Saturn's moon Titan. And by applying a sci-fi imagination to real geography, often located in the London suburbs, or in culturally altered American landscapes, Ballard, in his seminal novel, *The Atrocity Exhibition* (1970), condensed post-apocalyptic excerpts of dystopian modernity, split by iconic images of John F. Kennedy and Marilyn Monroe, into a bizarre synthesis of the fragile dissolve between imagined atrocities and realities. Using a method like William Burroughs of converting linear time into non-linear film frames, Ballard bounced narrative down into episodic vignettes in which obsessions with car sex, reconfigurations of Kennedy's assassination, B-movie psychiatrists, urban zombies, and the manipulable sexual images of Marilyn Monroe and Ronald Reagan occupy a confused, violent present. The novel, a blueprint for *Crash* (1973), in which Ballard explores symphorophilia and car crash fetishism, provides some of the most innovative poetry of its period, and I see Ballard as much as a poet as I do novelist, in his use of implosive visual imagery that leaves most poets a long way behind.

I'm not arguing that Ziggy Stardust comes directly out of Ballard, but Bowie's persona Ziggy occupies the same sort of post-apocalyptic ethos, particularly in songs like 'Five Years' and 'Moonage Daydream', that invent fractured mini-narratives riffed into immediacy by Mick Ronson's guitar weaponry. It's Ronson's playing that provides the often spooky soundtrack to Ziggy's alien posturing as transgender rock star, and in some ways we can credit the platinum-haired Mick Ronson with being the first sci-fi glam rock guitarist. And due to Ken Pitt having brought back an acetate of the Velvet Underground's *Banana* album, at the end of the sixties, as benchmark, drugs-driven garage, Bowie was not only performing Lou Reed's 'I'm Waiting for the Man', and 'White Light/White Heat' live ahead of his contemporaries, but clearly learnt from Reed how to construct songs about the urban underclass, and street culture written into the metropolis. Most certainly Ballard's visionary brokering of near futures in fiction, mixed with Lou Reed's cold lyric snapshots of the Warhol entourage at the Factory, were the inspirational prototypes behind Bowie's scary postmodern fiction theming: *Ziggy Stardust, Aladdin Sane* and the most ambitious concept of all, *Diamond Dogs*.

Ziggy Stardust, as the human manifestation of an alien channelling extraterrestrial info, as well as representing the definitive rock star consumed by burn-out and finally suicide, gave Bowie a persona that was bigger than him at the time of recording the album at Trident Studios in 1971/1972, when he was still a cult artist lacking a sustainable fanbase. He was now twenty-five, and like all aliens, including me, Bowie was a futures tourist, observed with suspicion; he still lacked a hit to endorse his increasingly spectacular androgyny. Whatever the origins of Ziggy Stardust, like Vince Taylor, the tragically eclipsed rock star with whom Bowie identified, Ziggy is, of course, an amalgam of Bowie's own real and imagined characteristics, and in that sense a clone or peripheral unleashed on the times, in the same way as Robert Vaughan in Ballard's *Crash* personifies the deviated extremes of his sexual imaginings. And the name 'Ziggy' perfectly accommodates onomatopoetically our received notion of what an alien or starman might perhaps be called, if we were to encounter an off-world contact. Bowie later suggested to *Q* magazine in a 1990 interview that the name Ziggy came accidentally from a tailor's shop, Ziggy's, that he passed on the train, and that the name had 'that Iggy Pop connotation, but it was a tailor's shop, and I thought, well this whole thing is gonna be about clothes, so it was my own little joke calling him Ziggy. So Ziggy Stardust was a real compilation of things.' There's never any specific cause of an imaginative creation, whatever it is, but more a cluster of dominant associations that synthesise in the process of developing a theme, singular, but integrating constellating motives as a plurality. Ziggy, dressed in brightly quilted zoot suits, made up by Freddie Burretti from sumptuous fabrics purchased from Liberty, or silk, patterned dresses, camping it as an effeminate queen, polarising the attention of both sexes, launched his transgender image at a wider public through his career-changing appearance with the single 'Starman' on *Top of the Pops* in July 1972. For a nation of pop viewers it was literally their first contact with the spiky flame-haired androgyne, playing an aqua-coloured guitar, dressed in patched Liberty ensemble with laced-up boxing boots dyed scarlet. The song, a gentle pop-rock, predominantly acoustic excursion into ET contact, and pre-empting the Ziggy Stardust album, describes Ziggy receiving a message from an alien through the radio as source of the signal from the spooky third kind. 'Look out your window you can see his light/If we can sparkle he may land tonight/Don't tell your poppa or he'll get us locked up in fright,' Bowie sings, looking again to children as more openly receptive to alien contact, and as a race set apart by active imagination, and likely to be locked up if they express truth about visionary experience. In an interview with William Burroughs for *Rolling Stone* in 1973, Bowie made it very clear that Ziggy is the recipient of the message and not the extraterrestrial carrier.

In Bowie's case of third mind category, *Starman*, although released three years later and peaking at No.10, is the logical successor to *Space Oddity* in terms of chart and planet-hopping his way to recognition. Made up as an interspecies, transgender rock-purveyor of alien speak, Bowie was a uniquely untouchable phenomenon, a Ziggy supernova arrived as the 'leper messiah' to an expectant generation looking out exactly for him. Bowie's moment had finally arrived; he'd put on what Ballard called his 'inner spacesuit.'

Patisserie Valerie, 3.30 p.m. The light outside's like a frosty green diamond, and the view through the window is like watching CCTV footage, only the images are sharper. I took time out from writing my Bowie document by doing a poem to feed my addiction to poetry, from which I can rarely separate. I speak to Teresa, a friend, rather than a waitress, and she tells me that after drinking two bottles of wine last night, she fell off the stepladder while attempting to paint her kitchen ceiling purple. Her right hip is bruised and sore, but she doesn't care, the booze was worth the fall, and her DIY a compulsive fetish, she likens to sex on an ironing board.

Released on 16th June 1972, the concept album *The Rise and Fall of Ziggy Stardust and the Spiders From Mars,* carried a title sounding more like a hard science sci-fi novel by Frank Herbert or Samuel Delaney, as lurid pulp evocation of interplanetary beasts crawling across scorched Martian canyons, depicted on the covers of early Ballard paperback novels like *The Burning World* (1964). In fact it's the dystopian, eruptive flameout of Ballard's *The Disaster Area* and *The Atrocity Exhibition* that bleeds into Bowie's urban spaceboy apocalypse, and particularly in the portentous opener, and my favourite track, 'Five Years', with the message come through that the planet has only five years, and with the echoes of 1984 incorporated into the package, Bowie's vignettes of condensed catastrophe were a first for pop.

> A girl my age went off her head, hit some tiny children,
> If the black hadn't pulled her off, I think she would have killed them
> A soldier with a broken arm, fixed his stare to the wheels of a Cadillac
> A cop knelt and kissed the feet of a priest, and a queer threw up at the sight of that

'Five Years' is a rock poem, a story of mutant cross-cultures and defiant edgewalkers that belong partly to Ballard and partly to John Rechy's hustler novel *City of the Night* (1970). I stay with it as Ziggy sights his alien contact, questioning and correcting what he sees:

> I think I saw you in an ice cream parlour, drinking milkshakes cold and long
> Smiling and waving and looking so fine, don't think you knew you were in this song
> And it was cold and it rained and I felt like an actor
> And I thought of Ma and I wanted to get back there
> Your face, your race, the way that you talk
> I kiss you, you're beautiful, I want you to walk . . .

It's intensely moving within the context of the song how Ziggy perceives his alien counterpart, who doesn't know he is in the song, doing normal in an ice cream parlour [or a Soho Wimpy, more likely] while Ziggy stands outside in the rainy cold. This is the moment in the song of cold alienation, the recognition of different races, and finally the physical union, '*I kiss you, you're beautiful,*' almost as an act of narcissistic conjugation.

Bowie conceived of his starmen as 'infinites' or 'black-hole jumpers,' who impartially planet-hopped across the universe, bringing news of catastrophe without any antidote or deterrent to survive it. Ziggy Stardust, inspired in part according to Bowie by Burroughs's *Nova Express* and *The Wild Boys* was originally intended to be a multimedia theatrical performance with forty cut-up scenes making the show radically different every night, the accidental accounting for the variant. In a *Rolling Stone* interview discussion between Bowie and Burroughs in February 1974, Burroughs punched home the point that 'the weapon of the Wild Boys is a bowie knife, an 18 in bowie knife, did you know that?' Bowie's sci-fi dystopia, or conceivable nightmare future, a fusion of Burroughs and Ballard, is projected as a glam rock endgame, the terminal point of his own youth, as well as the near para-suicide of the planet. In the rocky, fabulous 'Moonage Daydream', Bowie morphs Ziggy into a polymorphic humanoid, a shape-shifting space-shaman.

> I'm an alligator, I'm a mama-papa coming for you
> I'm the space invader, I'll be a rock 'n' rolling bitch for you
> Keep your mouth shut, you're squawking like a pink monkey bird
> And I'm busting up my brains for the words

Bowie was already discovering, much to his profound disillusionment, that rock was arguably too exhaustively superficial a frame for the concept in which he was engaged, despite the fame that it brought him as an ambiguously sexed rock alien. Although he was to pursue the theme further through the albums *Aladdin Sane* (1973) and *Diamond Dogs* (1974), *Rock 'n' Roll Suicide* off *Ziggy Stardust* is a sort of predictive finale to his trajectory as commodified rock star with an identifiable band. Writing these songs on which his own career in music acutely depended, Bowie saw himself as old in a modality exploited by youth, in other words he was five years behind his anticipated expectations. 'You're too old to lose it, too young to choose it/And *the clock waits so patiently on your song/You walk past a café but you don't eat when you've lived too long/Oh, no, no, no, you're a rock 'n' roll suicide.'* It's not overstating interpretation to suggest that something of Bowie literally dies in this song; the pop protégé Ken Pitt worked so hard to place commercially, when Bowie was unable to find hit songs and marketable focus throughout the second half of the sixties, had experienced celebrity and overdosed on its negative aspects. Looking back much later on the phrase with which the song opens, '*Time takes a cigarette,*' Bowie was to intellectualise it by saying, 'this was a sort of plagiarized line from Baudelaire which was something to the effect of life is a cigarette, smoke it in a hurry or savour it.' At the time of Ziggy, Bowie didn't have the luxury of time, just the intense awareness of now or never.

It's likely that Bowie's particular starman will never go away in the context of creativity, due to his singularly introducing the figure of the alien into pop, and through Major Tom the progressive reality of the astronaut not only brokering a moonbase, but creating micro-gravity industrialised systems in the near galaxy. But for me that trajectory into off-world demographics comes back to the song 'London Boys' and Bowie's sixties Soho, with frequent visits to the Wallace Collection in Manchester Square and Pollock's Toy Museum in Fitzrovia, the eclectic oddity of which fascinated him to the point of inspired distraction. At the time, surfing the Mod wave into its update of period-revival dress and psychedelia, Bowie was a questioning outsider, quizzing youth culture for a place to let him in, but remaining peripheral to its hub, his ambitions too big at the time for his immediate talent. We can imagine him sitting in Bar Bruno on the lip of Wardour Street, breathing into a frothy espresso and wondering if it would all ever happen for him, soaked in pop hits, but wanting inwardly and compulsively to pioneer new cultural frontiers that linked literary fiction to rock. 'London

Boys' seems to me the existential start of the extraterrestrially themed project that finds its culmination in the rock theatrical *The Rise and Fall of Ziggy Stardust and the Spiders From Mars.*

Soho again, Wardour Street, I finish writing and face into a mashed strawberry sunset finish over the Piccadilly point of Brewer Street. Writing about Bowie takes me back to Trident and St. Anne's Court, still a dark twist on the Soho compass, but with a constant stream of foot-traffic navigating north-south. It's rained while I've been inside writing, and there's a damp lick to the alley that Bowie would have known on rainy days, and that elusive smell of the city's wet skin exuding dirt. I stay maybe five minutes in thought, a sort of Bowie-directed zen, then hurry off for a drink.

OSCAR WILDE
AS DILLY PUNTER

A century before the shooting of the rent boy documentary *Johnny Go Home* (1975), they were already there at Piccadilly Circus, rent outside the department store Swan & Edgar, or slouched under the arches insolently with their slippery attitude, their punkish defiance, their hoodlum tactics, bashed in hats and tight suits, and their pocketed earnings, and Oscar Wilde was known to them in the polari they spoke as a tribal slang for commonality. Dilly trade, existing on the unstable boundary between visibility and invisibility (when the police showed up), covered a broad demographic from couriers to post office boys, newspaper sellers, sex workers, runaways, mean-hearted pretty young things, and were part of a fugitive gay demimonde to which Wilde grew increasingly addicted, as well as providing an underground source for the two novels he wrote between 1889–1891, *The Picture of Dorian Gray* (1890) and the scandalously homoerotic *Teleny*, published anonymously by Leonard Smithers in 1893 in an edition of 200 deluxe copies for subscribers only under the imprint of the Erotiken Biblion Society.

Swan & Edgar, a landmark department store constructed in the early nineteenth century on the corner of Regent Street and Piccadilly Circus, significantly targeted by the suffragettes in their window-smashing raid on November 21st, 1911, and surviving until 1982, when it was closed by the Debenham Group, was always integrated by rent into a convenient locale, largely because it had an exit directly into the underground. It was while waiting outside Swan & Edgar one day in 1888 that Wilde, according to his close friend Ada Leverson, first made direct contact with the lugubrious Dilly boys hanging on the corner. According to Leverson, 'as he stood there full of careless good spirits, on a cold sunny May morning, a curious, very young, but hard-eyed creature appeared, looked at him, gave a sort of laugh, and passed on. He felt, he said, "as if an icy hand had clutched his heart." He had a sudden presentiment. He saw a vision of madness, misery and ruin.'

We'll never know the boy's name, shuffling round the sunlit Circus, hands in his pockets, his contempt for Wilde, undoubtedly, the expression of his own repressed sexuality, but he was clearly the formative influence in liberating Wilde into an accelerated attraction to lowlife, and signposting the physical availability of rough trade at the Dilly. Leverson is in fact unintentionally describing Wilde's introduction to Dilly boys, an impromptu initiation that most London gay men underwent until the 1980s, in recognizing aberrant aspects of themselves in Dilly trade, and Wilde was, of course, no different. The place leads to dissociation, fascination, criminal impulse, and the weird spin of a circle, the Circus that is in fact standing still. If you stand on those black railings long enough, they spin, like you've got vestibular damage and feel motion sick and start quite literally seeing things.

Wilde's recreational London was specifically Piccadilly and Soho orientated, and his mapping almost a sexual psychogeography, focused on the Café Royal founded in 1865 by Daniel Thevenon at the bottom of Regent Street, near Piccadilly Circus, Piccadilly Circus for rent, the Lyric Club situated in the Prince of Wales Buildings in Coventry Street off Piccadilly Circus, the Hogarth Club at 36 Dover Street off Piccadilly, and Kettners, owned by Giovanni Sangiorgi, at 28–31 Church Street, renamed Romilly Street in 1937. There was additionally the St James' Restaurant at 24–6 Piccadilly, the London Pavilion, a music hall in Piccadilly Circus used by rent, the Florence Restaurant in Rupert Street, and, of course, his club the Albermarle at 25 Albermarle Street off Piccadilly, as well as the notorious Alhambra Musical Hall in Leicester Square, the Blue Lantern in Soho's Ham Yard and Charles Hirsch's Coventry Street bookshop Libraire Parisienne , where Wilde purchased gay erotica and deposited on a rotational basis with the rumoured collaborators the manuscript of the pioneering homoerotic novel *Teleny*.

During the initial period of Wilde's brokering of Piccadilly Circus, and his addictive gravitation to rent, London was rocked by the notorious Cleveland Street Scandal, given sensational reportage on 16th November 1889, by the North London Press, which implicated members of the House of Lords in a rent boy scandal based in a male brothel at 19 Cleveland Street in Fitzrovia, just off Tottenham Court Road. The rent boy scandal was precipitated by the arrest of Charles Swinscow, a teenage telegram boy accused of pilfering cash and suspected by police of illicitly pocketing eighteen shillings. When questioned, Charlie accounted for the cash by admitting that he'd been paid for sex at 19 Cleveland Street, and that he regularly sold his ass there to wealthy clients, including Prince Eddy, Duke of Clarence, second in line to the throne, and generally assumed, on account of his incurable misogyny and dandified appearance, to be unquestionably gay, as well as Lord Arthur Somerset, equerry to the Prince of Wales, and Henry Fitzroy, Earl of Euston, who successfully sued for libel. As a result of Charlie's confession, police inspector Frederick Abberline visited 19 Cleveland Street at 10 a.m. on July 6th, 1889, with an arrest warrant for the brothel's proprietor, 35-year-old Charles Hammond, and his partner, the 18-year-old Henry Newlove, the warrant stating that the two 'did unlawfully, wickedly, and corruptly conspire, combine, confederate and agree to procure teenage male prostitutes to commit the abominable crime of buggery.' Previous to issuing the warrant, Detective Inspector Abberline prepared a detailed report of his surveillance of the house. 'Observation has been kept on the house 19 Cleveland Street – and a number of men of superior bearing and apparently of good positions have been seen to call there accompanied by boys in some instances, and on two occasions by a soldier, but after waiting about in a suspicious manner left without gaining admission. Some of them arrived in separate cabs, but evidently met by appointment at the house for unnatural purposes. From inquiries I am satisfied that Hammond for a considerable time has obtained his livelihood by procuring boys and allowing persons to visit his house for unnatural purposes. Although at the present stage of the case (until Hammond is arrested) I have not deemed it prudent to interrogate other boys at the Post Office, I have every reason to believe that a large number have been defiled at this house . . .' Prince Eddy's involvement in the Cleveland Street Scandal was widely presumed to be the reason for the establishment whitewash and the non-prosecution of those aristos linked to paying for male prostitution. In a trial beginning on December 12th, 1889, Newlove's defence attorney, Arthur Newton, was spectacularly charged with obstructing justice by warning Charles Hammond of his imminent arrest, and assisting Hammond to leave the country in an effort to evade having to testify against his prominent clientele, and was sentenced to six weeks in prison. And from the Crown Counsel as prosecution we learn that the boys were usually paid a sovereign, of which they pocketed four shillings, the rest going to the proprietor Charles Hammond. The endemic sex panic that followed in the wake of press disclosures led, as a conciliatory act on the government's part in the same year, to Henry Labouchère's gross indecency law, in which a sentence of two years with or without hard labour was made statutory for homosexual offences, and gay sex criminalised, even in private amongst consenting adults.

We don't know Wilde's reaction to the hysterically punitive bill; Henry Labouchère was actually an acquaintance, but the description of same-sex relations as an 'act of gross indecency', coming at the time of the publication of his sexually controversial *The Picture of Dorian Gray* (1890), and while he was actively engaged in writing the pornographic novel *Teleny* as the B-side to *Dorian Gray*, must have fired panic signals into his nerves. There was, too, a rumour that Wilde may have been a regular at 19 Cleveland Street, and a potentially libellous review of his novel *Dorian Gray* by Charles Whibley in the *Scots Observer* compromised Wilde by suggesting 'if he can write for none but unlawed noblemen and perverted telegraph boys, the sooner he takes to tailoring (or some other decent trade) the better for his own reputation and public morals.' Wilde probably assumed that as a celebrity and married man he was above the law, and would never be found out, although the published law opened a gateway for persistent blackmail of gay people, and for Wilde personally, from Dilly drop-outs exploiting his regularly compromised sexuality, as well as the likes of professionals like William Allen and Robert Cliburn, who Wilde paid for the return of his potentially incriminating letters to Lord Alfred Douglas.

What we do know from Wilde's three trials, is not only the name of the notorious procurer Alfred Taylor, but also the identities of boys working the popular Swan & Edgar face of Piccadilly Circus, Freddie Atkins, Edward Shelley, Charlie Parker, Alfred Wood and William Parker, all of whom, and exempt from prosecution, admitted to having been rent to Wilde, as ambivalently sexed trade, using the West End as the lucrative arena in which to sell sex, often with blackmail as a secondary incentive. There were other boys, too, named in the trial, Alfonse Harold Conway, Walter Grainger, Sidney Mavor and Ernest Scarfe, dodgy little rough rhinestones, wised-up with optimal savvy and barcoded with sufficient street-cred to subject an essentially malleable punter like Wilde to their ratty systemised advantage.

Wilde was, of course, encountering and losing out to the fundamental Dilly paradox, that while punters drawn to the place are unquestionably gay, rent arguably could be straight, bi, homeless, or just criminally intentioned, although it's questionable how anyone indulging in same-sex relations isn't partially gay, or at least curious to experiment. It's the confused mixed motives characteristic of the place, given that plain clothes police were also a part of the milieu, that contributed to the extraordinary atmospheric of Piccadilly Circus as the epicentre of male prostitution hardwired to the resources of a Westminster pavement as its hard-edge focus.

Between 1893–1894, Wilde's testosterone seems to have been turbo-driven into coercing street rats into selling sex, and most often it seems to have been involuntarily. Everyone gets changed by contact with the Dilly, both punters and rent, the place radically eats into your nerves, but, like a drug, becomes a dangerous habit, and Wilde quite literally became a Dilly user, conspicuous by his preened, dandified look, vermilion ties and ostentatious green carnations purchased from a seller in the Royal Arcade in Mayfair, and smoking his customised brand of gold-tipped cigarettes bought from J.L. Fox in the Burlington Arcade. Wilde drew attention to himself by his regularity at the Dilly and quickly became a talking point amongst trade as someone who paid over the going rates, often bought dinner at Kettner's or the Florence, and gifted pretty boys with silver cigarette cases that could be sold on. Questioned about this in court by Charles Gill, Wilde confessed to great amusement amongst the lawyers in court: 'I have a weakness for presenting my acquaintances with cigarette cases. Rather an expensive habit, if indulged in indiscriminately, isn't it, but less extravagant than giving jewelled garters to ladies!'

Wilde and his Dilly boys represented in part the mapping of queer urban social inequality in a way that alerted the public to the fact that sexual difference as a subcultural genre was the more offensive for territorially invading the public domain by quite openly establishing local power-points on the street. While the bodies and spaces monitored by police surveillance were selective, the Dilly, with its transgressive dialectics, was quickly identified as a territorial zone in which queer contested normal and threw defiant shapes at the public – a zone coded into a continuously dispersed, but always resistant community. Dilly boys, no matter how often hassled, warned or prosecuted by the law, or violated by punters, invariably returned to the Circus, not only as an intransigent regrouping, but in part due to the addictive excitement generated by the place, in which almost anything can happen in the unpredictable chance encounter.

Urban queer, as an identifiable brand, is what the Dilly was to Wilde and all subsequent punters up until the late 1980s, drawn to its coded milieu, almost as the heartbeat of London's outlawed sexuality. Jack Saul, aka Dublin Jack or John Saul, who lived at 15 Old Compton Street, Soho, and was notorious rent, may well have been known to Wilde, who, according to Charles Hirsch, the proprietor of the Libraire Parisienne in Coventry Street, ordered a copy in 1890 from him of Jack Saul's pornographic rent boy confessions, *The Sins of the Cities of the Plain* (1881), published fugitively by William Lazenby in an edition of 250 copies, and reprinted by Wilde's publisher Leonard Smithers in 1902. Although the authorship of the book has been variously attributed to James Campbell Reddie and the street artist Simeon Solomon, Jack Saul was undoubtedly a Dilly hustler, who claimed he wrote his rent boy confessions for an advance of twenty pounds, and at the request of a rich patron. Supplying evidence in the Cleveland Street case, Saul claimed to have met one of his clients, Lord Euston, 'in Piccadilly, not far from the Albany Courtyard, near

Sackville Street – nearly opposite the Yorkshire Grey.' Saul detailed the encounter, reported in the Star, 26th February, 1890: 'He laughed at me and I winked at him. He turned sharp into Sackville Street. The Duke, as we call him, came near to me, and asked me where I was going. I said "home" and he said, "What sort is your place?" "Very comfortable," I replied. He said, "Is it very quiet there?" I said yes it was, and then we took a hansom cab there. We got out by the Middlesex Hospital, and I took the gentleman to 19 Cleveland Street, letting him in with my latch key.' Jack Saul was one of the male prostitutes selling sex for Charles Hammond at 19 Cleveland Street. Jack claimed to have met Charles Hammond in May 1879, and to have lived with him at 25 Oxenden Street, Haymarket, both of them earning their money as Dilly rent, and sometimes as much as £8 a week. Saul, at the time of the trial, gave his address as 10 Church Street, Soho, almost opposite Wilde's Kettner's rendezvous, and confessed to living with Andrew Grant, or Queen Anne as he was known at Piccadilly Circus. Supplying evidence that reportedly shocked the court by its unashamed explicit sexual details, Saul was asked, 'Have you any means of earning your bread?' –'No Sir.' 'I see you have a ring on your finger?' 'It's not my fault, or it would have gone long ago. It's only paste.' 'And a silver-headed cane?' 'Oh, that's not much – 1s 6d, no more. I bought it in the Brixton Road…The police and detectives have always been very kind to me here…'

Saul, who was in his thirties at the time when the Cleveland Street scandal broke, seems naturally to have resented Charles Hammond's ready supply of teen rent, and to have admitted importuning at the Dilly. 'I complained to Hammond of his allowing boys of good position in the Post Office to be in the house while I had to go and walk the streets for what is in my face, and that is my shame.' Saul's admission that the police had consistently shown moderation was corroborated by further questioning. 'Were you hunted out by the police?' 'No they have never interfered. They have always been kind to me.' 'Do you mean they have deliberately shut their eyes to your infamous practices?' 'They have shut their eyes to more than me.'

Saul was a tough little number who hustled and could hold his own, and wasn't above putting the frighteners on clients who were reluctant to pay. His attempts to sell sex were ostensibly directed not only by coding, but maintained by the fine-tuned instincts for self-survival that are basic to working the visibly policed West End streets. That he was known to the police as rent and adept at asserting control over his prospective client is powerfully conveyed in the expression and tone of his writing. Pursued across Leicester Square, and finally confronted by the man in that first paranoid edgy instant of contact, Saul's immediate response is to get out of the public eye. 'I am not at all delicate; but wish to keep myself out of trouble. Who can tell who hears you out in the street?' I said, hailing a cab. 'I don't like to be seen speaking to a young fellow in the street. We shall be all right in my own rooms.'

That Piccadilly Circus was already securely established in Wilde's time as a commercialized leisure zone hijacked by trade into opportunistic rent was corroborated by Saul's admissions in the Cleveland Street trial. Saul, in working the Dilly, had learnt instinctually to observe people's looks, and questioned as to whether he recognized Lord Euston from his photograph, he replied. 'Yes, by his face, and by his big white teeth and his moustache.' Asked, 'Where did you first learn Lord Euston's name?' Saul was emphatic. 'Along Piccadilly, not long after I first met him.'

What's significant about Jack Saul is his complete absence of apology for being rent, his attitude maintaining that his profession was normal to him, and that the police largely left him alone. Jack Saul and his associates at the Dilly adapted circus slang or palare, like Morrissey's 'Piccadilly Palare', into their coded vocabularies, with male prostitutes being called pejoratively Mary-Ann, pouf, fairy, tante, tapette, all terms known to Wilde and his milieu as family. A criminal slang vocabulary, known at the time as Parlyaree, as the prototype for the secret gay slang polari that coloured the repressive 1950s and 1960s, as a form of verbal drag, in which language is camped, was already in circulation with London rent, with some of its insolently spiked additives picked up from the nearby Alhambra Music Hall at 23–27 on the east side of Leicester Square, that was used as a pick-up place by both male and female prostitutes. The Alhambra had twice undergone radical repurposing in Wilde's time, once in 1888 by Edward Clark, and again in 1892 by Clark & Pollard, and was a convenient location for rent, as it had a promenade at the back of the stalls, where, for a small price, a standing ticket could be bought for the show. As the theatre bar remained open all through the performance, boys who had already made eye contact with likely punters would wait for them in the bar area, and if necessary have sex with them in the dark space behind the bar that acted almost as an early back room.

Wilde, in a black wool greatcoat with black velvet trimmings, or, more ostentatiously, an astrakhan maxi, was most likely first introduced to the gay demimonde at the Crown public house in Charing Cross, the Victorian equivalent of today's Quebec or Elephant's Graveyard at 12 Quebec Street, Marble Arch, where rent boys angled their availability to older men in a lowlife, bohemian, pub atmosphere. It was there in 1890 that Wilde met Fred Althaus, an office boy for a firm of city solicitors, and living at the time with his parents at Swiss Cottage, and quite clearly, from the tone of his letters to Wilde, looking for a suitably affluent sugar daddy. Fred wrote to Oscar, 'I have heard from Barnes that I can have a room there for two nights, and I feel quite pleased at the idea of going and hope very much that you will join me there after.' It's not without significance that, simultaneous with Wilde's first known assignations with rent, that on the first appearance of the unexpurgated *Dorian Gray* in *Lippincott's Magazine* in the same year, preceding the revised book publication of the novel by Ward, Lock & Co, the director of Ward Lock who were distributing *Lippincott's Magazine*, wrote to Wilde on 10th July saying, 'we have received an intimation from Messrs W.H. Smith & Son this morning to the effect that your story, having been characterised by the press as a filthy one, they are obliged to withdraw *Lippincott's Magazine* from their bookstalls.'

Wilde nowhere better conveys the randomised pull of the Dilly and its queer urban subculture than in *The Picture of Dorian Gray*, where he describes Dorian evidently cruising the place with the familiar look at me, look at you compulsion that its commercialized busyness presents to the punter. 'As I lounged in the park, or strolled down Piccadilly, I used to look at every one who passed me, and wonder with a mad curiosity what sort of lives they led. Some of them fascinated me. Others filled me with terror. There was an exquisite poison in the air. I had a passion for sensations.'

Wilde's metaphor 'exquisite poison' perfectly describes the Dilly ambience, with its questing streetwise pirates giving as good as they get in being stared at and staring back in the edgy dialectic of coercion and a necessary defensive hostility that characterises illicit importuning. Selling sex and turning a trick demands an implicitly unstable equation in that rent may find the punter physically unattractive, while the client usually resents having to pay for sex. It's the tension integrated into an illegal action on both sides that puts the defining moment at risk, the one in which payment is made or withheld for sex as the crucial deciding point. Wilde was known as a soft touch for his generosity, with Alfred Taylor, Wilde's regular procurer, telling William Parker, after Wilde chose his brother Charles, 'Your brother is lucky. Oscar does not care what he pays if he fancies a chap.' Freddie Atkins, a generic Dilly rogue, was taken by Wilde to Paris, and stayed with him at 29 Boulevard des Capucines, hung out in the Café Julien, and got his hair done by Pascal at the Grand Hotel in return for peddling his ass, and Wilde generally threw at rent money he didn't have, not only to broker sexual deals, but because as a hedonist he lived constantly in the optimally charged moment. It was Atkins who, on coming back to their hotel in Paris, discovered Wilde in bed with Maurice Schwabe, as an extra bit on the side. Freddie Atkins, who was seventeen when he met Wilde, had been variously a billiard marker, a bookmaker's clerk and a drag artiste working as a female impersonator at the Oxford Music Hall 14–16 Oxford Street, and at the Arches in Villiers Street by Charing Cross Station, under the travesti name Fred Denny, and at the time lived with a fifty something bookmaker, James Dennis Burton, who carried on a lucrative sideline in blackmail, employing not only Freddie, but Charlie and William Parker, to solicit men for sex, take them back to Burton's home in Coventry Street, and have Burton intrude on active sex scenes and blackmail the victims for corrupting his teen 'nephews.' Freddie Atkins lived at 124 Tachbrook Street, Pimlico, picked up at the Dilly and also at the Empire Promenade at the back of the circle at the Alhambra, and was part of a teen forum groomed by Burton for the purposes of entrapment and blackmail.

Freddie Atkins first met Wilde at the Café Royal on Regent Street, 100 yards from Piccadilly Circus, and was briefly employed euphemistically as Wilde's secretary, the job, according to Atkins, involving 'writing out only half a page of manuscript which took about ten minutes' before Wilde 'made improper proposals.' Atkins, who was thuggish was in the habit of robbing punters of money and gold watches, and had been apprehended previous to his criminal associations with Wilde by police constables 396A and 500A from Rochester Row Police Station, after an attempt to rob a punter from Birmingham at Tachbrook Street had gone wrong, with the man standing up physically to both Atkins and Burton after being persuaded to write out a cheque for £200 in the name of Fred Denny. The man had dropped charges in the interests of maintaining privacy, but extortion was for Atkins a lucrative and obligatory extension of rent. Questioned about the incident during Wilde's second trial, and quite clearly lying, Atkins claimed. 'I was not charged. I hit a man I'd met the same night at the Alhambra Music Hall and taken home to my room in Tachbrook Street for a game of cards.' Wilde, who paid on average between £2–£5 for sex, gave over the going rate probably to avoid intimidation from nasty nuggets like Atkins, although he couldn't circumvent the viral strain of endemic blackmail that rent used as weaponry to intimidate punters. Freddie Atkins was one of the numerous Dilly boys, including Charles Parker and Harry Barford, who Thomas Price, head waiter at the private hotel 10 St James' Place, where Wilde had rooms from October 1893 to April 1894, recalled as boys of 'quite inferior station' visiting Wilde there for sexual purposes.

Before CCTV surveillance cameras became operative in the West End, Dilly boys were the London eye who saw and heard everything from their monitoring posts at Piccadilly Circus, because so much of confidential London ended up getting dumped there as sensitive data on bitchy, gossipy kids whose rough street appeal polarised sex. And while Dilly boys have always comprised a destabilising mix of gay and straight sex adventurers, Freddie Atkins, who appears to have been gay, used his sexuality to exploit and intimidate vulnerable gays terrified of being turned into the police for their actions. Atkins was what Wilde called a 'street Arab', an early term for a Dilly boy, while other current street lingo was 'poof', 'fairy', 'mandrake', 'Nancy boy,' 'back gammon player.' And also 'gay', as evidenced by Jack Saul: 'I am still a professional Maryanne. I have lost my character and cannot get on otherwise. I occasionally do jobs for different gay people.' The word 'trade' adapted for usage as 'rough trade,' was also a street term when Wilde was an active Dilly punter, as instanced by the cross-dressing Boulton in a letter to A. Pelham Clinton. 'I am not going to apologise for being too solicitous today. I will confess I give you reason to think that I care for nothing but trade, and I think you care too little for it, as far as I am concerned.' Straight rent, like some of Wilde's dodgy pick-ups, were the most deviant, because they were motivated either by the need to eat, rob or, very often, blackmail.

Edward Shelley, who featured prominently in Wilde's second and third trials, was the second son of a blacksmith living in Fulham, and before starting work at the Bodley Head in 1890, the publisher conveniently sited at Vigo Street, off Piccadilly, had worked for Robert Bullock & Co, tea merchants, at 1 Dunster Court, Mincing Lane. Shelley, who wore a frock coat and was evidently an apprentice dandy, was seventeen when he met Wilde in the Vigo Street offices, and the two seem to have shared a genuinely sympathetic chemistry. According to evidence provided in Wilde's second and third trials from information supplied by Sidney Wright, porter at Wilde's Albermarle Club, Shelley, soon after meeting Wilde, went back to Wilde's suite at the Albermarle, drank whisky and sodas, got out of it, and was fucked by Wilde in the adjoining bedroom. Of the impropriety of the act in the prosecution's eyes, Edward Carson ventured:

C: On that occasion did you have a room leading into the bedroom?
W: Yes.
C: Did you give him whiskies and sodas?
W: I suppose he had whatever he wanted. I do not remember… He did not stay all night, neither did I embrace him.
C: Did you ever give him money?
W: Yes, on three occasions – the first time £4, the second time his rail fare to Cromer, where I invited him to meet my wife and family, and the third time £5.

C: Did you think this young man of eighteen was a proper companion for you?

W: Certainly.

C: Did you give him a signed copy of the first edition of *Dorian Gray*?

W: Yes.

It's noticeable how Edward Carson's line of prosecution follows very closely methods of entrapment employed by plain clothes in the fifties and sixties in the attempt to convict for a suppositional crime that remained purely hypothetical. Carson's attempt to implicitly colour a set of facts with the corollary that gay sex inevitably followed from giving Shelley drinks, and the fact that there was a bedroom attached to Wilde's suite at the Albermarle, is intended to suggest that Wilde paid for rent. Wilde's inscription in the copy of *Dorian Gray* he gave Shelley read: 'To Edward Shelley, poet and friend, from Oscar Wilde, poet and friend.' You can read 'friend' how you like.

The artist's impression of Edward Shelley in court suggests a morosely introspective individual with short-styled hair and the sad look of someone who really isn't sure of himself, possibly confused by his sexuality, and not streetwise like Freddie Atkins, Charlie and William Parker, Alfred Wood or whoever Wilde got at Piccadilly Circus. Who exactly is Edward Shelley to 21st century readers, a sleazy fact molecularized by neural pathways into the configurative idea of one of Wilde's rent boys, who may have hung out outside Swan & Edgar to supplement his income as a publisher's assistant. I'm thinking of an abstract, a celeb-obsessed wannabe writer, a kid on the make whose life got irreparably messed up by the Wilde trial and who was bought for £20 to give evidence against Wilde. That Shelley was inveterately duplicitous and used his position at the strained partnership Elkin Matthews and John Lane to continuously supply Lane with pejorative information on Matthews, and that his tone was sticky, and knife-twisting, can be evidenced in his undercover letters to Lane. 'I should like to have a few minutes conversation with you, nothing very important, that can be used to advantage. If I see you, before I can receive a reply, make some sign to me, in which I shall know where to meet you. If you cannot do that with safety, please shut the door if I am to meet you at the coffee-house but leave the door open (as you come in) if you cannot meet me.'

Shelley's iffy mind-set, like a dodgy snoop, manifests the potential for blackmail through surveillance, and has all of a Dilly boy's conniving gymnastics in informing and exploiting. Shelley may have had something sexually going with John Lane, and Wilde, in picking him up and taking him to the Albermarle in Piccadilly, was putting himself immediately in danger, in the same way as punters picking up Dilly boys in the 1970s and taking them to the nearby Regent Palace Hotel often met with unstable personalities, systemised into denial of their homosexuality, and selling sex as the incentive to intimidate, exploit or work on the punter's vulnerability. According to Shelley, 'Mr Wilde kissed me. He also put his arms around me. I felt insulted, degraded, and objected vigorously.' Shelley claimed that his resistance didn't stop Wilde handling his cock and that the two ended up in bed, and that he returned the following night for more sex. We learn too from the prosecution Edward Carson, the physical places in the capital's West End where Wilde took Shelley as a personalised topography, the Independent Theatre in Soho's Dean Street, the Earls Court Exhibition, the Lyric Club at Piccadilly, the Café Royal on Regent Street, Kettner's in Church Street, Soho and Wilde's own house in Tite Street, Chelsea.

Edward Shelley, who was paid fifteen shillings a week by John Lane, dressed and lived beyond his means, and was most certainly on the game. He was also a serious depressive, delusional at times and violent, too, in that he was arrested for assaulting his father and had to be bailed out by Wilde. Clearly pathologically self-loathing and torn up by what he thought of as his aberrant sexuality, his psychology fitted closely with a category of Dilly rent who were essentially homophobic, but willing to sell sex along complex pathways motivated ultimately by revenge. Edward Shelley's fuckedness quotient grew in proportion to his realisation that he was simply one of Wilde's many boys, and he clearly had aspirations to be the only one and to being kept. Something about Shelley's depressive-anxiety symptoms warned Wilde away, but he must have known Shelley would come back at him. 'I would have called on you this evening,' Shelley wrote, 'but I am suffering from nervousness, the result of insomnia, and am obliged to remain at home.' Shelley had been kicked out of home by his father – quite possibly for being suspected gay – telling Wilde in a letter, 'I have had a very horrible interview with my father and been told to leave the house.' A distinct strain of Dilly boy has always been the teen runaway who ends up on the meat rack after being thrown out of home, traumatised, on the rebound, often, of domestic violence, and doing rent both to eat and in a perverse way to make their rejection public by taking it to the centre of the world – Piccadilly Circus – and rubbing their outraged banditry into people's faces.

From correspondence read in court, we know that Shelley was now living at 3 Hildyard Road, Earls Court, had lost his job with Matthews and Lane, and had clearly been ridiculed for his relations with Wilde, referring to 'the stupid brutal insults at Vigo Street,' and his apparent poverty. 'Here I am stranded and without hope. I do not ask for more than sufficient to live upon, and by strict economy I can live on six pounds per month, but even this I cannot obtain . . . I am in torture and do not know what to do.' Shelley was fired from his Vigo Street publishing job due to rumours of his prostitution to Wilde, a link that had the staff injuriously call him 'Mrs Wilde and Miss Oscar.'

Things collapsed fast in Shelley's life. His best friend Charley

Hinxman died, he and his one time employer John Lane were at enmity, and the reasons may have been sexual – 'the loss he has put me to is beyond his power to repair' – and geographically Shelley was hanging out in the East End. 'I am frequently in the East End and have traversed the region known as Leman Street, Whitechapel. The sight of those poor hungry souls is a never to be forgotten one. I am afraid sometimes that I am not very sane. I feel so nervous and ill.'

What exactly Shelley was doing hanging out in Whitechapel we don't know: was he selling sex or, in his breakdown state, identifying with real losers? But the tone of his letters lean on Wilde financially without directly resorting to blackmail. Edward Shelley wasn't homeless, but he was understandably desperate, and wanted what he thought Wilde had – flashy bling. That he could be bought to testify against Wilde suggests he was open to being paid by both sides and fundamentally corrupt. Speaking about the first time he had sex with Wilde, Shelley admitted to his profession: 'I was entrapped…he took advantage of me, of my admiration, and of – I won't say innocence – I don't know what to call it.'

What Wilde couldn't predict, of course, was what Shelley was really thinking when they had sex; and the complex nature of guilt compounded into the boy's dangerously vulnerable personality that had him both on the make and at the same time despise himself for being rent. Shelley was toxic to Wilde because he had the street savvy of a cultural wannabe and a sufficiently subtle know-how to bring him down. Of the rent boys who surfaced in Wilde's trial, Shelley was by far the most damaging, not only because he was generically Dilly, but because his fringe association with one of Wilde's publishers made him appear fractionally more credible in supplying evidence bought by the Crown, than the blackmailing trio Alfred Wood, Charlie and William Parker. Wilde's romantically real conception of rent was colour-saturated by underworld mythology.

According to his friend Vincent O'Sullivan, in his book *Aspects of Wilde*, 'one day about a year before his trial, I met him at the Café Royal. He seemed rather upset. "There is a dreadful youth waiting for me in Regent Street. He is pacing up and down before the door like a wonderful black panther. I think he must be there still. Do go and see. If he is, I shall go out by the side door."' What O'Sullivan saw when he went outside was Dilly rough trade looking undoubtedly to blackmail Wilde or extort money in return for shutting up. And in relation to Wilde's fixation with Piccadilly as the rent epicentre, he relates how the poet Ernest Dowson, on visiting Wilde early one evening at the Berkeley Hotel in Piccadilly, found Wilde in bed propped up with pillows and engaged solipsistically in pasting newspaper clippings about his celebrity into a large scrapbook. It should be remembered, too, that Wilde was fixated on icons like Rejane, Sarah Bernhardt and the punkish, drawlish English music hall singer, Marie Lloyd.

Charlie and William Parker were wised-up butch-looking teens who first met the procurer Alfred Taylor, and his partner Edward Harrington, at the rent boy pick up bar at St James' Restaurant, 24–26 Piccadilly in 1893, broke, unemployed, wanting to hustle, and already experienced as rent. On meeting Alfred Taylor Charlie recalled him 'drawing attention to the prostitutes who frequented Piccadilly Circus,' saying, 'I can't understand sensible men wasting their money on painted trash like that. Many do, though. But there are a few who know better. Now, you could get money in a certain way easily enough if you cared to.' Charlie had been fired from his position as a gentleman's valet, William had been a groom (their father was a horse-dealer) and Taylor, knowing they were homeless, gave the brothers a room in his house at 13 Little College Street, in return for sex, and with the knowledge he could easily pimp the boys to his apparently affluent clients like Oscar Wilde. According to Charlie, under prosecution, 'I said that if any old gentleman with money took a fancy to me, I was agreeable. I was agreeable. I was terribly hard up.' Alfred Taylor, who occupied a four-room permanently shuttered first floor above a disused bakery in Westminster's 13 Little College Street, rented from Mrs Ellen Grant for £3 a week, and did his own cooking on a gas stove, had rapidly burnt up an inherited fortune of £45,000 from a father who was a wealthy cocoa manufacturer, and effectively pimped rent he picked up on the street or in bars. Taylor's floor, a sort of quasi-bohemian squat, contained a mattress on the floor, low lighting from coloured lamps, incense burners, a drag wardrobe, harboured a miscellany of continually renewed boys, and was ostensibly a safe house for gays like Wilde looking to pay for casual sex.

The introduction to Wilde came on 10th March 1893, a forensically cold blue Soho evening, when, ostensibly to celebrate Alfred Taylor's birthday, Wilde took Taylor and his two butch escorts dressed in tight-fitting suits to his preferred restaurant, Kettner's in Church Street, Soho, where the manager, Giovanni Sangiorgi appears to have been sympathetic to Wilde's habit of taking rent there for dinner, always in a private room with red-shaded lamps and a piano. It must have been as obvious to Giovanni that Wilde was using his restaurant for rent assignations, as was for staff at reception in the Regent Palace Hotel in the nineteen seventies and eighties, when punters, having picked up (usually at Exit 1 Piccadilly Circus underground), would hire a room at the hotel for immediate sex.

Wilde, it seems, instantly took to Charlie and they had something going from the start, a gelled sexual chemistry, with William observing that the solicitous Wilde, drunk as always, 'often fed my brother off his own fork or out of his own spoon,' and that the two French-kissed a preserved cherry from mouth to mouth several times, as a smoochy prelude to the oral gymnastics Wilde already anticipated.

Wilde, who was living dangerously on credit, took the incredulous Charlie back to the Savoy, to rooms 361 and 362, where, after drinking Perrier Jouet champagne, they had oral sex. According to Charlie, who claimed to be resistant, 'I was asked by Wilde to imagine that I was a woman and that he was my lover. I had to keep up this illusion. I used to sit on his knees and he used to play with my privates as a man might amuse himself with a girl.' And according to Charlie's contradictory statements on other occasions, referring to Wilde as punter, 'I tossed him off and he would do the same to me. He suggested two or three times that I would permit him to insert it in my mouth, but I would never allow that.'

Charlie Parker's initial statement provides valuable insight into one of Wilde's role-playing demands as a punter, for which Charlie claimed he was paid £2 for two hours. Wilde, it appeared, had sex with Charlie Parker at a number of addresses, given as the Savoy, No. 7 Camera Square, No. 50 Park Walk and No. 10 St James' Place. In the second of Wilde's three trials, Charlie, under interrogation, claimed that Wilde had sodomized him, with Jane Cotta, a chambermaid at the Savoy, supplying graphic corroborating evidence as to the lubed state of the messy linen sheets, still sticky with Vaseline. Charlie was generic Dilly street dodgy, and under examination in Wilde's trial by the defence as to the unreliability of his character, he defended himself against blackmailing charges with the sort of confused sexual motives common to so many Piccadilly hustlers. 'I have accepted money, but it has been offered to me to pay for the offence. I have been solicited. I have never suggested this offence to gentlemen.' Charlie's notion of being the disinterested passive party in what he called 'the offence', and to being solicited rather than importuning was, of course, designed to have him appear a victim of sexual predators, like Wilde, but the duplicity of his statement is apparent in the lie that he never importuned. Asked about Wilde's gifts of a silver cigarette case and a gold ring, Charlie's feminine aspects showed through quite clearly in his reply. 'I don't suppose boys are different to girls in taking presents from them who are fond of them.' Charlie also confessed to going back to Wilde's Chelsea home to stay the night. 'We went to Tite Street. It was very late at night. Wilde let himself and me in with a latchkey. I remained the night, sleeping with the prisoner, and he himself let me out in the early morning before anyone was about.' They additionally had sex at Parker's room at Park Walk, an act overheard by his landlady who threw him out the next day. Wilde was pushing his luck with hustlers, and according to Charlie, 'he came in a cab and drove away after staying about a quarter of an hour, having kept the cab waiting outside.' Charlie gave the time specifically as about eleven-thirty or twelve. Wilde was a night person, an outlaw who cabbed across the capital with rent, but who was always watched by the ubiquitous London eye.

Whatever Charlie's deceptions, Wilde was very clearly a benign punter, and none of his rent ever met with the sort of aggro, brutality and humiliation they probably encountered elsewhere along the way. Wilde's problem was that his innate generosity was met with testy suspicion by the confused personalities of boys used to hard bargaining for cash, and he was additionally physically vulnerable, and knew that rent could turn nasty and paid over the odds to compensate. Alfred Taylor, who was entrepreneurial in selecting suitable types for Wilde – they had to be clean-shaven pretty boys with some attitude – also introduced Wilde to Sidney Mavor, having picked Sid up at the Gaiety Theatre in September, 1892. Sid, who lived with his mother in South Kensington, and went under the name Jenny, worked for a small business manufacturing and supplying lamp-wicks, as well as acting as one of Taylor's male escorts. Sid or Jenny, according to smoke and mirrors reinvention, was introduced to Wilde at Kettners on October 3rd, 1892, by now the accepted HQ for Wilde's assignations. According to Sid, who arrived with Taylor at the private room at Kettners on an abruptly showery

October evening, Taylor characteristically remarked, 'I'm glad you've made yourself pretty. Mr Wilde likes nice clean boys.' Sid went back later that night with Wilde to the Albemarle Hotel and had sex with Oscar in his room, got paid £2, and a few days later was gifted with an expensive silver cigarette case inscribed, 'Sidney from O.W. October 1892.' Sid, despite being coerced into bringing allegations against Wilde, denied when summoned as a witness for the Crown that any improprieties had taken place between him and Wilde, perhaps wanting to save his own face, or as an act of defiance against the systemised abuse of justice being used like a handgun against Wilde. It was Sid and not Jenny who was in denial, and, by his stand, fucking with the snakebite of Carson's venomous line of enquiry.

It was, in fact, Sid's courage that provoked Wilde's principal partner, the sexed-up blond aristo, Lord Alfred Douglas (whose father the Marquess of Queensbury had threateningly bribed Sid into making a statement), to make one of the most powerfully crunching defences of male prostitution in a full-on attack at W.T. Stead's sensationally vilifying reportage of the Wilde case in *The Review of Reviews*. Writing from Hotel De La Poste Rouen, 28th June 1895, where he was in hiding, Douglas projected a controlled, eloquent fury at discrimination in sexual politics. 'I am not pleading for prostitution, but I think if a man who affects female prostitutes is unmolested it is disgraceful that a man who prefers male prostitutes should be thus barbarously punished. The only difference is that the man who brings bastards into the world, who seduces girls or commits adultery does an immense amount of harm, as you have yourself pointed out, whereas the queer does absolutely no harm to anyone.' Detractors of Douglas as a duplicitous, shape-shifting trickster, partly instrumental in Wilde's catastrophic ruin, and absent from his defence, sometimes overlook Douglas' volatile temerity in attempting to broker equality for same-sex relations. 'Why on earth in the name of liberty and common sense a man cannot be allowed to love a boy, rather than a woman when his nature and his instinct tell him to do so…is another question to which I should like to hear a satisfactory answer.' Douglas' spray-canned hissy invective in this letter, effectively criminalising himself by his own admissions – he had shared most of Wilde's rent – went unnoticed in the consensus of acrimony directed against Wilde; but the tonal gesture is one of an impacted fist rather than a derisory, limp-wristed fizzle. Impotent to effect change, and socially degraded by Wilde's conviction, Douglas remained unapologetically shameless in his slashing at moral hypocrisy, and toxic in that he knew the inside track of Wilde's story, what was true and what was manufactured to stitch him up indefensibly by a prosecution intent on shattering.

I'm concerned with Wilde's London boys, rather like David Bowie's 'London Boys' (1967), as a lyric opening a gateway into runaway deprivation, homelessness, drugs, discovering Soho's Wardour Street, and finding solidarity in what for Bowie was the Mod look as axiomatic of a lifestyle themed by sexual ambiguity.

On trial, Wilde, facing Carson's insidiously slippery tone, confessed to having been introduced to 'six-seven-eight' bits of trade by Alfred Taylor, who had moved to 3 Chapel Street in Soho, after quitting his blacked-out floor in Little College Street; and these were all London boys or Dilly boys. Asked about whether he knew Charlie Parker was only seventeen, and clearly rent, Wilde in denial responded, 'You cannot ask me a question about which I know nothing. I don't know his age, he may be sixteen or forty-five, don't ask me about it. I think he was about twenty. If you cross-examine me on the question whether he was seventeen, I have never asked him his age. It is rather vulgar to ask people their ages.'

The other London boys of interest in Wilde's case were all hustling blackmailers – the nineteen-year-old Alfred Wood, living at 50 Medina Road N. London, who lived by prostituting himself with a view to extortion, and the notorious blackmailing duo William Allen and Robert Henry Cliburn (a.k.a. Harris, Collins, Stephenson, Robertson and Carew), both of whom hung out at changing addresses in Broadstairs, handled stolen goods, sheltered criminal offenders and generally mixed with lowlife and the underground. No matter that Wilde was on the receiving end of Allen and Cliburn, he perversely admired their invidious skills as blackmailers, noting in *De Profundis* that 'Cliburn and Atkins were wonderful in their infamous war against life. To entertain them was an astounding adventure,' while Wilde's friend George Ives, who founded the Order of Chaeronea, the secret society of homosexuals to which Wilde belonged, described Cliburn in his diary as 'one of the biggest blackmailers in London,' and as having 'a beautiful but mad face, the face of a tiger though very handsome.' It's interesting that to Wilde the likes of rent and blackmailers were referred to as panthers, and to Ives as tigers, with both men captivated by the predatory looks of the boys squeezing them for money. Alfred Wood, Charlie Parker and William Allen sometimes worked together as a ring to trap unsuspecting gays, with Wood admitting his involvement with the other two in extorting money from a man in the second and third of Wilde's trials.

Alfred Wood was one of Taylor's groomed Dilly boys, a blond butch teen who was introduced to Wilde at the Café Royal, given drinks and taken to dinner at the Florence Restaurant in nearby Rupert Street, where according to him, Wilde 'put his hand inside my trousers beneath the table at dinner and compelled me to do the same to him.' What's interesting here is not only the association between queers and criminals, but the smoke and mirrors confusion of queers turned blackmailers, in the sense that there was no way that Alfred Wood, Charlie Parker or William Allen were straight. On the contrary, they were rogue operatives exploiting the minority to which they belonged, either from homophobic or criminal motives, as part of the B-side Dilly consortium of confused issues that have consistently involved potential damage on both sides as the outcome of sex. It was, of course, the fact that the Dilly was criminal that so appealed to the aspect of Wilde who was turned on by his opposite, mean scheming little Johnnies who lived off the grimy street.

With Wilde's wife away, he took Alfred Wood back from the Florence to his house at 34 Tite Street, Chelsea for sex. The two drank Wilde's favourite hock and seltzers before having sex, during which, according to Wood, Oscar ejaculated on his bottom without penetration. According to Wood, the liaison continued over a couple of weeks at Chelsea, with Wilde regularly waiting for him under a lamppost between 10 p.m. and midnight on the corner of Tite Street before taking him home. Wood's admission, and a serious one, was that 'it was a long time, however, before I would allow him to actually do the act of sodomy,' suggesting that Wilde's objective all along was to fuck him on a financial scale ascending from two to three to four pounds in the pursuit of optimal pleasure.

Wilde's relations with Wood, though, were only the half of it, because Lord Alfred Douglas' kick was usually to share Wilde's Dilly boys, and Wood, after Wilde had dispensed with him, joined Bosie at the Mitre Hotel in Oxford, where Douglas, attempting to make Wood look less street, loaned him a suit with a highly compromising letter from Wilde still in the pocket. Securing the letter, Wood, with his blackmailer's nose, sniffing like a coke addict for a line, discovered while Douglas was sleeping a handful of sensitive letters concealed in a scarlet morocco box, mostly from Wilde to Douglas, and stole them, aware immediately of the potential for lucrative blackmail.

Through Alfred Taylor, and being one of his pimped boys on the game, Wood had met the blackmailing duo central to the Cleveland Street scandal, William Allen and Robert Cliburn, both of whom were smartly adept at stealing any incriminating letters or documentation from their clients, and often instigated sex specifically in the interests of blackmail. Wilde had unsuspectingly got into a network of underground operatives, sticky as a spaghetti parcel-looped on a fork, and Wilde, independently of Alfred (was he Alf or Alfie in bed?) had to admit to his counsel, Edward Clarke, 'some time ago I was turned out of the Albemarle hotel in the middle of the night and a boy was with me. It might be awkward if they found out about that.'

Alf Wood, though, was in return being screwed by Allen and Cliburn, and while he had no option but to hand over the most compromising of Wilde's letters to Lord Alfred Douglas to the firm, he managed to keep back three of Wilde's letters, as well as some particularly toxic ones from D'Oyly Carte to Douglas, all of which were saturated with pointers to teen rent, and Wood now found himself in an underworld of vicious Piccadilly queers working connivingly against each other for financial advantage with Wilde as their fall man. Wood panicked. As rent and a thief he couldn't go to the law, and he couldn't any longer hang out at the St James' bar or the Crown or the Alhambra selling sex because Allen and Cliburn were on his trail. Wood was running scared and his procurer, Alfred Taylor, wasn't strong enough to stand up for him against the firm. Wood moved to Langham Street and was in hiding after being chased across Leicester Square at night by one of Allen's gang. Wilde, meanwhile, consulted George Lewis, a solicitor who specialised in blackmail cases and who wrote a sufficiently threatening letter to Wood, the outcome of which was, after weeks of delaying tactics, an arranged meeting between Wilde and Wood at Alfred Taylor's Little College Street flat, where Wood was in hiding. Alf handed back to Wilde three of his compromising letters to Lord Alfred Douglas in return for £30, two £10 notes and two £5 notes, with another fiver to follow the next day, to assist Wood to get away and start a new life in America. Wood was hunted and in a state of panic, as Allen and Cliburn's network trawled the familiar bars, urinals and pick-up places looking for him, and he managed to hold up for another three weeks before sailing for New York on the SS Servia on April 15th, 1893, much to Wilde's inestimable relief. Unfortunately for Wilde, though, the principally incriminating letter of his to Douglas, the one containing the phrase 'madness of kisses', remained in Allen and Cliburn's possession.

Wilde was inextricably locked into a criminal subculture in which he could understandably trust no one. The boys he fucked were sometimes queer and sometimes straight, identified with neither, stole, and with Queensberry's former Scotland Yard private detectives, Inspector Littlechild and Frederick Kearley, diligently searching the West End for Wilde's Dilly boys, the heat was palpably on. The gateway, of course, through underground signposting, led to Alfred Taylor, who very negligently, on leaving his flat at 3 Chapel Street, Belgravia, owing money to his landlady Sophia Gray, had left behind a hatbox of letters including a number written by Wilde to the likes of Freddie Atkins: 'Obliged to see Tree at 5 o'clock so don't come to the Savoy. Let me know at once about Fred.'

Retrieved as evidence, and used by the prosecution against Wilde, the word 'Fred' used in this implicitly importuning context smacked of rent, with Wilde clearly placing an order for Freddie Atkins like a takeaway.

As sticky was a letter from Taylor's partner, Charles Spurrier Mason, asking for money as trade had been slow. 'Soon as you can afford it to let me have some money, I shall be pleased and obliged. I would not ask you if I could get any myself, you know. Business is not so easy as one would think. There is a lot of trouble attached to it.'

The Marquess of Queensberry's two private eyes, together with the militantly interrogative Charles Russell, now concentrated on Piccadilly and its Dilly boys as their investigative focus. They dragged them all in, threatening to rough them up if they didn't make statements, Alfred Taylor, William Allen, Robert Cliburn, Freddie Atkins, Sid Mavor and Charlie and William Parker, a boy known as Hades, countless gossipy, hissy and breakable little Dilly rough rhinestones who had seen and heard, like Ginger; and went additionally to staff at Wilde's places, the Savoy, the Albemarle, Kettner's, the Florence restaurant, assembling facts from the underbelly of Wilde's life that could be consolidated trickily into impacted prosecution. Wilde's sticky network of underworld contacts was put under additional scrutiny, as the result of a midnight police raid on a house in Fitzroy Street in Bloomsbury in August 1894, when eighteen men were taken into custody, including Alfred Taylor and Charlie Parker, for what was described as a gay orgy. Bound over after a week's remand, Taylor and Parker were referred to by the magistrate as men of 'the vilest possible character.'

That Wilde had reacted so indignantly to the Marquess of Queensberry's card left at the Albemarle Club on 28th February 1895, with the hall porter Sydney Wright, on which he had scrawled, 'For Oscar Wilde, posing somdomite,' and decided to criminally libel Queensberry for the indictment, was only part of the reason for the Dilly round-up of rent by the thuggish quasi-legal authorities. A bigger cover-up was in operation to protect Lord Rosebery, the Prime Minister, currently undergoing both chronic influenza as a physical symptom and an acute nervous breakdown as a mental one, of a soupy undertow of gay allegations going all the way back to his involvement in the whitewashed Cleveland Street scandal. The suicidal Rosebery, clearly scenting in Wilde's case his own potential ruin – Queensberry had referred in a letter read by the police to 'snob queers like Rosebery' – attempted to resign on Tuesday 19th February 1895, only to have his resignation blocked on the grounds of illness. Rosebery was at the time suffering from chronic sleep disorder and clinical depression, triggered in part by the assumed suicide of Francis Drumlanrig, his secretary and Lord Alfred Douglas' brother, found dead of a single shot in a turnip field at Malsey Cross Farm, Over Stowey, near Bridgwater in Somerset. It was widely suspected that Rosebery and Drumlanrig were lovers, and the Marquess of Queensberry had paid undercover to stalk Rosebery, as he had done Wilde, finding conclusively from the state of the sheets that the two men had fucked after a party at Bourne End on the Thames. While Drumlanrig's suicide was attributed to a shooting accident, or death by misadventure, Rosebery must have had inside knowledge of the facts and blamed himself in part for his friend's death at a time when the heat was on in London and its gays were getting collared and dragged into the spotlight.

Rosebery was sweating fear on his skin anticipating arrest, while Wilde's poker-face attitude in taking the offensive against Queensberry looked suspiciously more like effrontery than cool.

Wilde, like most Dilly punters, got locked into the confused notion of making a public space private, and of attempting to rehabilitate a commercialized precinct to a subcultural queer dominance. While the distance between the Café Royal in Regent Street, where Wilde drank absinthe, or the Lyric Club on Coventry Street to Piccadilly Circus, was only a matter of five minutes walking distance, the space crossed was charged with sexual possibilities in the randomised, maxxed-up compression of place into a coded sexual arena. At the Dilly, there's no yesterday or tomorrow, the past is as unreliable a source as the future, there's only the optimal present in all its observable risk to both punters and rent. The person you mistook for a regular, wasn't he plainclothes all along, and the other one Jim, a lawyer, isn't he really Richard who works in a Soho bar? The continuous morphing of identities into alternative states of coercion and threat was the Dilly dialect, and most Wilde biographers are understandably ignorant of the catastrophic dangers entailed by hijacking a public place to broker sexual deals. It's the speed and visual aggression of the place that throws you – all those anonymous strangers in your (Wilde's) face and nobody cares who drops down from impacted velocity.

You've only got to look at the drawing of Wilde's arrest at the Cadogan Hotel that appeared in the illustrated Police Budget, captioned, 'Pet of London society and one of our most successful playwrights and poets, arrested on a horrible charge,' to observe how the two Scotland Yard detectives are integrated into smoke and mirrors. Dressed in standard streetwear, long grey overcoats and top hats, and essentially undifferentiated from the nondescript, no-colour public, their style-less dress dissolves into the pedestrian. The two men look like Dilly watchers who could also be punters, and that was always Wilde's risk, being arrested by police pretending to be public. There's something shocking when somebody looking ordinary reveals themselves as an authority figure: it's like skinning an apple to find a twisted, blackened core.

Piccadilly Circus, created by John Nash in 1819 as part of the future King George IV's plan to connect Carlton House – where the Prince Regent resided – with Regent's Park – lost its circular form in 1886 with the construction of Shaftesbury Avenue. Wilde's Circus was a busy traffic junction connecting six roads, incorporating the Shaftesbury Memorial Fountain, erected in 1893 to commemorate the philanthropic works of Anthony Ashley Cooper, 7th Earl of Shaftesbury, and topped erotically by Alfred Gilbert's iconic nude statue of an archer, popularly called Eros, but lacked the Piccadilly Circus Tube station that opened on the 16th March 1906 on the Bakerloo line, and on the blue Piccadilly line in December of the same year. Wilde's Dilly included advertising hoardings, red roadsters, hangers out, homeless, rent, ubiquitous tourists, sex tourists, the law, the endless crunch of foot traffic churning into a six-way gateway into the West End – the radical inequality between rich and poor instantly apparent like contrasting colour blocks – you know the poor by their clothes, their smell, their TB cough, their bad diet, their acute resignation to irredeemable poverty. Wilde, on a run for a time, was dandified and had a cash flow from his popular plays, but was liquidating his earnings by spending excessively on Lord Alfred Douglas, who bled Oscar as a sugar daddy – onhotels, dinners, champagne and rent – and knew by the company he kept he could just as easily lose it all, and did. When you're a bohemian hedonist oxygenated by cash you invariably attract your opposite – lowlife – partially because they can be bought, but more significantly because the dodgy aspects they've cultivated in themselves to survive seem to manifest the bad luck that comes after good as a sort of correction in the natural order of chances. It's the idea you don't get nothing for nothing that sustains the dialect of gain converted into loss and money into sex. If Wilde was too generous for his milieu, then he actively got high on danger as a dopamine chemical flooding the brain, and because the Dilly was coded in secrecy he longed to draw attention to what he did as a cocksucker, to shock the public into an awareness of his double life. For Wilde as an attention-seeking celeb, it wasn't sufficient to be rumoured gay; he somehow wanted the public to have access to his sex life with Dilly boys, because he invited scandal, like Elvis Presley blasting his TV screens with automatics; and although he feared the criminal consequences of his actions, Wilde wanted the iconic, scandalous myth-making that came of being a notoriously intrepid Dilly punter. It wasn't enough to be rumoured gay, and to actively be seen with trade; Wilde secretly wanted the facts made public so as to shock. In 1895, the celeb Wilde hit the headlines – his contagiously hot play *An Ideal Husband* opened on 3rd January, while *The Importance of Being Earnest* was due for its West End premiere in February, a bonus that encouraged him to take up residency in Piccadilly's Albemarle Hotel, perfectly situated as a luxurious HQ in which to fuck rent.

Wilde's young friend George Ives, the founder of the Order of Chaeronea, invited to an ostentatiously camp dinner at the Continental, was the first to anticipate danger on his finely tuned same-sex radar. 'I wish they (Wilde and his 'set') were less extravagant and more real,' he confided in his diary, 'so gifted and so nice, and yet here is this terrible world waiting for the word of truth to set it free.'

Ives realised that Wilde was being watched by plain clothes police, and that his openly taking rent boys to dinner at places like Kettner's, the Florence and the Savoy was inevitably inviting not only hostile scrutiny, but forming the basis for arrest. Piccadilly Circus would come back at Wilde like slap off the walls picked up by mics as reverb. On Wednesday morning, 3rd April 1895, Wilde was telling his story at magistrates' court proceedings, Great Marlborough Street, Soho, after the Marquess of Queensberry was arrested at Carter's Hotel on a warrant from Wilde's solicitor, Charles Humphrey. According to Wilde, Queensberry reportedly, in reference to his alleged affair with Lord Alfred Douglas, said, ' "You were both kicked out of the Savoy Hotel at a moment's notice for your disgusting conduct." I said, "that is a lie." He said, "You have taken furnished rooms for him in Piccadilly." I said, "Somebody has been telling you an absurd set of lies about your son and me. I haven't done anything of the kind." He said, "I hear you were thoroughly well blackmailed last year for a disgusting sodomitic letter that you wrote my son."'

It was the first time that Piccadilly as a specific location had been mentioned in proceedings, as reported conversation on Wilde's part, but as the physical nucleus of his trouble, the rent centre from which news travelled. Wilde had earlier in the trial explained to the judge what the word 'rent' meant, giving far too much away in the admission of his involvement with Dilly boys. 'R-e-n-t. A slang term.' 'There is no use trying to "rent" you as you only laugh at us.' The fusion of Piccadilly and rent on Wilde's part, and his insider's knowledge of slang – rent was also a term for blackmail – seems to suggest he'd picked up the street lingo: ass peddler, cocksman, fag boy, commercial queer, man cunt and foot soldier, all being common usage.

Wilde's involvement with the Piccadilly milieu also extended to being a regular customer at Charles Hirsch's bookshop, Libraire Parisienne, in Coventry Street, where, according to a highly contentious account given by Charles Hirsch in his introduction to the first French translation of the pornographic novel *Teleny* (Paris, 1934, 2 vols, 300 numbered copies), Wilde, the assumed author, and his ring of collaborators deposited handwritten sections of the novel in the shop for safekeeping and anonymity in a sealed packet, each using Wilde's personal card as ID for accessing the manuscript. According to Hirsch, the manuscript was called for four times before it was returned to Wilde; and Hirsch, despite allegedly promising not to do so, read the highly compromising manuscript, noting it was in different hands, including Wilde's. The book's proto-gay-activist sections, and its explicit descriptions of same-sex acts, including one in which a wine bottle lubricated with paté and used as a massaging dildo breaks inside the protagonist's rectum, future-forwards the book more into the 1980s than the late nineteenth century, with its unapologetic tone of hardcore written into Soho that the publisher Leonard Smithers, for fear of being tracked, changed topographically to Paris. According to Hirsch, the book was extensively edited by Smithers, who added the subtitle, 'Or the Reverse of the Medal', and omitted the prologue. Written without financial incentive, and clearly for sexual kicks, and published by Leonard Smithers in an edition of 200 copies for subscribers only from the Smithers-Nichols imprint in Soho Square, *Teleny*'s putatively collaborative evolution began almost simultaneously with Wilde purchasing from Hirsch in 1890, 'obscene little books bearing an Amsterdam imprint,' with the carefully concealed manuscript trusted to Hirsch, and called for, according to his account, by each of the collaborators. 'I could easily see why,' Hirsch tells us, 'with his wife, children and servants, he [Wilde] could not leave this compromising extra-licentious manuscript at home.'

Why, then, did Hirsch, a noted translator of French pornography into English, want *Teleny* in his shop, given the shockwaves of homophobia transmitted by the Cleveland Street scandal, and the fact that he could have been prosecuted for its possession, jailed and shut down? Why did Charles Hirsch take the risk of acting as go-between in this matter? Was he paid by Wilde, or was he involved in the same gay subculture of rent and mean little street kids up the road at the Dilly? Hirsch tells us of Wilde's visits that, 'He rarely came alone. He was usually accompanied by distinguished young men who seemed to be writers or artists. They showed him a familiar deference. In a word he seemed the master surrounded by his pupils.' As a camp attachment to Wilde, his celebrity was used at the time to sell Gilbert & Sullivan's *Patience*, Madame Fontaine's Bosom Beautifier and Straiton & Storm's cigars.

Any dispute of Wilde's involvement in *Teleny* seems redundant, given that the majority of the descriptive writing so obviously carries, in its sensuous cataloguing, his individual signature, and quite clearly comprises the underbelly outtakes to Dorian Gray maxxed up to sensory overload. As a form, though, the novel didn't suit Wilde; it demanded the sort of self-disciplined, sustained writing to which he was characteristically disinclined; but writing for kicks, the lexicon of masturbatory fantasies that drives an explosive groove through *Teleny*, coincided with his surge of sexual activity in the early 1890s, when he became obsessed with rent, who, once having been used, came back at him like the backthrust of Boeing 747s queuing to take off at Heathrow on runway 26R.

Wilde's case presented a typical vice demographic: the apparently moneyed punter and the incongruous nature of his relations with rough trade, and, at first in denial of his obvious sexual activities, Wilde seems, as the case developed into a vicious network of irrefutably sticky content, to have accepted his role as disgraced punter, offering in return no criticism of the boys paid to drag him down morally to the bottom of the stairs, despite seeing his generosity spat back at him collusively, coercively and forensically factually, like an altered recreation of the past played back in the present, with bits of fiction added like nuts pitted in nougat pieces. Listening to what he'd supposedly done through other people's distortion of the facts wasn't easy, because, of course, their unreliable interpretation of events differed radically from his own, with what both had forgotten, or photoshopped mentally to appear credible, additionally confusing the mix. There was the problem, too, in court, of Wilde's dandified look, so that when libelling the Marquess of Queensberry, and reporting Queensberry's insulting queer allegations, 'I don't say that you are it, but you look it,' the disruptive laughter provoked by this comment had the judge threaten to clear the court. Wilde had dressed down for the occasion, wearing a black frock-coat, wing collar and black tie fastened with a diamond and sapphire pin, and elegant grey suede gloves. It was his affected camp gave him away, his manner of playing to the audience in defiance of the question, so, too, the provocatively gestural coloratura of his affected voice. Diffidence, arrogance and an unfaltering belief in his own unimpeachability did Wilde few favours in court, with the *Morning* reporting, 'His affected manner meant his replies were rather difficult to catch.'

Wilde's case occupies my time in a different century – I'm messaging from an iPhone while writing this at Patisserie Valerie on Soho's Old Compton Street – because it's written into a subcultural topography – the dirt like the polymer tooling on a pill that leaves signs, tracks, traces of slang and its underground coding on Piccadilly Circus. Wilde's fascination with the place was arguably like that of so many punters, motivated more by the awareness that this could be me selling, rather than buying sex, if the social equation was different. Invariably the rent boy is what the punter would like to have been at nineteen, but didn't dare, and buying his ass was the substitute in age, preventing the realisation of the need to go totally public as Dilly meat.

Wilde couldn't be rent so he fucked Dilly boys so as to be identified with them as scandal. It's the self-destructing symbiosis that put men on men in one of London's most conspicuous public spaces with the unconscious realisation that the sexiest thing isn't orgasm, but being caught.

Wilde, who used to visit his close friend, the quasi-Masonic George Ives, at his booklined apartment at E4, the Albany Piccadilly, also helped out with the cult's general policy of financial help and advice given to punters blackmailed or ruined by the law. Ives' personal papers suggest a consolidated proto-support-line, a place where disaffected gays could find safe refuge, and if not counselling, then a system of emotional backup that involved community, and to which Wilde personally contributed.

Jack Saul admits a constant in his rent boy memoirs, when he confides, 'the extent to which sodomy is carried on in London between gentlemen and young fellows is little dreamed of by the outside public.' Writing his book in a café at the Haymarket, and using the slang term 'mancunt' for arse, Saul, and if he'd met Wilde he would certainly have let us know, tells us: 'There isn't a girl about Leicester Square but what would like to have me for her man, but I find it more to my interest not to waste my time on women. These clandestine games pay so well, and are quite more enjoyable. I wouldn't have a woman unless well paid for it.' Again there's the twist of ambiguity, like a lemon slice in gin, of an achievable bisexuality, like most of Wilde's rent, as though the orientation can be switched to heterosexual gigolo if the money's right. Wilde must have known that, perhaps with the exception of the delusional Edward Shelley, most of his boys were in the Dilly tradition of straight/bi, but sufficiently ambivalent to sell themselves on the rack as criminally gay.

It's not without significance that Piccadilly as a London commercial zone got its name in 1717 from a designer called

Roger Baker who lived in the area, and created a popular frilled collar called a piccadil; and got rich from retailing his design to period dandies wanting to get in on the look. If Wilde's psychogeography of the Dilly was predominantly subcultural, then access to a secret mapping of the precinct began to show in his dissipated look – he was drinking all day to cope with his controversial celebrity: hock and seltzer, absinthe, cognac, wine, champagne, incessantly chain-smoking for nicotine hits, wearing green carnations bought from Goodyear's the florist in the Royal Arcade for queer coding, and assuming the defiant attitude of punter identifying with rent, as an almost symbiotic association of criminality in which the respective roles take on significant interchangeable visual aspects of each other. If you work the Dilly you can recognize punters outright, no matter their nationality or profession, and that's an intuitive-radar thing; you know them by their singular concentration on not wanting to be obviously recognizable, the fugitive look in their eyes, the often downturned lip, the slightly arrested slo-mo approach, and an attempted self-assertiveness trying to cover tracks for guilt. Most come at you tangentially, as though they really aimed somewhere else, and have suddenly been startled into accidental awareness you're there, having most likely been watching you dodgily out of sight for a long time. It's that time-lag that sometimes gives you the feeling you've met this person somewhere before, even if they are a stranger. I mean, of course I know you, as you've been soaking me up with surveillance for half an hour, and now you've surprised me.

Wilde would have had his own strategy for tricky Dilly boys punking it outside Swan & Edgar's. One bit's there to attract the other, and neither have rights to hang out in a public space monitored by the Met. And if I didn't meet you today, I'd meet you tomorrow, and leave you singing 'Baby Come Back'.

It's the sense of betrayal, too, that's endemic to the place, as nobody's going to stand up for rent. Four years before Wilde's arrest, the North London Press had carried the headline, 'The West End Scandals: Names of Some of the Distinguished Criminals Who Have Escaped', in reference, of course, to the Cleveland Street raid and arrests. The distinguished criminals hinted at were, of course, aristo punters like Lord Arthur Somerset and the Earl of Euston, described as 'inculpated in disgusting practices' (i.e. cocksucking and fucking). Most of the rent involved migrated from Fitzrovia to Piccadilly Circus, where Wilde was starting to look like a physical extension of the place: a faggy Alhambra out-take camped in foppish astrakhan. Wilde, whose image was pop, had a way of offending the public through his look. After the premiere of *Lady Windermere's Fan* (Feb 1892), Wilde had taken to the stage by way of an ostentatious encore, a fag insolently drooping from his mouth like Ronnie Wood, 'a metallic blue carnation' badged on a lapel, to pitch a piece of suitably camp impudence. Wilde smacked the audience with quips that were leather-cuffed: 'I congratulate you on the great success of your performance, which persuades me to think almost as highly of the play as I do of myself.' Wilde's tartish affectation was sent up by the media and he couldn't have cared less.

But Dilly blackmail was corkscrewed into the urban underbelly, and Jack Saul relates something of its vicious tone in his rent boy confessions, through citing a professional blackmailer, the teen Dilly boy, Yonny Wilson's method as, 'Don't I know too well that little boys only get five or ten shillings after it's all over? But that won't do for me, no shell out at once, or I'll raise the house, and a pretty scandal that will be. That frightens them at once, so I always get five pounds, and sometimes more, as I take care to write and borrow as much as I can afterwards. There's nothing like bleeding one of those old fellows, and young ones better still – they are so easily frightened.'

That was Wilde's pit; the fundamental denial and self-hatred of rent for selling sex, directed at the punter for buying it, with the opposing tensions proving irreconcilable. You can't just be turned on by anyone, and Wilde was starting to bloat from booze, lack of exercise and hydrogenated fat-saturated restaurant food. Acutely hedonistic, a gastro-enthusiast who would have welcomed Helmut Blumenthal, the haute-cuisine Hitler to his profession, Wilde's physical body was clearly unattractive to some of his pick ups as sex workers – he was climbing into his late thirties, was physically unfit, and got sex because at the time he could pay. But what if you don't feel attracted to a 34/36" waist, if you lack aesthetic and any intellectual take on sophisticated repartee, what do you do with this oversexed same-sex bon viveur, who weighs 200 lbs, is probably an STD carrier, is monitored by plain clothes, and who believes in the unimpeachable right of artists to defy the law? We don't have it on record that Wilde was ever gay-bashed, mugged or abused, but there must have been a dangerous flip-side, other than blackmail, to his liaisons with rough trade. Wilde, partly through his rejection of inherited class, had dipped into the city's grimily networked underworld, and was fascinated by his romantic conception of criminals, fraudsters and queers as dose-sensitive to money however illegally it was obtained. While Wilde believed 'art is rarely intelligible to the criminal classes,' paradoxically he lived as a sexual criminal attracted to the same, as well as the ambiguous rogue outlaws linked to the manipulatively complex pattern. Wilde was, for instance, particularly attracted to one of his principal blackmailers, the good-looker Robert Cliburn, and, according to diary records from George Ives, questioned Cliburn about being rent: 'Did you ever love any boy for his own sake?' to be given the reported reply: 'No, Oscar, I can't say that I ever did.'

Cliburn's dissociation from emotional involvement with clients brings us back to the conundrum of apparently straight rent that always characterised the Dilly ethos, the morphing of sexual identities into monetised roles – bodies that are queer for trade, then revert to being quasi-straight. But straight men usually can't do same-sex without a physical resistance, or antipathy to the act, unless they're doing drugs or curious to experiment. A century before the 1985 founding of Streetwise Youth, a London-based charity targeting young, male, often homeless rent boys, as a drop-in day centre for those selling their bodies as illegal resources, Dilly boys slept rough, but still reverted to prostitution often as a singular source of income. And even if you're selling to stay alive, and some of Wilde's rent boys were doing just that, it's still problematic to bend orientation into altered states, unless there's some propensity for same-sex encounters, an undercover repressed gene signalling gay.

It's often the sense of irrational fear that hits you at Piccadilly Circus, and Wilde, for all his attitude and dexterous verbal front, must have experienced shock-waves of fear in approaching and sometimes being rejected or menaced by rent or 'panthers.' We know through the documentation of Wilde's three trials only his relations with boys who were either procured for him, or came through a third-party introduction, and not those picked up on the street or in bars that were tough, mean and trouble.

The evening when Wilde was arrested at 6.20 in Room 53 at the Cadogan Hotel by Detective-Sergeant Allen and Detective Inspector Richards, the floor littered with evening newspapers' sensationalizing headlines of a warrant issued for his arrest, and with Wilde boozed up on brandy and soda, a customised fag drooping from his mouth, his friend Robbie Ross was despatched to Tite Street, broke into Wilde's locked bedroom and cleaned up all the incriminating letters and papers he could find relating to Wilde's indiscriminate involvement with rent. Like most seriously sex-addicted punters, Wilde had accumulated evidence of his guilt, almost as the attempt to chronologize his actions.

In court on 3rd April 1895, under hawkish questioning from the aggressively homophobic Edward Carson, Wilde attempted to dissolve preconceived social boundaries of differing education and means in his relations with Alfred Wood, by saying outright, 'I don't care about different social position. If anybody interests me or is in trouble and I have been asked to help him in any way, what is the use in putting on airs about one's own social position?'

And, of course, indirectly rent is always in trouble, and in need of help, the social problems often being homelessness, lack of money, drugs, STDs, family relations etc. – Wood lived variously at 36 Langham Street and 14 Russell Street, both conveniently near the Dilly as rent-operation, and Wilde as a named punter could be considered as someone giving him a living in return for paid sex. The illegal contract between the two was the barrier, the law refusing to acknowledge the moral rights of the individual to monetise their body, and Wood, apart from engaging in prostitution, also admitted in the second and third trials that he was an extortionist into blackmailing gays, that he had set up with the help of the two lawless professionals, William Allen and Robert Cliburn, further confusing the issue over motives for rent, as though ambiguous sexuality used to advantage, i.e. selling sex, was also a gateway to into the more lucrative resources of blackmail, to which Wilde, like most queers of his generation, was repeatedly subjected. Wilde's problem was in part his attraction to the individuals who ruined him; referring to his dubious relations with Allen and Cliburn, he said, 'to entertain them was an astounding adventure,' and it was to a large degree Wilde's inability to separate corruption from its fictionalised counterpart, decadence, that led by inevitable stages to his arrest and imprisonment. Rent was invariably and inextricably attached to blackmailers, who also pimped, and Wilde was attracted to both in equal proportion, as part of the testosterone bombs activated by 'feasting with panthers,' for dare and cock. Wilde's exceedingly controversial green carnation from the Royal Arcade in Mayfair was, as a gay badge, the precursor to the pink triangle, the rainbow pride flag, the lambda symbol, and the red

Aids awareness ribbon as a sign adopted by homosexual men to identify themselves, and it was an easy one for Dilly boys to spot when hanging out on the Circus or trawling the backroom bars at the Lyric, the Alhambra or St. James' at Piccadilly Circus.

What's left of Wilde's reconstructed Piccadilly Circus in the 21st century, or of the specific precinct associated with rent, up until 1990, is – apart from the facades of the Criterion and Lillywhites on the southern side, and the Shaftesbury Memorial Fountain, relocated to its present position in the south-western corner – only an imaginative recreation of the place as a continuous random sexual opportunity and calculated possibility. The LED ads still promote Samsung and TDK, as well as Sports Direct.com and Chicken Legend 'I'm lovin' it' from Mcdonald's, and on the Glasshouse Street side, there's Donuts, Jewel, Barclays, Boots pharmacy, and, above it, Barclay Bikes free App text Bikes 67777, and opposite, on the site of Swan & Edgar, there's The Sting, selling innocuous casual wear to opportunistic shoppers. The subversion of the place into spatial disorder, by rent commanding a permanent place on the Tube station itself, in a space authorised to be travelled through, or on the street above designated a commercial zone, again to be used transiently in passing through, was a form of overt territorialisation, challenged by the authorities as contempt of its individuated flows. You can't command any public space in the capital, particularly the street, without coming under surveillance for obstructing the highway, and as an unstable domination of administrable zones intended for work, home or leisure. Once you hang in a side-street, subterranean Tube concourse, or, as it was, on Piccadilly itself, under the LEDS, you're somehow commandeering queer potential, in that straight people don't usually challenge public space in the way of loitering, as queers do very often in public toilets, streets, and urban cruising spots. Wilde must have been, by his imposing size, a standout at Piccadilly – if you're not moving you attract attention, because rent is also standing still, and the fusion of two suspicious immobilities invites scrutiny from the curious and, in particular, the authorities. Wilde invited arrest because he was always immobile, either sitting in a club or bar or standing still looking for Dilly boys with conspicuous attitude, whereas most Londoners are transient in passing through and on the move.

There's no way of hiding yourself at Piccadilly Circus. Even without the invasive CCTV, you're a conspicuous focal object if you hang in the pathways of its assaulting foot traffic. Wilde would have been seen and known by his celebrity and infectious camp. He estimated that in the brief period in which his plays earned, 1893–1895, he spent £5,000 on his boyfriend Lord Alfred Douglas, a lot of those popstar's earnings going into procuring rent, since they often shared the same boys, and into paying off associative blackmailers, hotels, restaurants, champagne and gifts for Douglas. And most of that money was spent in and around Piccadilly, as the epicentre of Wilde's activities.

The urban dynamics of Wilde's corrosively illicit dealings with Dilly boys ate into him like the oxidised railings. People who see you there, more than once, click on to what you're actually doing, because you shouldn't by rights be there, subverting a public space for sex often linked to tainted cash.

Twenty-eight London newspapers gave sensational, sleaze-grabbing accounts of Wilde's vindictively prejudicial trial, including *The Evening Standard, Evening News, News of the World, Observer, St James' Gazette* and *The Times*, and the complete contents of Wilde's house, 16 Tite Street, were auctioned by order of the sheriff, by Mr. Bullock, on the premises, on Wednesday April 24th, 1895, at 1p.m. These included Wilde's library of valuable, often signed first editions, Carlyle's writing table, old Persian carpets and rugs, Moorish and Oriental curiosities, a valuable ormolu clock, and his art collection, an asset-stripping, morally hypocritical, ignominious sale, conducted with acute malice, that only raised £285 against Wilde's escalating debts as a consequence of the trial.

Out on bail, and hunted across the capital by plain clothes and the gutter press, Wilde, after being turned out of the Midland Hotel, St Pancras, as a branded queer, took refuge with his mother and brother Willie at 146 Oakley Street, Chelsea, but grew suicidally depressed at the family's lack of psychological backup, the tense atmospherics of the house where he was essentially unwelcome and drank heavily in the attempt to wipe out, however temporarily, the impending prison sentence he anticipated. Wilde, who was dragged down, dispossessed and without credit, seems, despite his vicious Dilly slapback, to have deepened his conviction that he was quite all right about being gay.

A brightening, mood-shifting move to stay with the gay-friendly actress and novelist, Ada Leverson, at her sparky partying house in South Kensington, restored something of Oscar's characteristic chutzpah and intellectual bounce, before his facing trial by the seventy-seven-year-old Mr. Justice Wills on Wednesday 22nd May, 1895, with the knowledge that the previous day his friend and rent procurer, Alfred Taylor, had been found guilty of gross indecency with Charlie and William Parker, and sentenced to two years with hard labour.

Wilde was adeptly, agilely, contentiously and intrepidly defended by Sir Edward Clarke, who tried repeatedly to draw attention both to the unreliability and inconsistency of the evidence given by rough trade, and to the essentially conspiratorial nature of the trial, reminding the prosecution, Sir Frank Lockwood, that he was not in court 'to try to get a verdict by any means possible.' Clarke's incisive efforts for Wilde nonetheless ran up against a wall, despite his pointing to the irregularity of witnesses who 'in testifying on behalf of the Crown, have secured immunity for past rogueries and indecencies.'

Clarke couldn't turn it round, despite concerted brilliance: the whole dodgy, lugubrious tactics of rent, not only paid by the Crown to give evidence, but, exceptionally in this case, immune from prosecution, as the injured parties, contrived to set Wilde up as the inevitable fall man. The same fabricated Dilly stories of boys being corrupted by a decadent celebrity came up again for four exhaustive days, slippery as lube, and Wilde, his defences stripped, capitulated. The dissolve between importuning and soliciting had been purposely obscured throughout the trial, and Wilde, with the jury out for two hours, was joined in the dock by Alfred Taylor, to face sentence on seven counts, Clarke having successfully demolished the eighth, when Freddie Atkins perjured himself under oath.

Screwed up with anxiety, what was Wilde imagining in the most focused moments of his life, his face white with fear, and shaking convulsively, as the first of the seven verdicts of guilty was delivered? 'It is the worst case I have tried,' Justice Wills maliciously commented, and, of the spaghetti tangle of Dilly lowlife involved, Wills didn't doubt, in sentencing Wilde, like Alfred Taylor to two years with hard labour, that Wilde was at 'the centre of a circle of extensive corruption of the most hideous kind amongst young men.' Dilly rent.

WAITING ON A FRIEND

Supplications: Selected Poems of John Wieners, *edited by Joshua Beckham, CA Conrad and Robert Dewhurst, Enitharmon Press, 2015*

Perhaps no other poet writes with such persistently acute anxiety in his nerves as John Wieners, and correspondingly with so little apparent motivation to be rewarded for the singularity of his lifelong pursuit as a poet. Unlike his Boston neighbours, Robert Lowell and Anne Sexton, who made self-consciously confessional literature from recurrent breakdowns, something monetised by its absorption into academe, Wieners wrote above all, and desperately, for company, as soundtrack to an incurably pathological loneliness. If Wieners answered to no other identity than poet, so the use of poetry as vehicle to autonomously navigate his mostly distressed, fractured, junk-habituated vulnerability, did little or nothing to remedy the real issues of poverty and social alienation in which he lived. The rawness of Wieners' emotional response to a systematised world of corporate institutions in which he was unemployable, and the discrimination that sometimes comes with being gay, placed him increasingly in the role of unhelpable casualty in an American poetry renaissance he was so instrumental to reviving. As a non-careerist, Wieners, like all truly committed poets who stay outside the rewards system, cultivated extreme originality – there is simply no poet like him – rather than the essentially derivative style of mainstream contenders snuck into imitation of each other. A John Wieners poem is an event rather than simply another competent poem popped out of a Baked Beans can.

Supplications, an excellent, sensitively informed Selected Poems, is, of course, only a partial overview of Wieners' poetry, omitting a mass of uncollected work to be found in manuscript form, small press magazines, private ownership, archive dispersal, and, of course, his journals *707 Scott Street for Billie Holiday 1959* and *Stars Seen in Person*, which contain a wealth of poetry often in draft or variant forms. This book provides an ideal introduction to an essentially uncategorisable, harassed and marginalised poet, but disappointingly adds little for hardcore fans by way of fingering so much that remains uncollected to date. What can a poem do for a poet? Arguably nothing: what can it do for the reader? Potentially everything. It's this qualitative disparity that so often leads to profound disillusionment on the part of the poet, and negligence on the part of the reader for failing to recognise it. And the dilemma's insoluble and has a lot to do with why poetry has such limited generational appeal. Effectively, Wieners gave up publishing original collections of poetry after the publication of *Behind the State Capitol: Or Cincinnati Pike* in 1975, a resolution compounded by disappointment and the growing awareness that the word reaches maybe five hundred people in a continent. And as much as Wieners' work imports a mapping of his own personal survival as a poet through building a lyric architecture out of acute psychological damage, so his epochal tracking stands as much for the survival of poetry itself, as it does for the physical extension of his body. And on a sexual level, Wieners' often frustrated pursuit is to be loved by a man as a woman; his consistent identification with ruined glamour icons like Garbo, Dietrich, Billie Holiday, Jackie Onassis etc., is by empathy the desire not only to adopt the characteristics of a diva, but inwardly to be taken for one. 'I died in loneliness/ for no one cared for me enough/ to become a woman for them.'

If Wieners' initial start in poetry with the publication of the seminal *The Hotel Wentley Poems* in 1958, when he was part of the emergent Californian poetry scene initialised by Spicer and Duncan, admitted junk, cocksucking and insanity quite openly as subject matter for a new poetry, then the lyric beauty of his writing provided a rich textural aesthetic to its dark prohibited corners. Living at the time at 707 Scott Street, San Francisco, heroin-addicted, but with the tidal shifts of the Pacific, and the ubiquitous Californian sunshine as influence on his writing, Wieners wrote poems of lyrical transparency flavoured with a mysticism picked up from his reading of Tarot and kabala. In 'July 27' he writes of his immersion in blue oceanic light, 'Wrapped up in an Indian blanket/with the mist falling on this paper/ I could see miles out on the Pacific Ocean/ but fog blocks up the view.' There is, too, a hallucinated saturation of imagery, sometimes induced chemically as altered state that floods poems like 'Dope' with torrents of lapidary imagery.

> Gold-blue jewels of the day. Opalescent rubies
> of the moon. Amethyst of the sun. White marbles
> at noon, when the rain falls out
> to our ankles. Grey tourmaline. Topaz from Mexico
> brought back as booty, a golf ball to adorn
> your little finger, can you lift your hand now to fuck the sun?

What Wieners employs to natural advantage is that he isn't writing for a publisher's list, or anyone at all but himself and the intimate circle of friends who cared about his poetry. And no matter the continuously professed influence of Olson, filtered through Wieners briefly attending Black Mountain College in 1956, Wieners is in most ways Olson's sensibility opposite. His emphasis is invariably on deeply personalised subjective lyricism, whereas Olson's insistence on geographic place as praxis often comes over as pedantic, alyrical, and too factored into topography at the expense of poetry. Wieners predominantly lists as a desolate romantic bohemian, whereas Olson, with his isolated spill into alcoholism, is essentially a cerebralised avatar to poets, and his epic *Maximus* often more historic exegesis than inspired poetry.

Apart from an abundance of broadsheets and chapbooks, Wieners, for so prolific a poet, published surprisingly few books in his lifetime, *The Hotel Wentley Poems* (1958), *Ace of Pentacles* (1964), *Nerves* (1970), *Selected Poems* (1972), *Behind The State Capitol* (1975), and two selections of his work edited by Raymond Foye, *Selected Poems 1958–1984*, (1986), and *Cultural Affairs In Boston : Poetry and Prose 1956–1985*, (1988). Brutalised by psychiatric incarcerations, run into the ground by drug charges, and often a homeless itinerant transitioning between hotels without ever paying the bill, Wieners finally settled in Boston in 1970, living for the next thirty years in an apartment at 44 Joy Street on Beacon Hill, a reticent recluse to poetry, and a vocal gay activist helping to spearhead Charles Shively's Good Gay Collective – Shively who published *Behind the State Capitol*, the last book in which Wieners actively participated, leaving the arrangements of future publications of his work to the devoted editorial intercession of Raymond Foye. What exactly Wieners wrote during the last three decades of his life is unclear due to its remaining unpublished and it is rumoured that he periodically destroyed work in progress.

It's a fact that critics take poetry far more seriously than poets, because as a poet you care nothing for what you've left behind, but everything for what creatively engages your present. For Wieners and for most prolific poets, poems are transitory marks in time, made into objects of attention by a faculty sold on finding in them what was never implicit in their building. A poem most usually occupies a small intense space of time, a bite on experience; I could call it a love bite on time, and it is as soon gone. By the time of Wieners' return to Boston in 1970, coincidental with the publication of *Nerves*, his health both mentally and physically was seriously compromised by drugs, booze and a series of nervous breakdowns to which *Asylum Poems*, published by Angel Hair in 1969, owes its scrambled origins. *Asylum Poems*, only marginally represented in *Supplications*, is as seminal a documentation as Lowell's *Life Studies* in courageously navigating the infrastructure of breakdown and family as its poetic resource. Published as loose-leaf unpaginated sheets in a folder, *Asylum Poems* as an entirety remains mostly unknown outside of a small circle of John Wieners' fans. Contemporaneous with this collection, and inexcusably omitted here, is 'With Meaning', the poem giving basis to *Nerves*, and professing Wieners' total affiliation to outlaw status, as one of the terminally disaffected unlikely ever to come in from the societal edge he occupied. It's a poem central to Wieners and to his fellow associates like Jack Spicer and his one-time lover Steve Jonas. 'The multitude of martyrs,/staring out of/town houses now on Delaware Ave/in the grey mist/of traffic circles, taking LSD/then not holding up/in rooming houses, Berkeley and motorcycles.'

There's arguably no book of poetry so saturated in absorbent human loneliness than *Nerves*, in which, stripped of human defences, Wieners confronts material greed from which he is inexorably excluded by employing poetry alone as his weaponised defensive tool. Wieners' affiliation to queer subcultures is the extra differential to being penalised in a book in which zero apology is offered for subversive resistance to the State. In the absence of polemic, Wieners uses delicate lyricism to convey awareness of feeling abjectly unwanted by anyone anywhere.

> In a bus station
> listening to voices
> pretending they're yours.
> Poetry is a trance
> Of make-believe.

For Wieners, poetry, even if it doesn't provide a gateway out of existential dilemma, and the associated ontological repetition of the mundane, is nonetheless the only resource that can provide some sort of consolation for suffering.

> Best to get away from one's self
> one's own life
> for it leads to frustration
> no matter who one is,
> or what he has done.
> The loneliness of hotels lingers
> in grey mid-Manhattan
> in mid-morning mist
> as taxis splash through rain.

By nature immersed in subcultures, ideologically, culturally and sexually, Wieners is arguably by default the most original American poet of his generation, exploiting a subject matter natural to him, but often shockingly alien to his contemporaries, and completely outside the conservative remit of mainstream British poetry. And because Wieners is so naturally a poet without necessarily wanting to be one, rather than competitively forcing the issue, as is the way with careerists, his work is organically, unapologetically there, take it or leave it. In other words, it's indubitably the real thing, something given to few. His themes are often close to those of torch singers like Libby Holman, Billie Holiday, Nina Simone, Shirley Bassey, k.d. lang, in the sense of integrating unrequited love and collapsed emotions into his essentially wounded lyricism.

While *Supplications* reaffirms Wieners' cult status to a principally American readership, and in many cases introduces his work to a British one, what is called for is a *Collected Poems*, the condensing of a lifetime's brilliantly maverick, deviant, consolidated lyric genius into an indispensable Wieners monolith. There'll never be another poet like John Wieners, and crowded out of attention by outnumbering interchangeable poets, how many are there you can you really say that of?

AN APPLE WITH ORANGE SIGNATURE

John Ashbery, **Commotion of the Birds,**
Carcanet Press, 2016

A new book by John Ashbery is always for me like discovering a new colour that didn't exist before; its high levels of pigment creating something like the distribution of borrowed light, as the precise colour of sunlight across shade. *Commotion of the Birds*, his twenty-seventh collection, is as hip, modern, mirage-tinted and domestically chatty in burying gay slang as an abstract into lyric idiom, as its three equally brilliant predecessors, *Planisphere, Quick Question* and *Breezeway*, as an affirmative diagnostic of a late poetics of energised iridescent pursuit. What so distinguishes all of these books is in part their refusal to make age the subject of poetry. Ashbery's work is tonally refreshed by existing now, in the immediate, like the arrival of light, or the lick of Farrow & Ball high refractory finish on a street door. Ashbery, like all good poets, is more interested in being a tourist from the future than a curator of the historic past, and where history does theme poems like 'Days of 1948' and 'Cribbage, 1954, Utica,' it's not so much an exercise in looking back as an allusively scrambled narrative belonging intuitively to the present. The bits related could have been anytime, and Ashbery as an events-mixologist stays totally modern by filtering whatever happened into happening now. And his apparent depersonalisation of subject only serves obliquely to engage the reader more closely, as though confessional hints, immediately sponged by dissociation, shine brighter for their opportunely elusive shimmer. And when Ashbery, as subject, does enter the spotlight in the sublimely beautiful title poem – a retro appraisal of cultural evolution – the eloquent halftones of self-portrait are dissolved into rainy moments of pure evaluation of his singular involvement in a movement.

> It's good to be modern if you can stand it.
> It's like being left out in the rain, and coming
> to understand that you were always this way: modern,
> wet, abandoned, though with that special intuition
> that makes you realize you weren't meant to be
> somebody else, for whom the makers
> of modernship will stand inspection
> even as they wither and fade in today's glare.

That none of us are intended to be somebody else, and the taking of responsibility for our own individual signature, is, of course, deeply integrated into the creative sensibility, is fundamental to the process, and catching it happening is, to a point, what we call poetry. Nobody writing today does it better than John Ashbery, whose new collection could be mistaken for his first, only that the facility to push poetry into places where it shouldn't go, or hasn't been before, is now a naturally perfected reflex. What's central to Ashbery's poetic drive, and its consistent undertone resembles the hum of a fridge buried in the kitchen, is the ability to import spontaneously observed visual detail to corrupt linear flow, in other words, facilitating the brain's mechanism that seamlessly patches fragments of vision into a singular unified background image. Ashbery's pathways-in are worked out by having the poem partially copy routes of consciousness, with interruptions inclusive in the process.

> At Opium Bridge
> an apple with orange signature.
> No, but a cat came in,
> rushing around as though its life depended on it
> and lets you deal with
> all of that.

It's the abrupt transitioning here, like one thought pattern breaking up simultaneously into another, achieving the vital disconnect between initial image and the cat's mercurial arrival, almost writing by snapshot, that keeps Ashbery's resource always one step ahead of modern. His effort often seems the direct attempt to notate consciousness, in what it selectively grabs of significance, something significantly wide of most British poetry with its resolve to somehow make a poem mean, rather than happen. And what Ashbery won't do at any cost is let you have anything directly personal on him or his close circle. While he writes brilliantly characterised prose on his contemporaries in art and literature, you can't at the same time imagine him writing elegies for dead friends, or poems about specific people, it's simply not his way. It's not that people are things in his work; it's more that the recurrent 'you' he addresses in his poetry is particularly an aspect of himself. The ambiguity is always near perfect. In 'Cooler Temperatures', which hints at the need for a bed companion, the character is rinsed into photoflash anonymity.

> You look nice,
> giving away like that.
> I'll buy you this and buy you that:
> a closer look, a nice warm bed
> to hide under
> in the event that...

That's the annihilation point, the stealthy subjectivised transforming of character to a no-person, but totally fascinating for what Ashbery does and doesn't give us. This is a person (male) he's evoking, not a spook or a holo; but he's featureless. If you breathe on a good poem the lines should smoke, and Ashbery's best do that. Like all his books, *Commotion of the Birds* brims with crypto-erotic imagery, as a submerged gay ethos clandestinely filed in the corners of his life. It's so well done that the self-reflective suppression of sexuality in his poetry as an ongoing dominant works characteristically in his favour: 'The volcanic entrance to an antechamber,' as a standout sexual line in the epic 'Fragment' (1970), is a little more, but only fractionally, revealed in this much later collection. In 'A Disservice' he writes of the hormonal fizz of youth, 'You had just gotten so young/it was all I could do to contain you/in the linen dishtowel we kept for that purpose/the doctor prescribed bed rest.' Of course, in reading Ashbery, and that's the thrill of it, you have to reappoint notions of time, space and geography to a non-polarised compass. What happens in the poem could be now or decades ago, and it's part of his method to blur all boundaries and never let on. So, too, big city poetry, largely written in his New York apartment, is also offset by rural landscape lifted from his upbringing on a farm in Rochester, New York State, the juxtaposition of territories providing the often filmic sweep of domain occupied by his poetry. And always it's this odd contradiction between intimate subject matter and the detached alienation of the narrator that makes Ashbery so compelling as a poet and the work so continuously open-ended, like driving into a constantly expansive skyline on a road that goes on forever. And what's so heroically wonderful is that Ashbery has never come off the highway, one marvellous sustained slab of it being 1991's *Flow Chart*, a book-length poem built architecturally out of bits synthesised into something so ineffaceably magical that it appears like a giant drug, a film-coated granular solid, blocked into poetry's rapidly changing skyline. You could arguably connect all of Ashbery's books into a word-metropolis, compressing six or seven decades of work into one cellular skyscraper, with *Commotion of the Birds* the latest floor added to the innovatively isolated benchmark. Philosophic, casual, lyrical, the humour standing out like a flavour of gin mixed into the context, there's still also bite and kick towards the heteronormative in this new collection, expressed through anger at exclusion. The outstanding 'Prayer Not To Touch' slashes rather than grazes the knee of the opposition. This is Ashbery getting into his stride:

> I tell you, it was when I knew you were chasing me,
> mockery on your lip during the morning meet-and-greet.
> Others than I saw the vast
> punch pushing love up to the surface. To do nothing
> was our ancient privilege. And though we'd talked about it later,
> it always felt unacknowledged, as though we never met,
> only passed each other in some narrow alley, where brushing
> against one's neighbour was unavoidable, not putrid.

It's hard not only to recapitulate such deeply traumatising events, but to lyricise them, and live with the residual traces, like watching a Boeing contrail thicken in vaporous tracks before falling away. But it's all part of reading a book that liquidates the inept backwardness of nostalgia common to so many poets in their later years. Ashbery's sunshine moment remains the present as operative modality, and his sense of cool maintained through each decade leaves him totally open to the new continuously shaping his profound literary sensibility. The analogy for me is with Warhol, and the masking of autobiography in the interest of art as impersonally instructive autonomy. It's this particular faculty that gives Ashbery a timeless sameness, as though no book of his specifically attaches to its time, but could arguably have been written anytime modern. We could call the textural surface monochrome in its luminous wash over time, but centrally lit by an emergent personality with the glow of late afternoon sunlight. That's the quality of light I associate with an Ashbery poem, and *Commotion of the Birds* confirms that qualitative glow, a halo of sadness tingeing light beamed up from eclectic inspiration. In the obliquely titled 'The Upright Piano', he writes:

> If things darkened afterward, that was no one's fault
> except the self-appointed guardians of civility's,
> who nattered on, dense with the realizing it.
> We knew it before. So many flowers washed up on the beach
> it was pure chaos, or fun. Now it's time to pray.

What is in fact a throwback to a generation of gay friends summering on the beach ends with this perfectly pitched measure of enigmatic loss. The greatness of this collection throughout is its investment in poetry as celebratory of the good, the bad and everything incorporated into the poet's idiosyncratic remit of experience. It's a book that belongs now in Ashbery's life, and my feeling is it will read as modern in thirty or forty years and keep on staying that way.

ROBERT DUNCAN:
THE H.D. BOOK

There's no living British poet who would have the imaginative scope, visionary mapping or full-on celebratory generosity to work with a single poet, in this case H.D., as the basis for so intensely focused a 600-page book. The book is about and comes from the view of poetry as a total commitment that gives itself precedence above all other experience while fully integrating itself into the dynamic of living.

Duncan's random episodic figures – and I'd call the music of his language 'dance figures' – in reflecting on the neglected poetry of H.D., and establishing an almost telepathic empathy with his subject's hypersensitive sensibility, sustained for much of her life by the wealthy female shipping magnate and novelist Bryher, is arguably the greatest book written on poetic imagination as a voyaging probe, like the Mars rover Curiosity, currently scooping Martian soil for particle analysis. I mean, Duncan travels that far inwardly, pushing frontiers of inner space to link with their organic external correlatives. As Duncan comments so insightfully, 'Poetry, like dream reality, is the juncture of the experienced with the never experienced,' and the thrust of his book, written between 1959-1964, is precisely reading sensory experience through its imaginative equivalent to discover a reality altered by language as a ground of suggestion and association.

Robert Duncan and his hard-drinking friend Jack Spicer, both unapologetically gay, were the instigators of the San Francisco Bay Area Renaissance, releasing an essentially homoerotic freed-up poetics into the Bay, before famously taking up with Charles Olson and his Black Mountain colleagues, falling under the influence of Olson's projective verse, , in which syllables, viewed as the smallest particles, united in accentuating form as an extension of content, and, via Ezra Pound and William Carlos Williams, forging the adaptation of words, not as thoughts we have, but ideas in *things*, so that the poet 'must attend not to what he means to say but to [what] what he says means.'

The force of Duncan's dazzlingly original thesis is rebellion, never more apparent than here in his attempted rehabilitation of H.D., but manifest always in his unstoppable, uncompromising writing of the new, like he was always the first to find that individual poetic moment. Erudite, mystical, Duncan as one-off maverick is marvellously anti-academic in his command of the spontaneous moment of creativity, looking to Pound's wildness as prototypical avatar in roughing up literature, compared to Eliot's formal writing, 'adapted to the convenience of an accepted culture.'

Duncan, with his idiosyncratic, un-moderated enthusiasm, worked hard to rehabilitate the ageing, largely forgotten and out of print H.D. (Hilda Doolittle) to a new sixties generation of American poets, and was instrumental to having James Laughlin publish a new expanded *Hermetic Definition* (1972), from his forward thinking New Directions imprint, and to generally getting H.D.'s work reappraised through his accelerated chutzpah for support.

Passionately anti-war, and more than Allen Ginsberg responsible for the most eloquently lyrical condemnation of Johnson's unsanctioned war effort in the meltdown of Vietnam, and as directly pro-gay in his support of liberation, Duncan argues humanistically, 'The poetic urge, to make a poetry out of the common language, is to make room for the existence of the poet, the artist of free speech.'

I read Duncan like I'm addicted to benzos, breaking up the work like I shred a dusty blue or white 10 mg Valium into fragments of crumbling granules. The drug feeds my writing curve, and in this case my reading notes taken while writing. Duncan, in his interactive consensus of sharing, reminds us of what we all often take for granted, the reader's, and in this case his, – with H.D. as his focus –increase of imagination in proportion to the work read. 'The poet and the reader, who if he is intent in reading becomes a new poet of the poem, comes to write or to read in order to participate through the work in a consciousness that moves freely in time and space.'

What Robert Duncan consistently communicates in both his euphorically visionary poetry and courageously motivated prose, is a hyperactive enthusiasm to morph whatever he sees into its imaginative counterpart, always with the heightened sense of the relatedness of everything as a facility that sets poets apart. He expresses the faculty perfectly in his perception that, 'The Universe is a book of what we are and asks us to put it all together to learn to read.'

Duncan's H.D. book is essentially autobiography; it's one of the closest reads we'll ever experience, as to what it means to live poetry as the principal gateway to interpreting the universe through complex neural associations mediated by language. It's also a book in which Duncan acknowledges his avatars, most notably H.D., Pound, Williams, Spicer, Creeley, and, monumentally, Charles Olson, who entered Duncan's life as a poetic and physical giant, and, given the close union of the two men, Duncan movingly records their first meeting as the necessary collision of impacting poetic sensibilities.

'The figure of the giant hunter in the sky brings with it, as often, the creative genius of Charles Olson for me. Since the appearance of *Origin* I a decade ago, my vision of what the poem is to do has been transformed, reorganized around a constellation of new poets – Olson, Denise Levertov, Robert Creeley – in which Olson's work takes the lead for me. The man, himself a "giant" – six foot seven or so – has been an outrider, my own Orion.

'It was this same time of year, with Olson overhead, in 1955, when Olson read aloud to Jess and me the beginnings of a new sequence of poems, O'Ryan. The scene in the bare room at Black Mountain, with its cold and blazing winter sky at the window springs up as I write. The fugitive hero of that sequence was drawn from Robert Creeley, but he is also the humor of the poem Hercules the Sun or Son who must pass through the twelve houses of the zodiacal initiation.'

Duncan's epic meditation on H.D. as a seminal mover in his adopted community of poetic influences, was partly grounded in their shared occult matrix, H.D. having been raised in the Moravian Church of Count Zinzendorf, while Duncan had grown up in a family with connections to theosophy, as the basis for his exploratory readings in Hellenistic neo-Platonism, gnosticism, the troubadours, Arabic angelology, and inevitably Blake as the focus for poetic thinking as orgasm or mediated altered state, making real what is only real in a heightened sense.

Although the *H.D. Book* Part 1 was prepared for publication by John Martin's Black Sparrow Press in 1971, having been turned down by mainstream publishers, the project was dropped, partly due to Duncan's obsessive holographic revisions of successive manuscripts, sections of the book were published in five influential small magazines of the period, *Aion, Caterpillar, Coyote's Journal, Stony Brook* and *Tri-Quarterly*, lending the proposed book a suitably hermetic underground flavour, while Duncan continued to amend and expand the potentialities of his accretive work in progress.

Arguably an extended conversation with the reader – 'I am a

student of, I am searching out, a poetics' – Duncan's *H.D. Book* is an inimitable original that can be opened for reward at any page, given the quality, depth and allusive sparkle of the writing, as charged with optimal active imagination, in every digressive expression. There's no line of Duncan's that could be written by anyone else, as the signature of a unique stylist, rather than an interchangeable copyist.

Robert Duncan's forcibly individual pioneering wouldn't make compromises with material priorities or with a society that discredited individual creativity in the interests of collective conformity to the state. With his own poetry largely published by individuals like John Martin at Black Sparrow Press, James Laughlin at New Directions, small West Coast publishers, and often in self-published limited editions, illustrated by his partner Jess Collins, Duncan operated on the edge and stayed there as his naturally chosen poetic module. His interest in restoring H.D. to a small, select readership was, of course, partly motivated by the fact that her inherent gravitation to beauty as an almost lapidary aesthetic, kept her work apart from any popular readership. Duncan writes passionately of the courage to live with fine-tuned sensitivity, as poets do, often risking breakdown and acute human alienation in the process. 'The beauty of the poem, the poet's sense of beauty,' he writes, 'in itself, that cannot be bought and sold. Beauty, in a society based upon commodity-profit is ambivalently praised and despised. The popular mistrust, the industrial and commercial mistrust, opposes and destroys where it can individual sensitivity, as out of place in the democracy of big party politics or in the community of the modern city as individualistic architecture with its romantic and expressive form, even ornament, is in the plans of the new functionalism.'

What I personally value in this defiantly committed book that brings the poetic process up for psychological evaluation on the nerves, is its strong anti-literary bias. Duncan isn't interested in forensic criticism or competitive careerist rivalries, or the sterile work created by safe lives programmed by convention, but only in the risk undertaken by edge-walkers who burn like re-entry flares from rocket parts, at no matter what cost.

The writing of the H.D. book unfolded in Duncan contemporaneous with a trio of poetry books, *The Opening of the Field* (1960), *Roots and Branches* (1964) and *Bending the Bow* (1968), in which he peaked in the advancement of his instantly recognisable poetic voice wherein the apparent discovery of the marvellous completely deletes all notion of the predictable.

Duncan's attraction to H.D., whose work could be described as frigidly crystallised into glacial images of highly concentrated beauty and lacking in emotional resources, was due in part to her early involvement with Pound and the Imagists, and was clearly also operative on a level of compassion, concern and interest with her traumatised life, the smash-up of her marriage to Richard Aldington, her near destitution, her almost dying from the flu pandemic in London, and, contemporaneous with her desertion, her rescue and patronage by her lesbian lover Bryher (Annie Winifred Ellerman). These damaged bits of her life all got integrated into Duncan's essentially romantic conception of the poet as heroically resistant and as the projector of a work rooted in the recognition that what is seen is already fully informed, full of form that determines what is seen and how it's seen, even though the forms may remain hidden and only visible to the poet.

There's generally in every generation a surplus of mainstream poetry that all reads the same in its interchangeable limitations, in which restrained vision is usually the focus, and social thesis the directive, but Robert Duncan, Charles Olson, Jack Spicer and Robert Creeley radically broke up formal poetics, like smashing a linear road, an innovative thrust singularly blocked by British poetry to its lasting detriment, its persistent locking out of the weird and imaginatively scoped from its remit, its backwardness; and every line of Duncan's shimmering, acutely original prose is remedial to the cause. What Duncan writes of Eliot and Wallace Stevens' formality is central to his belief in pushing frontiers into a distressed remit, the outlaw territory adopted by the likes of John Wieners, Ed Dorn, Frank O'Hara, John Ashbery, and all contemporary bandits who fuck with respectability.

'The voices of Eliot or of Wallace Stevens do not present us with such disturbances of mode. They preserve throughout a melodious poetic respectability, eminently sane in their restriction of poetic meaning to the bounds of the literary, of symbol and metaphor, but at the cost of avoiding facts and ideas that might disturb. Both the individual and the communal awareness are constricted to fit or adapted to the convenience of an accepted culture.'

Historically, Duncan sides with Pound as the progenitor of ripping up respectability – the Cantos are a torrential diatribe against accepted culture, a fusion of eclectic beauty and raw polemic and linear shattering that bashes poetry like a street gang.

Duncan's pivotal attraction to H.D.'s poetry dates back to the sensual associations of his youth, and his personalised response to her richly synaesthetic imagery is simply the basis for perhaps the greatest extended meditation on poetry ever written by a poet, a book in which we follow the neural micro-circuitry of Duncan's awareness of poetry existing in almost everything his electric impulses dictate. Duncan's magic, in that his exuberant personality is his writing, there in the heliotropic pull of his poetry into orange glow, and in his writing out in the *H.D. Book* the events of poetry in his deeply personal reading, is nothing less than altered state marvellousness.

'The power of the poet,' Duncan writes, 'is to translate experience from daily time where the world and ourselves pass away as we go into the future, from the journalistic record, into a melodic coherence in which words, sounds, meanings, images, voices, do not pass away or exist by themselves but are kept by rhyme to exist everywhere in the consciousness of the poem. The art of the poem, like the mechanism of the dream or the intent of the tribal myth and dromena, is a cathexis: to keep present and immediate a variety of times and places, persons and events. In the melody we make, the possibility of eternal life is hidden, and experience we thought lost returns to us.'

Poetry is a record of personal experience given some sort of form for time-travel; if it's good it meets whenever it does, or it just disappears into the huge impermanence of things as a forgotten fact, like most things and poems do.

Duncan's *H.D. Book*, published posthumously, appears without him present to oversee its publication, but with the work sparkling off his nerve-tips with a generosity that keeps it impactingly, durably alive, and as original as a Martian microbe.

"JOHNNY, REMEMBER ME": HART CRANE'S SUICIDE

If suicide is in part the attempt to create an imaginary rather than biological death, and one in which control is retained over the method of dying, then the imaginative autonomy involved in both processes may help explain why the creative sensibility is so attracted to suicide. Imagination, which Hart Crane possessed to an extraordinary degree, not only dissolves the boundaries between inner and outer realities, but also invests the poet with the power to recreate the world on his own terms. Living antisocially, the poet may choose to die in a similar way, his death shaped by configurative inner design and not the dictates of nature or the intervention of medicine.

Hart Crane lived and wrote like liquid explosive. The only child of a broken marriage – his father was a candy manufacturer in Ohio – Hart's conflictual and traumatic early years were spent siding with a highly strung, hysterical mother in a distraught marital arena. Encountering his first gay experiences in his teens, ironically, it is suggested, with a friend of his father's, he renounced formal education to pursue poetry and his ideal of the perfect sailor with all the reckless abandon of someone resolved to burnout fast.

It could be argued that the incandescent momentum of Crane's life wouldn't anyhow have allowed for the prospect of longevity. Crane, with his Rimbaudian belief in self-induced altered states, ran at life with the same dedication to overkill that had him, at the age of 32, pitch over the stern of the SS Orizaba into the Caribbean. The reputation for bingeing that earned him the sobriquet "the roaring boy", in imitation of Christopher Marlowe's infamous drunken brawls in London pubs, pursued Crane from New York to Paris to Mexico, via innumerable beatings, degradation and prison cells.

Crane's dynamic was a visionary one that attempted forcibly to smack poetry into a projected spiritual dimension. Hyping himself up by listening to Ravel's *Boléro*, or Sophie Tucker records played on endless repeat, his system fired up by bottleneck slugs of Cutty Sark, Crane's early poems collected in *White Buildings* were the product of big city excitement launched from an inherently romantic sensibility. The work is charged with the ability to compress sensory experience into its exact metaphorical equivalent. If Crane's book-length poem *The Bridge*, begun in the mid-1920s, sometimes finds tangential comparison with T. S. Eliot's *The Waste Land*, both writers transforming the long poem into a bitty collage of cultural references, then Crane's investment in the epic is heroically subjective, whereas Eliot's is almost unfailingly culturally objective.

Crane, like his prototypical model in visionary poetics, Arthur Rimbaud, was a distinctly neural poet, by which I mean he adrenally wired the poem with his own highly idiosyncratic nervous signature. All of his generosity as a person, his omnivorous sexual appetite, his hedonistic demands of life as continuous optimal sensation, together with a sensitivity constantly shattered by financial anxiety and the chronic instability of personal crises, come together in a poetry that polarises the contemporary moment as the nuclear core of its energy. Crane sometimes gives the impression of entering a poem like someone testing the edge of a tower drop and being thrown back inside by the sonic roar of edgy traffic. The slightly displaced perception infusing many of his poems gives them a sense of having been written while the poet was nursing the residue of a severe hangover, before drinking again to get out of it.

Crane organised his largely chaotic personal life around his poetry. Working variously as an advertising copywriter, a private secretary to a wealthy Californian businessman, and travelling whenever the opportunity permitted, the pattern of his fragmented, discontinuous existence finds its interface in the equally upended structure of his epic poem *The Bridge*, in which dazzling lyricism often compensates for lack of a historically realised theme. Crane's particular mindset was best suited to working in short periods of intense hypercreativity, rather than through the sustained methodology he attempted to achieve in writing a long poem to give voice to his vision of the American Dream.

Crane's life as we know it, documented by his letters, was burnt by continuous worry over financial instability, as well as the exacting demands made on his time and emotions by his mother's second divorce in 1926, and her authoritarian reliance on him for psychological support. Grace's parasitical emotional dependency demanded of him that he wrote to her every day. There was additionally the problem of his criminalised sexuality and how best to accommodate it to the society in which he lived. In 1924 he had fallen in love with a young, blond Danish naval officer, Emil Opffer, who was to be the inspiration for 'Voyages', Crane's extraordinarily beautiful sequence of poems published in White Buildings, in which his love of maritime imagery is fused to an elegiac homoerotics of desire. Expanding on the nature of the relationship in a letter written to his friend Jean Toomer, Crane wrote, 'I have never been given the opportunity for as much joy and agony before. The extreme edges of these emotions were sharpened on me in swift alternation until I am almost a shadow. But there is a conviction of love – that is the only way I can name it – which has somehow arrived in time, and which has (now so much has proved it) an equal basis in the both of us.'

It's the catch of honesty in Hart's account that jolts one into an awareness of his highly evolved individuality, as well as the sense of him seeking the same qualities in love as he does in art. Writing to his friend Waldo Frank about the visionary experiences imparted by his love for this handsome sailor, Crane wrote, 'It will take many letters to let you know what I mean when I say that I have seen the Word made Flesh. I mean nothing less, and I know now that there is such a thing as indestructibility. In the deepest sense, where the flesh became transformed through intensity of response to counter-response, where sex was beaten out, where a purity of joy was reached that included tears.'

Crane's letters are so directly complementary to his poetry that they provide a continuous biographical commentary on the circumstances under which individual poems were written. The entire force of the man is present in both, his elated visionary and agonised moods contending in a volatile cocktail of disruptive sensory experience. The arc of his poetry built into attempted transcendent vision is like his response to love, no matter how short-lived or brutal. The request is ultimately spiritual or transhuman, as in 'Voyages II', to 'Bequeath us to no earthly shore until/Is answered in the vortex of our grave/The seal's wide spindrift gaze toward paradise.'

The intimation of suicide here in the reference to being swallowed by a marine vortex was to prove self-prophetic, as though Crane, even at the time he was celebrating his love for Emil Opffer, was clear as to what form his end would take. There's every reason to believe that by living with the inner configuration of his death, Crane moved inevitably towards its physical resolution. If you decide you're going to take your own life, you're usually aware not only of how you will do it, but also of having in the process activated an impulse that may or may not gather dangerous momentum. Crane's did, and his suicide may have been as much motivated by the need to be free of the spooky presentiment, as it was an act of liberation from a set of acutely unresolved emotional problems.

What Crane took with him into the ocean was that rare thing, the self-transcendent vision of the artist prepared to sacrifice himself unconditionally for his vision, a conviction nowhere better pronounced than in a letter written to his father about his artistic intentions. With characteristic generosity, Crane wrote, ' try to imagine working for the pure love of simply making something beautiful, – something that maybe can't be sold or used to help sell anything else, but that is simply a communication between man and man, a bond of understanding and human enlightenment – which is what a real work of art *is* . . . I only ask to leave behind me something that the future may find valuable, and it takes a bit of sacrifice sometimes in order to give the thing that you know is yourself and worth giving. I shall make every sacrifice toward that end.'

Crane's 32 years carried with them all the compressed power and impact of someone attempting not only to make sense of himself in relation to his age, but also of the absolute themes favoured by the Elizabethans that he read, like Marlowe: life, love and death. Any life, no matter how long or productive, offers no more than a quick, close-up bite of the apple, and Crane took his lick fast and clean.

Gifted with a Guggenheim fellowship of two thousand dollars in March, 1931, ostensibly to write a long poem on Cortez, Crane headed to Mexico on the SS Orizaba, the same ship from which he would jump into the Caribbean on his return journey a year later in 1932. Once in Mexico, and dressed unequivocally to cruise in a red sweater, white sailor pants and a blue silk handkerchief, his recklessness increased in proportion to his drinking. According to his friend and neighbour, Katherine Anne Porter, Hart was desperate to live out the full spectrum of his sexual fantasies. 'He confessed that his sexual feelings were now largely a matter of imagination, which drove and harried him continually, creating images of erotic frenzy and satisfactions for which he could find no counterpart in reality . . . He said, he now found himself imagining that if he could see blood, or cause it to be shed, he might be satisfied.'

Already facing burn-out due to heavy drinking and literally risking his life in picking up men on the streets, Hart, suffering from acute loneliness and having drunk away the first instalment of his grant, turned both paranoid and suicidal. Faced by a paralysing creative impotence and still lacking any clear focus on his intended Mexican epic, Crane found himself nailed by his old self-destructive habits. To the poet Leon Felipe Camino, who discovered him drunk and emoting to records by Marlene Dietrich, 'He was tall and had an angelic face, with large blue eyes filled with asombro: fright, astonishment, amazement.'

Crane's terror was, of course, of himself and the often unmanageable contents of his imagination, as much attuned to the sexual underworld as it was to the light. It wasn't easy to be Hart. His acute sensitivity had him live outside his skin most of the time, and there is a limit, for anyone, to how much of this can be tolerated. Death 'with a bang' was what he had predicted for himself, and in Mexico he worked himself towards the explosion.

Taking up with Malcolm Cowley's estranged wife, Peggy, who had also joined Mexico City's expatriate colony as a Guggenheim fellow, Crane, driven by extreme loneliness, attached himself to Peggy, first as a companion and later as a confused, distraught lover. Their mutually alcoholic and incongruous relationship was to accelerate Hart's sense of guilt at betraying his mother's affection by contact with another woman. At once wanting to reform his same-sex habits and at the same time deeply resentful of any changes made to his sexual orientation, Crane oscillated between the desire to prove his sexuality to Peggy and the need to cruise for sailors after dark. 'She thinks she can reform me, does she? I'll show her. Why, God damn her, I'd rather sleep with a man any time than with her!' he railed in a letter, while informing his old friend William Underwood that, 'The fluttering gait and the powder puff are unheard of here, but that doesn't matter in the least. Ambidexterity is all in the fullest masculine tradition.' But the climate wasn't quite as accommodating as Crane made it sound, and on 28th January 1932, he spent a drunken night in jail for having sex with a servant boy in public, and with Peggy refusing to visit him, he was released the following day with a severe warning and a ban on him ever entering Taxco again.

Peggy Cowley's memories of her short-lived liaison with Crane are additionally interesting for the light she throws on his frenetic moods of creativity. Hart's year in Mexico triggered little more than one completed poem, 'The Broken Tower,' but Peggy was witness to its creation and the combustible assault Crane made on his material. Elated by the pre-Christmas festivities, in which tribal rituals had been performed in the early hours before the cathedral, and by the pyrotechnical firework displays on Christmas Day, to celebrate which he had bought 200 scarlet and green poinsettias, Crane was inspired to work on what was to be his last poem. Rather like Jackson Pollock's dynamic of running at the canvas, or Francis Bacon's habit of throwing paint at it to initiate a work, Crane furiously scribbled fragments on sheets of paper that were torn up and discarded. Writing to the sound of music played at full volume, and fired by the rush of tequila as it came up, Crane worked at the sort of manic pitch that burnt. Endlessly trying and changing phrases out loud, he was in Peggy's words, 'the instrument on which he played the words, changing each perhaps a hundred times before retaining a small fragment.'

For three days Hart's energies raged as the poem began to be licked into tentative shape. With Peggy integral to its direction, Crane was interrupted in his work by having to return to Mixcoac to address practicalities connected with the disappearance of his passport, and by the need to be vaccinated against typhoid. Unable to sublet his house, and in urgent need of immediate money from his father's trust, he returned to Peggy and Taxco, with the poem still big and loud in his head. It was there like a fireball when, unable to sleep, he went out on a night walk to the town plaza and stumbled across his friend the old Indian bell-ringer, who was on his way to the church to announce the dawn. He requested Hart assist him in his epiphanic work, and the two men climbed the turrets of Santa Prisca and released the bells, or, in Hart's poem, 'Oval encyclicals in canyons heaping/ The impasse high with choir.' The triumphant physical act of bell ringing became for Crane the symbol of his return to a visionary dynamic, his reawakening to the call of poetry. The tower, a metaphor in Crane's mind for the one in which Danae in hiding had been impregnated by Zeus' golden shower, was now the receptacle of a poem brought powerfully alive by his memory of light breaking over the mountains as he had manipulated the bell ropes. With the act forming a gateway to the rebirth of his poetic talents, Crane considered himself 'healed, original now, and pure . . .' All his rich language and allusions to a world inherited from his affinities with the Elizabethan poets flooded back as he collided with his theme in an act of ecstatic overreach of the kind at which he excelled.

But regardless of his return to poetry, and the high esteem in which Peggy held his latest creation, writing to her husband on 27th January that, 'He is by no means finished. It is a magnificent piece of lyric poetry that is built with the rhetorical splendour of a Dante in hell,' the poem's execution wasn't sufficient to re-establish a working rhythm in the irrevocably bibulous poet. Strung out by the anxieties connected with having disgraced the Guggenheim by reports of his drunken behaviour in Mexico, by the imminent financial crash of his father's estate, and by the equally intolerable state of sexual confusion created by his fling with Peggy, Crane began to disintegrate in the weeks leading up to his suicide. He made a half-hearted attempt to kill himself by drinking iodine, an offence that the doctor summoned had to officially report, thereby placing Crane under threat of deportation.

Investigating options for their return to New York, and given Hart's love of the sea and ships, the couple secured berths on the SS Orizaba, where it quickly became clear to Peggy that Crane's reputation was common knowledge amongst the uniformed crew. That Crane had made a number of the men was obvious, and when the Orizaba stopped off at Havana for six hours, Crane, becoming separated from Peggy, and failing to keep their rendezvous at a café called the Diana, instead went off on a solitary binge with a sailor.

When Peggy anxiously returned to the ship, Crane, she was told by the captain, was already on board, and drinking in the bar. Understandably disappointed in his behaviour, and additionally so, in that she had gone to the trouble of purchasing him the gift of a number of new jazz records in Havana, Peggy went to the bar to look for him. Not finding him there, she ordered a cocktail, put on a record and lit a cigarette, only to have the box of Cuban matches explode in a violent flare that scorched her wrist and arm. Blacking out from the pain, she was carried to the surgery to have her arm treated with a solution of tannic acid. It was there, while she was being treated by the ship's surgeon, Richard Newman, that a belligerently disruptive Hart appeared, interrupting Newman's work and loudly threatening to sue the Ward Line itself. Ordered out by the doctor, Crane waited outside, and attempted to escort Peggy back to her cabin. Peggy had been told to take a sleeping pill and go to bed, but her rest was periodically interrupted by the distressed figure of the poet forcing his way into her cabin to continue his confused, self-accusing monologue laced with a drunk's recriminations against everything and everyone.

It was Crane's last stand. He was sailing back to a city that offered him no expectations, and no future. His ideal of the poet as visionary had been disowned by a society in which he had no place. At some stage in the night, Crane was forcibly restrained and locked in his cabin, only to break out and go on a rampage in the sailors' quarters that resulted in him being badly beaten, before attempting to climb the ship's rail and being wrestled to the deck by the watch at 3:30 a.m.

When Crane resurfaced at 10 a.m., the steward reported that he was drinking copiously from a bottle of Cutty Sark whisky. Dishevelled and nursing a black eye, he found his way to Peggy's cabin an hour later, and contritely confessed that his ring and wallet were missing and that he had no memory of the previous night. With Crane still in his pyjamas and a light topcoat, Peggy persuaded him to eat a large breakfast of grapefruit, cereal, eggs and bacon and toast. Advising him he would feel better after he was shaved and dressed, Peggy did her best to persuade him to return to his cabin and put on clean clothes. 'I'm not going to make it dear. I'm utterly disgraced,' he told her, before leaving the room.

A few minutes later, and shortly before noon, Crane reappeared on deck. A large number of the Orizaba's ninety passengers who were assembled waiting for the results of the ship's pool watched Crane walk rapidly towards the stern. In the words of an eyewitness, 'He walked to the railing, took off his coat, folded it neatly over the railing (not dropping it on the deck), placed both hands on the railing, raised himself on his toes, and then dropped back again. We all fell silent and watched him wondering what in the world he was up to. Then, suddenly, he vaulted over the railing and jumped into the sea . . .'

Hart's drop into the ship's white detonative wake, in waters policed by cruising sharks, 275 miles out of Havana, didn't, however, result in instant death. The same witness, running to the rail, reported on Crane's instinctual fight for survival: 'Just once I saw Crane, swimming strongly, but never again. It was a scene I am unable to forget.' Whether he was sucked under by the explosive churn of the ship's four-turbine engines, or lacerated by killer sharks, the four lifeboats lowered for rescue found no sign of Crane's body in a diligent two-hour search. By the early afternoon the ship's captain, James Blackadder, was forced to conclude, 'If the propellers didn't grind him to mincemeat, then the sharks got him immediately.'

Crane died with the same projected intensity with which he had lived. Unconventional, uncompromising, he maintained his visionary belief to the last impacted second. More than any other writer of his generation, he believed in living poetry to the full, not as an occasional practitioner, but as the total embodiment of the romantic ideal. If, as Peggy Cowley commented, he had no other credentials in life but his gift, then his death may be seen as a courageous defence of a talent that he considered worth taking into the ocean, rather than having it degraded by financial humiliation and the jobless future he faced. Crane literally disappeared into the blue, on a day when the Caribbean was the serene colour of lapis lazuli, and with the ship riding the Tropic of Cancer. Hart's drop was the raw physical smash of 170 lbs of plasma colliding with the blue-skinned Gulf of Mexico, a propulsive impacting detonation that would have shocked him, however momentarily, into the blinding realisation of solid immersive unbreathable cold before being dragged under.

AS YOUR EYES ARE BLUE: LEE HARWOOD'S *COLLECTED POEMS*

Lee Harwood's extreme individuality as a writer of soft focus, American-influenced lyric poems that dissolve the boundaries between dream and reality happily breaks all the rules of how conventional British poetry is conceived. An extraordinary one-off, he contrived to shape a body of poetry so individual as to carry not the least trace element of the Larkin-Hughes-Heaney triumvirate who have been the ubiquitous role models for most post-1950s mainstream poetry.

Everything about Lee Harwood's poetry is original: its form, diction and engaging sense of sexual ambiguity that frees the work of the constraints of a straight poetry harnessed to familial ties, and places relationships in a flexible space – one in which the possibilities to be explored are both exciting and open-ended. There wasn't anything like Lee Harwood's first two books, *title illegible* and *The Man with Blue Eyes*, in British poetry at the time of their appearance in the mid-1960s, and there still isn't anything remotely comparable in terms of a poetry written directly from fluid sensory associations rather than from the attempt to organize experience into an artificially constructed linear event. And the poem that signalled Harwood's arrival, 'As your eyes are blue', is not only one of the great love poems in the English language, but is in every way the blueprint signposting his finely tuned method of streaming synaptic cut-ups into floating visual imagery. While the poem is clearly written for a man, the question of gender nonetheless remains enigmatic to the reader.

> your shirt on the top of a chest-of-drawers
> a mirror facing the ceiling and the light in a cupboard
> left to burn all day a dull yellow
> probing the shadowy room   "what was it?"

The clues are in the objects scattered around the room. The shirt isn't necessarily the giveaway (women wear shirts), but it's a pointer in a poem that is so abstractly modern that it changes the direction of poetry altogether with its mix of charged, urban beauty. What is apparent in staying with this poem as a sign of the flavour of work to come is Lee Harwood's facility to dissolve inner landscapes into the realities of city life happening in the moment outside his window. He can jump effortlessly within the space of a line from imagining a mountain scene to the immediate perception of a brilliant red bus travelling down Gower Street. His mapping comes close to recreating the continuous processes of thought in which we invariably morph between the past and the future to the exclusion of the present. He is in this respect more immediate than John Ashbery, who together with Frank O'Hara forms the more obvious influences on this and Harwood's early poetry. But who, other than Harwood, could get the spaciness of love so right, together with the questioning network of conflicting emotions that it calls into being? Underneath the poem's surface tranquillity is an undertow of anxiety surrounding separation.

> yes, it was on a hot july day
> with taxis gunning their motors on the throughway
> a listless silence in the backrooms of paris bookshops
> why bother one thing equal to another.

The poet's judicious edits that continually prevent resolution are handled with exemplary cool. His imagery comes up bright as Swarovski crystals, and the tone at once casual and implicitly committed resonates with a young poet's idealistic vision. 'As your eyes are blue . . .' is, to my mind, a love poem as important to its time as Shakespeare's androgynously sexed sonnets were to his.

The major thrust of Lee Harwood's poetry, in which dream autonomy is linked to fragmented narratives, is to be found in the three books *The White Room* (1968) *Landscapes* (1969) and *The Sinking Colony* (1970), all published in quick succession by Stuart Montgomery's Fulcrum Press, their momentum establishing Harwood's reputation as a leading poetic voice in the heady, transitional climate of the late 1960s, when poetry was for a short time loosely federated to an ethos in which drugs and rock music were its coefficients. And for a brief period a gateway opened in the narrow strictures of post-war British poetry letting vision in. The subject matter became suddenly modern and explosive rather than retrograde and commonplace in line with the criteria established by the Movement, and Lee Harwood's work was central to the hope that a new poetry, taking its firepower from imagination and its lead from the crazy dynamic of pop, would replace a rigidly endemic conservatism.

The disruptive social milieu, contributing to his growth as a poet and the need to express the times in a poetry that was wholly new, in part explains why Lee Harwood's poems written in the period 1965–70 are still so exciting to read. He is liberated in ways that make his mainstream contemporaries feel dated and free in the sense of going wherever experience takes him, rather than narrowing his remit to the essentially ordered domestic world road-mapped by the Larkin generation. It's all the more marvellous that we have poems like 'As your eyes are blue . . .', 'White', 'Plato was right though', 'Pullman', 'Cargo',

'The Sinking Colony' and 'The Words', to mention only a few of the memorable early successes, or a poem like 'Linen' in which Harwood's characteristic emphasis on the sensual is complemented by a typically deconstructed narrative.

> Waking on the purple sheets whose softness
> The streets heavy with summer   the night thick with green leaves
> drifting into sleep we lay
> The dazzle of morningthe hot pavements
> fruit markets   "The Avenues"
> "You and I are pretty as the morning"
> on the beaches
> machine-gunning the fleeing army
> the fighters coming in low "at zero"
> the sun behind them and bombs falling all around
> "Jah Jah"   CLICK CLICK   Jah Jah"

This poem exemplifies Harwood's ability to shift rapidly from private to public worlds, from the intimately personal to the political arena in the space of eleven lines. The poem reads like footage, jumping from the languorous atmospherics of waking on purple sheets to the dazzle of an intensely hot day to the war-zone of a beach raked by fighters flying out of the sun to bomb an army in retreat. What might look casual in his work rarely is so, and a mark of Lee Harwood's originality is that there are no imitators of his style in British poetry. You don't open a magazine or anthology to find Harwood clones, because it's risky working in his sort of space, whereas most mainstream poetry is a variation of recognisable sources, or, in pathological terms, a weaker strain of the virus.

There is no radical rerouting of Lee Harwood's poetic objectives after 1970, the poems remaining consistent with the poet's personal sense of geography, his gravitation to American rather than British influences on his work, and to the creation of quiet, allusive poems that document the significant experiential changes in his life. In 1970, Harwood moved to Brighton, where he lived up until the time of his death in 2015, and the importance of the town and the adjacent south coast became a significant factor of his work, not in provincial terms, but in the sense of colouring his poetry with the referentials of a lived psychogeography and a colour design equal to the luminous marine shimmer of the coast.

The section in *Collected Poems*, 'Boston to Brighton 1972–73', records the beginnings of the poet's association with the seaside commuter town, almost but not quite a suburb of London's sprawling metastasis, that has featured so prominently in his work. You can picture the poet with his perennially slim, boyish figure, dressed casually in jeans, a Ben Sherman shirt and sneakers, making the Brighton topology his own as he retrieves visual detail from a tomato red sunset over the beach, or the extended shutdown of a mirage-like summer's day to the virtualised space in which he works on the page. In fact, Lee Harwood's increasing preoccupation with sea voyages, something begun with poems like 'The nine death ships' and 'Death of a pirate king' from *The Sinking Colony*, was to be continued with 'Sea Journals', a sequence in which direct personal observation of shipping is linked to allegorical narratives whose storylines blur between fact and fiction. There is a raw descriptive faculty displayed here, too, that is absolutely physical in its recreation of life on the deck of a ship lying off the coast of Shoreham.

'The sound of the waves slapping against the side, the black iron plates thick and heavy with many re-paintings; the wind rattling the metal lines against the metal masts.

'A clear bright day, the sun hot on your arms as you sit outside the galley taking a breather, the deck in front of you littered with potato peelings and a few egg shells. All the clutter of the stern. The smells of the galley, the deck, the ship. The engines quiet, still.'

The sniff of the real and of the stripped down practicalities of galley and deck are the necessary counterpart to Harwood's otherwise free-associated perception, and when the two energies mesh as they do in the perfectly realised 'Gorgeous – yet another Brighton poem' from the much later *Morning Light* (1998) collection, then the poet achieves a transparency that is like a window shining on consciousness. This poem, in its appraisal of the physicality of beach life on a summer's day – no other poet would dare use the word gorgeous – is quintessential Harwood, bringing refinement to a method in which an almost naive simplicity is matched by a rare descriptive aesthetic. The poet asks nothing more of the poem than that it turns the reader on to the sensory exuberance of a summer's day.

> The summer's here.
> Down to the beach
> to swim and lounge and swim again.
> Gorgeous bodies young and old.
> Me too. Just gorgeous. Just feeling good
> and happy and so at ease in the world.

At first look there's nothing much happening here on the surface, other than the pursuit of recreational pleasure, but what is amazing is how close the poem comes to windowing direct experience. It's as if there's no separation between the language and the physical happening, no differentiation between the seen and the known. And it's this easiness of tone, this never straining after the unnatural, that makes Lee Harwood's poetry so immensely pleasurable to read. You go its way as a co-journeyer in an act of sharing that invites the reader into the poem. It's a given that runs throughout his *Collected Poems*, imparting an openness and generosity to the work that is in strict contrast to the inflected irony and self-deprecation that underscores so much careerist British poetry. Harwood is a romantic in his use of the self as pivotal to expression. The 'I' in the poem is the honest narrator taking the beach scene back in his head in 'Gorgeous' to meet the experience of a day out with words.

> I walk home.
> the air so soft and warm,
> like fur brushing my body.
> The dictionary says
> "gorgeous – adorned with rich and brilliant colours,
> sumptuously splendid, showy, magnificent, dazzling."
> That's right.

For Lee Harwood, the building blocks of the poem attract and organize themselves into a pattern through the almost unmediated autonomy of personal experience. There are a number of moving poems written in memory of his friend, the poet Paul Evans, whose death Harwood witnessed when he fell on a joint mountain climb, in which the loss felt, no matter how acute, is translated into the familiar and known landmarks they shared in and about Brighton and also in scaling the Welsh peaks. In other words, grief is given a topology and made tolerable through the recognition that what was once shared is still vitally alive to the poet in the here and now, as in 'Coming out of Winter.'

> suddenly slammed up
> against a wall by memories of the dead
> loved ones completely gone from
> this place
>
> shafts of sunlight cutting through the clouds
> onto the everchanging sea below
>
> How many times we discussed the sea's colours
> all beyond description   words a mere hint
> of what's before our eyes   then and now

There's little encouragement to any poet, other than an inner prompting to keep writing in the face of neglect and zero financial reward; but poets do, and Lee Harwood's *Collected Poems* speak of the persistence of a vision that has grown contemporaneous with his life. Whatever of real value that has happened to him has found its way into the poetry, allowing the life and work the sense of cohesive unity that comes of unconditionally giving oneself to one's art.

It's a weird thing what makes poets fill in their time with words, and adjust their lives, usually to their detriment, to the anti-social nature of their work. Few occupations demand so much and outwardly give so little in return. But the reward in Lee Harwood's case for both poet and reader is not only the exceptional gift of his writing, but more that the resource continued to inspire and deepen growth within the poet right up to the time of *The Orchid Boat*, published in the same year as his death. Later poems like 'Young woman in Japanese garden', 'Orchids' and 'Dear Joe' are as perfect as his aesthetic can get in working out ways of seeing that are always distinctly new. The sparkle of his imagery often catches like the sudden flare of a diamond accompanying an unobtrusive hand gesture, visible across the room: the light raying out as a brilliant starburst. And always we go back to this deep quiet centre from which Lee Harwood works as an instructive source. 'Young woman in Japanese garden' exemplifies to the full his gift for tranquillity arrived at by a zen-like notation of the present.

> The day so cold. Your breath white,
> coming out in small trailing clouds.
> The trees snow laden in the Snow Garden.
> A pause in the ritual, step by step.
> The pale late afternoon like that
> makes you think you're there, so present
> crunch of snow and the red gate post –
> but you're not.

The trick, of course, is in the seeing. You could be misled into thinking little is happening here other than the creation of a mood and atmospherics, whereas, in fact, the poet has established the prelude to a small fiction, a frozen novella in which the detail is the happening. The poem is in this instance an act of re-photography in that the poet is taking his subject from a young woman observed in a photograph and inventing her probable story.

For Lee Harwood as for John Ashbery, writing is never a means of trying to nail a subject into an artificially conclusive resolution, but more a way of pointing up not only the plurality of seeing, but the inexhaustible potentialities available to the poet in documenting his material. Whereas someone like Thom Gunn concentrates his energies on focusing the poem into a singular motive that argues its metaphysics as right, Harwood prefers to keep his options fluently, questionably open. It seems to me that any poem carries the inherent potential to be reworked in any number of ways by the poet, and Lee Harwood's work in particular seems to lend itself to this experimental facility. There's arguably no end to how a poem can be remixed in the limitless creative permutations available to the likes of a Harwood or Ashbery in their open-ended rather than conclusive invitations to have the poem adopt its own preferred direction.

On bad days poets often wonder why they ever bothered to traffic with their fundamentally unrewarding craft. The loneliness built into the pursuit, the ever-deferred practical issues, the time invested in the work, all seem counterproductive to material advancement, and the book, when it finally appears, usually goes unnoticed or receives minimal reviews. In a better world, some of the real originals in British poetry like Lee Harwood, Harry Fainlight, Asa Benveniste, Keston Sutherland, Tom Raworth and Christopher Middleton would at least be elevated to public awareness rather than consigned to cult status.

But poetry travels always best by word of mouth, and the people responsible for its survival, rather than the self-appointed autocrats who legislate over its internal politics, are usually the ones in the know. In poetry the viciousness of its factions rarely allows for any honest assessment of what is happening outside of the elected hierarchy, and while this in the short term may compromise the more pioneering and liberated it cannot, in the long term, destroy the importance or the durability of truly original work. Lee Harwood's *Collected Poems* are there as a sure thing, their substantial 500 pages brimming with constantly inventive flair and palpable durability.

It's an odd thing, too, how work written 40 years ago still catches on the nerves. Lee Harwood's 'first real love scene' as he recounts it in 'Rain journal: June 65', written at a time when he was working at Better Books in Charing Cross Road, communicates rather like an old home movie watched on a rainy Sunday afternoon. Describing lovers sitting naked together on a bed, drinking vodka in a state of post-sex euphoria, the poem runs time back to the moment of writing, in which separation is an immediate issue.

> but John
> now when we're miles apart
> the come-down from mountain visions
> and the streets all raining
> and me in the back of the shop
> making free phone calls to you
> what can we do?

The writing here is as open as a pop lyric and doing something completely new, not only in directing the poem to a man (John), but in the perfectly relaxed tone in which it addresses separation. It's confessional in a way that's unnervingly modern and could well have been scribbled down in the back of the shop, but is curiously, quizzically moving in its question 'what can we do?' As with most situations presented to lovers who are living on opposite sides of the world, there isn't anything than can be done except recreate the other through the figure in the imagination.

> whole days spent
> remaking your face
> the sound of your voice
> the feel of your shoulder

Lee Harwood was in his mid-twenties at the time of writing this poem and much of the work that would go into *The White Room* (1968), and what is so impressive here is that he borrows nothing at all from inherited British poetry, but writes as though he is inventing the language and starting out new. Harwood's early love poems are like nobody else's; all the familiar clichés of a recycled heterosexual repertoire are dropped in favour of streaming often dissociated fractured memories into the everyday awareness of physical separation and loss. If love is ideally magical, then it follows that a poem should try to approximate the same effects imaginatively. The almost hallucinatory free fall of imagery in 'No – all the temple bells' recreates perfectly the sort of dreamy space-time that a lover virtualises in the attempt to be with the other.

> whoever you are
> let me shelter you
> and with this
> drumming rhythms grew
> until the entire planet was woven
> into
> an elaborate stringball
> rolling across a green desert

whose orange and humid night
I now eat and offer you
"let us reconsider . . . I mean these
mountain problems"
a car starting in a quiet side street.

These love poems are all the more marvellous for existing in the inspired mental spaces their originality creates. A good poem should, to my mind, have something of the qualities of altered state in its mapping of the poet's brain chemistry. It's a simple criterion. If you can't get into the visionary present then what you are relating is most likely pedestrian, and of little help in shifting the reader's consciousness to different realities. The problem for Harwood and all poets who actively subvert the accepted status is that most British poets are conditioned to do little else but reaffirm the ordinary nature of their lives. The generic fear of delinquent imagination coded into so much of the poetry that takes its lead from Larkin holds those who differ at ransom. I suppose the criterion for any poet who has reached a point in his life where a *Collected Poems* seems a necessary assessment of what is most durable in his or her work is: how could it have been done differently, if at all? The absolute homogeneity of Lee Harwood's poetry suggests that for him it could only have been achieved one way, and the consistency of his writing affirms the resourcefulness of a lifetime's endeavour to articulate his highly individual way of dissolving the frontiers of inner space into his own perceived reality. Part of Lee Harwood's outstanding originality is that he stands out too much as different. Poets who lack easy comparison with their contemporaries are likely to be neglected at the expense of the ubiquitously derivative. Lee Harwood, apart from his links to the early, more lyrical Tom Raworth of *The Relation Ship* and *Big Green Day*, and to aspects of FT Prince's quieter, disarmingly allusive moments, and David Gascoyne's visionary surreal spearheading, is almost singularly isolated in British poetry. You can't easily imitate his style or leech his kinetic broken narratives, which you can quite easily with the predictable formatting of Larkin, Hughes or Heaney in various degrees of dilution.

Lee Harwood's progression over the transitioning decades, and that implies the biological changes brought to his poetry by inherited heart disease, can be picked up on in a late poem, 'Classicism (Satie, Finlay, et Cie . . .)'. The approach isn't essentially different from his early poems; it's the references that have changed and deepened.

> Afternoon light slides through a Paris apartment
> The white walls and few furnishings
> Simple and bare and elegant
> Piano music now
> The books   the couch
>
> Timeless moment
> we would stare into each other's eyes
> almost frightened so intense the love

The constituents of this Paris interior are characteristically aesthetically pleasing with music coming up to shape the light arriving through a window. What appears simply descriptive in the arrangement of domestic things within the poem is given a radical dislocation.

> "No fear. No harm."
> say Chinese sages 3000 years ago
>
> Caravans depart the oasis
> Roman mottos grow mossy

The associations that began with the quiet order of a Paris apartment are reversed 3000 years to connect with events that themselves press down on the moment of writing. It's a transitional dynamic the poet has perfected into an instantly recognisable method in which present tense also includes both the past and the future.

Lee Harwood's *Collected Poems* exist to bring optimal pleasure to the reader. Elementally they have the smell of the beach about them, the bittersweet tang of summers on the South coast, and of high places – mountains and sky-coloured lakes. They are also witness to the urban spaces in which much of our lives go on, taking in love, loss and the things we do indoors like listen to music, reflect on our relation to the world and evaluate those special moments that in Harwood's case become the reason to write poems. They're also a superb affirmation of individuality rooted in something much deeper than literary fashions and that is the persuasion of the self to write independently of reward and just for the giving. In this respect, Lee Harwood's poems are gifts to the reader, sometimes quiet as a Rothko and nearly always celebratory in their impulse. I personally need their shine in my life and made my association with his books and person a long time ago into a meaningful thing. And reading a poet is another sort of love affair, demanding give and take and the persistence that comes with trust. Poet and reader often coexist through a lifetime without making contact – who knows who carries lines of poetry around in their heads in big city life – but writing about another poet is at least a form of communication and a way of acknowledging gratitude for something given that can't be taken away.

WASN'T IT A STRANGE WAY DOWN: PETER PERRETT AND THE ONLY ONES

Part of the attraction that Peter Perrett, as a ruined enfant terrible of a specifically dysphoric genre of rock, continues to assert over his admirers, is a quality of timelessness of image. The idiosyncratically drawlish voice, redolent of Lou Reed's monotonal delivery, the dark shades, the implacable cool adopted as attitude, and, above all, the imperturbable belief in rock music as a mode of redemptive expression, are all components that help make Perrett into a composite of the irredeemably wasted rock star. You can't age Peter because of the indelible rip his image has made in time: the searingly elevated cheek bones, the poutishly androgynous lips, the forbidding fringe and the emaciated figure are all part of our received notion of dissipated glamour, as the archetype instructing a pop genealogy who have taken drugs and performance to a committed edge. The man dressed, even in midsummer, in raffish wolf or fox fur coats, or splashy Biba leopard print jackets, was, of course, in the context of his music, a romantic without ever consciously aspiring to that role. I'm quite sure that Peter has never read Baudelaire, Rimbaud, Genet, Burroughs, or that glacially evocative drug classic, Alexander Trocchi's *Cain's Book*, because he was never in conscious need of assimilating influences to his natural tendency to write romantically charged lyrics celebrating loss, crime, drugs and the vicious aspects of an underworld milieu; but he shares with all of these writers a disposition to explore the darker aspects of the psyche as the dynamic central to fuelling his creativity.

I would argue a case that from the 1960s onwards, that is, with the advent of lyricists like Bob Dylan, Leonard Cohen and Lou Reed, the literate songwriter has assumed precedence over the poet, as the voice speaking for the psychological needs of youth, a role that poetry has done little to challenge in losing its ascendancy to the more direct communication of pop. And it's essentially as a lyricist that Peter Perrett would like to be remembered, the peculiarly nocturnal flavour of his songs standing out as resistant narratives of the individual living on the edge, at a dangerous angle to society, or in his own words, 'out there in the night.' All of Peter's lyrics, originating on the page, and later put through the laconic instrument of his dejected voice, and fed heroic arpeggios by John Perry's guitar, write the outsider into the role of decadent hero, the disaffected protagonist of the song having absconded from any pretence of normality.

When The Only Ones arrived on the punk-inflected music scene in 1977, they were already out of time with their contemporaries. Their musical influences, upgraded to accommodate some of the more flagrantly anti-social aspects of punk, were, however, rooted in the melodic hooks and articulate guitar riffs of 1960s pop. It was not surprising that the drummer Mike Kellie had been in 60s outfits like Spooky Tooth, and Camel, that the bass player Alan Mair had been nurtured in the same decade by the Beatstalkers, and that John Perry owed his spectacular guitar pyrotechnics to the saturated influence of iconic legends like Hendrix, Townshend and Clapton, as the virtuoso practitioners of stratospheric guitar figures. Peter's image, too, was visually and sartorially a throwback to an era in which dressing for the stage was integral to a singer's role.

Internally warring, and outwardly angular to the musically ravaged punk ethos in which they found themselves caught up, disdainfully signed to a major label – CBS reputedly offered them an advance of a quarter of a million for ten albums – The Only Ones had the air of a maverick band living from posthumous recognition almost before they had begun. Despite their attraction as a live act, who no matter how substance disorientated, or in individual conflict with each other, were nonetheless consummate professionals, the subject matter of Perrett's songs, and the downbeat rendition given them by his invariably narcotic delivery, were always inclined towards heroic failure rather than the incentive of commercial success. Even their spectacularly accelerated debut single for CBS, 'Another Girl, Another Planet', with Perry's riffs compressing the entire history of rock into an anthology of meteoric chords, and Perret's skewed vocal chasing a trajectory across the song's chemical references, barely managed to graze the Top 50. The song's immediate declaration of defiance, 'I always flirt with death/I look ill but I don't care about it/I can face your threats and stand up tall and shout about it', seemed unconsciously designed to alienate mainstream listeners. The confession driven by a tone of streetwise contempt, and coloured by a flat, South London drawl, had about it all the arrogant credibility of the youthful Mick Jagger, poking an older generation into enraged abeyance by his candid sexual posturing.

Critically acclaimed as a paradigm of the synthesised energies needed to create a great pop single, the band's disappointment at the failure of 'Planet' to chart, was in part responsible for the aura of disillusionment that subsequently invested their profile. It was as though, having revealed themselves at their best too early and been rejected by the record-buying public, the injustice done them could never be fully reversed. According to Alan Mair, the single's failure went deep into the band's collective psyche. 'I think that took the edge off the band. It affected

Peter deeper than he ever said. Radio One wouldn't play it. They thought the lyrics were too heavy. "Space travel's in my blood" wasn't quite to their taste in 1978.'

What Perrett had discovered, to his disadvantage, was that his code of normality, when it was made public through a song, was viewed with suspicion and moral hostility by the conventional. The heavy black eyeliner, the retro clothes and attachment to drugs that were accepted currency in his circle, were not so easily translated into the daylight world of Margaret Thatcher's voraciously materialist Britain. Perrett and his band were, in fact, the antithesis to the prevailing reactionary climate of British politics. Perrett, as the defiant frontman of a band so radically displaced in time that they appeared always to have existed, while creating the impression of having just dropped in, literally from another planet, quickly became the singular focus for a cult who advocated defection from society as a chosen lifestyle.

The reality of Peter's chemical life, as both a lucrative dealer and progressively dysfunctional user, was on a daily basis to lead to a disruptively unreliable lifestyle in which appointments were rarely kept, and in which heroin time came to replace real time, as the precinct in which he existed. But despite becoming habituated to chasing the dragon, Perrett nonetheless managed to maintain a demanding tour schedule with The Only Ones, his compelling stage presence and the rapid fire of his adept rhythm guitar playing, projecting a visual magnitude that set him apart from his contemporaries, by the adoption of a careless aesthetic that always seemed right. The studied hair, backcombed like the fashion obsessed Small Faces at the apogee of their Mod popularity, the pink leather trousers and fur coats that seemed outtakes from the Rolling Stones' wardrobe, circa 1967, and the black shades with their Warhol, Lou Reed and Dylan connotations, were all referential components integrated into Peter's distinctly modern, but alienated personification of the pop star as someone set apart by looks, mystique, and a self-regulating hedonism that defined its own laws.

Laired up in the labyrinthine maze of his big house at Forest Hill, South London, the interior decorated with antiques bought from the King's Road on impulsive spending forays, Peter and his managerial wife Zena became locked into an interior zone where drugs were prioritized over the basics of everyday living. Disappointment at the failure of The Only Ones' eponymously titled debut album to make commercial headway, rather than stall as a cult classic, was an additional reason for Perrett to retreat into a state of pharmaceutically induced introspection. The album, with its unremittingly dystopian vision, a lyrical triumph of submerged dreams in conflict with reality, washed over by John Perry's atmospherically edgy guitar, deserved a lot better, and remains to this day one of the great lost records of its time. And if the fascination surrounding artistic failure invariably gives rise to cults, then the hard facts of rejection were not so easily dissolved into Perrett's life of total identification with music as a justification for living. By projecting his own private mythology on to the public in songs like 'The Beast', 'Creature of Doom', and 'The Immortal Story', lyrics written as heroin analgesics to the raw ontological pain of living, Perrett had made himself vulnerable to interpreting resistance as a refutation of his personal obsessions. The plaintive warning in songs like 'Breaking Down' and 'The Beast', of a fragile nervous sensibility close to shattering, were slowly becoming realised in a life in which oblivion appeared preferable to a discredited system of poetics. 'The Beast', a metaphor for smack as Peter's psychological tool of degradation, was prophetic not only of his fall, but of the lives of some of his close milieu. 'As soon as I took smack,' he told Nina Antonia, 'I knew how dangerous it was, just the fact I could like something that much. But I genuinely believed I wasn't going to succumb to it…I wouldn't have carried on with it, if I'd really believed it was going to happen to me. I've known a couple of people who wanted to be junkies, who thought it was glamorous, but I never wanted to be a junkie at all.' In 'The Beast', the dealer/user, in inevitably symbiotic union, is conceived as a redoubtably vampiric figure. 'Out in the streets the modern vampire prowls/He's been spreading disease all around/ There's an epidemic if you don't believe me/Take a look at the eyes of your friends.' The signposts were all there for Peter to follow, chasing the intangible dragon all the way to his brain's reward centre through the dopamine rush delivered by heroin melted on to foil and inhaled.

Dispirited, but invariably reaching an optimal creative peak in the studio, The Only Ones were to record the darkly hypnotic *Even Serpents Shine* as a follow-up album to their first excursion into the subterranean corridors of empathising with the addicted, terminal, disaffected outlaws who occupied Perrett's songwriting imagination. Recorded at Central Recorder and Tony Visconti's Good Earth Studio, the album was in some ways a still darker continuity of Perrett's obsession with perversely turning his back on life in order to accelerate his fascination with the rituals of drug-induced self-destruction. The band's formula of dystopian monotonal vocals, matched by Perry's onomatopoeically vertiginously spiky guitar, differed little from the preceding album, and, if anything, reaffirmed the band's resistance to any sort of commercial compromise. The entrenchment was perversely heroic, right from the album's initial line, 'I see a woman with death in her eyes,' sung by Perrett with the detached cool of someone living in an interzone between flickering consciousness and sleep. 'From Here to Eternity', the album's opening track, about a young woman selling sex and going under, sets the mood for an even darker repeat prescription of alienated death-bound themes than those explored on their preceding album. It's in the lyrical concerns manifested on *Even Serpents Shine* that Perrett comes closest to the influence of Baudelaire in consolidating a pervasive mood of irreparable melancholy. I would argue that

Perrett, as a lyricist, is unquestionably the Baudelaire of pop, his raw, untutored poetry confronting a generation of rock enthusiasts with an index of self-loathing and delight in pathological decay every bit as shocking as Baudelaire's ability to outrage the mid-nineteenth century bourgeois sensibility with a poetry that had him prosecuted for obscenity. The analogy extends deeper in that Baudelaire's dependency on opium as the co-partner to his increasing creative lethargy, and his neurotic obsession with death, are in many ways paralleled by Perrett's heroin addiction contributing to an only intermittently broken musical silence since the demise of The Only Ones in 1981.

The songs collected on *Even Serpents Shine* are some of the darkest written in the history of rock and represent Perrett at an emotional nadir, but one from which he still considers it worthwhile communicating. Fatigue, disillusionment with the messy ups and downs of relationships, a prevailing anomie – 'Sometimes when I wake up it's like I never woke up at all' – the substitution of night for day as the precinct in which to live, and the misanthropic reversal of life for death as the desired state in which to be, are all themes given shape by Perrett's inimitably despondent voice that takes Lou Reed's characteristic flatness down five flights of stairs and sits on it, it's that low. Songs like 'Flaming Torch', 'No Solution', 'Miles From Nowhere', 'In Betweens' and 'Curtains For You' play nihilistic endgames with the idea of exiting from life through the gateway to addiction and impartial functioning. In none of the lyrics does Peter ever give the sense of truly relating or connecting to either people or things, and the nonchalantly disturbed 'In Betweens', with its sense of total lack of commitment to any aspect of living, nursed by Perry's eloquently cooked guitar figures, finds the singer, in his late twenties, already vacillating over whether to live or die, his conception of failure in both his personal life and music blocking the road forwards. In fact, most of *Even Serpents Shine* sounds like a timeless lament for what was so early on denied The Only Ones as a band – recognition as the quotient of commercial success. Perrett and Perry's musically disruptive partnership seems, in embracing terminal ennui as a theme for their music – and few guitarists can meet Perry in his ability to celebrate loss through heroic guitar figures – to have conspired to initiate band defeat even before the idea of fame could be entertained as an option. Perry's guitar, chord by chord the sonic translator of Perrett's opiated chemistry, seemed always to be played directly from his neurology rather than the guitar stem, as though he was plugged into a metabolic core he shared with the singer rather than the studio's electricity. *Even Serpents Shine*, as a black-mooded suite of misanthropic songs, is a truly visionary rock statement, an Orphic journey of retrieval from the bottom and the end of the night. It's a solid black diamond of an album mined from the subterranean arteries of South London. 'I've had enough of all this poison and decay,' Perrett sings on 'You've Got to Pay', as an admission of the chemical and moral toxins flooding his precariously fractured sensibility. And, almost as prophetically, he was to recognise in the lyrics of 'Miles From Nowhere' his innate propensity to shrink geography to the circumscribed radius of a single room. 'I wanna die in the same place I was born/Miles from nowhere/I used to reach for the stars/But now I'm reformed,' he intones with the conviction of someone accelerating his own removal from life to the constrained physical space needed by the user to sit on the same mattress in the same room day by day in the monotonous inertia of the junky conscripted to existing in heroin time. On a psychological level, one could argue that Perrett's conversion of the written word into the compressed medium of a pop song – 'space travel's in my blood' – was his way of compacting experience to a reduced quotient – the two to three minute duration of an Only Ones number.

The demanding Serpents tour, taking in Britain and Europe, did little to redeem the album's low commercial profile.

Increasingly phobic, Perrett would refuse to go out on stage if the food wasn't arranged to his liking in the dressing room, or if chocolate cake hadn't been provided to appease his sweet tooth. Despite the manic activity surrounding the tour, the band could make no inroads on the expansion of their marginalised status, idealised by a cult, but ignored by the general record-buying public. Limited appeal fed the worst of Perrett's and Perry's respective dependencies, refuge in narcotics cushioning the two from the reality of the band's failed commercial expectations. Two albums into their lucrative contract, and hot with the voltage of live energies, The Only Ones were increasingly viewed by CBS as potentially irredeemable casualties. In a way, Perrett had already sounded their epitaph with the line 'I'm always in the wrong place at the wrong time' from 'Flaming Torch', and the acute realisation that his tenable position in music was visibly and irretrievably slipping away was a reason to precipitate an inexorable habit. But more than just addiction, Perrett's descent was taking him deeper into the criminal underworld of dealers. According to Alan Mair, 'It was reaching the stage where instead of arriving in Amsterdam and rehearsing for the gig, Peter and John would end up trying to score some dope and end up in the heaviest places with the heaviest people, who Peter would bring to the gig.' The consequences of using for Peter were indolence, increased mental dissociation, loss of projection on stage and the retreat into a world of solipsistic disregard for the band's credibility with its label.

A third album, *Baby's Got a Gun*, reflecting not so much the frenetic energies of their live stage act as Peter's slow-burn habit, only reaffirmed the band's lack of commercial viability and their unwillingness to compromise. Despite Perrett's claim that a number of the songs remained unfinished fragments and that his dislike of Colin Thurston being brought in arbitrarily by CBS to produce the album in part deadened the band's edge, the overall feel of *Baby's Got a Gun* is often melodically uplifting, notwithstanding its lyrical preoccupation with death and drugs as the gravitational field towards which Perrett was instinctively pulled. Chaotically rehearsed in Romansleigh, North Devon, in an 8-track Langley Farm studio, before going into Utopia Studios, London, to begin work in earnest with Colin Thurston in September 1980, for sessions that were disrupted by the band's 26-date tour of the US to coincide with the release of *Special View*, a compilation lifted especially from their first two albums, *Baby's Got a Gun*, was arguably the quintessential Only Ones album. Perrett's twisted declaration on the seminal number 'Why Don't You Kill Yourself', 'This ain't no missionary speech/Just some friendly advice/Why don't you kill yourself?/ You ain't no use to no one else', are lyrics literally metabolized by Perry's symbiotic fretwork into the sonic equivalent of overdosing. Having experimented in the States with fixing in order to secure a quicker rush, Perrett had eschewed the needle in favour of chasing the dragon, because the slower effects of inhalation were less likely to result in an overdose. 'With smoking,' Perrett commented, 'if you put a quarter gram on a piece of tin foil, it takes 10 or 15 minutes to get to you. It's a much slower way of taking it into the system, whereas with an injection it is much easier to OD. Luckily I've always had enough. That made it easier to resist fixing. I'm not saying that I'm stronger than other people just because I didn't fix, I was just luckier in that I didn't have to resort to it.' 'The Big Sleep' was lyrically and musically an end to it all, a song that stops time in its abyssal nosedive into going rock bottom with drugs. Something of Perrett's deep sense of disappointment at his music being wastelanded comes through in the telling lines, 'As soon as someone told me there's no such thing as glory/Changed my life completely it's a whole different story', taking 'The Big Sleep' into the shattered fragments of autobiography frozen in time by heroic crystallization. Again, Perry's guitar maps the song's neural evolution from Perrett's by now drug-compromised commentary on his habit, with the consummate ache of chords retrieved from his viscera and transferred to his brain. There's a case to be argued for 'The Big Sleep' comprising the ultimate smack song, a lyrical atlas open on a white plateau across which Perrett had started to walk in lunar gravity.

The edgy psychic landscape crossed by Perrett's inveterately nocturnal imagination inevitably threw up 'Deadly Nightshade' as a lyric, a flower that carries the poison belladonna. Perrett's dodgy paranoia as a user and dealer becomes apparent in the lines, clearly addressed to himself rather than the indigo-coloured flower, as the assumed subject of the song : 'Stars are your companions/And the darkness is your friend/It protects you from the gaze of any would-be hired assassins.' Living as he was behind a system of heavy fire doors acting as a deterrent to opportune police raids, and mixing on a daily basis with gofers and dealers, Perrett had every reason to fear being murdered. His total immersion in underworld drug dealings accounted not only for the fragility of some of the songs on *Baby's Got a Gun*, but also for the sense of incompletion that he felt inhibited the album's potential. 'There are some good songs on it but it doesn't seem complete. The first and second albums seemed rounded and finished, whereas that album, maybe because I knew how it was made, seems a bit up in the air. There is nothing to take it to its conclusion. It just reflected the disintegration.'

But, as always with The Only Ones, dissolution was a defiantly subversive gesture with Perrett's vocals sounding relentlessly disinterested and Perry's guitar reaching for sublime phrases to commit an extended last rites over the irremediably down-mooded lyrics. And as with their two previous studio excursions, the material recorded for *Baby's Got a Gun* lacked any song light enough to prove a charts contender as a single. The absence, too, of give in Perrett's voice, no matter the attempts on the part of Koulla and Pauline Murray to colour a number of songs with ethereal backing harmonies, created an inevitable impasse. 'Trouble in the World' simply wasn't the right single to make headway in the charts, nor one of the album's more memorable numbers, and disappeared on its release in November 1980, without any significant trace. The fascination for fans was once again with listening to the band commit career suicide with such uncompromising style.

Looking for a way out of the band's etiolating internal frictions, Perrett starting turning up at the studio with a coterie of adulating teenage musicians as a way of provoking dissension in a band already stretched to the limits of tolerance by his immersion in drugs. Perrett, of course, blamed it on Perry. 'I was worried about my relationship with John. We just weren't getting on well, mainly 'cos whenever I stopped using, he'd bring stuff on tour or whatever.'

A 23-date British tour on the back of the April 1980 release of *Baby's Got a Gun*, found the band's ability to create live desultory pyrotechnics on stage undiminished by their essential lack of camaraderie. The end, deferred by contractual obligations, was to come on the skewed American tour that followed. After they were dropped as the support act to The Who's 1980 summer tour of the US, the band's essentially impecunious fragmentation happened fast. Marooned in the American desert without the funds to return, and with Perrett wanted on an attempted murder charge in San Francisco for driving his getaway car directly at a car park attendant, and, to add to his problems, having contracted hepatitis B, the band's dissolution happened fast. Three final gigs at London's Hope & Anchor, Dingwalls, and at the Lyceum Ballroom extended their duration sufficiently to be iconized by the music press as the last shambolic purveyors of the romantic legacy of the rock star turned hero by default.

Anticipating a solo career that never happened, and seriously ill with hepatitis, Perrett literally de-realised, his withdrawal from the world deepening over the years to a state of almost terminal disconnect. Post-hepatitis depressed and out of sync with a new decade busy deconstructing the image of the archetypal rock star as confessional ruined hero, orchestrating his own self-destruction in an existing four piece band seemed an easier option than attempting to make music. Unable to continue to motivate himself, Perrett went down with his drug into the basement of himself. Contracted into a perpetually stooped lotus posture on his mat, Perrett's radius shrank to the width of a foil. In his visits intended to retrieve Perrett from a state of terminal addiction, John Perry was a witness to the singer's lapse into a permanently comatose state. 'There were two visits about six weeks apart and I noticed when I got there the second time that he hadn't actually shifted from the part of the floor he was sitting on, or changed his clothes, or apparently moved in the six weeks. The pile of tin foil around him had grown, but otherwise he hadn't moved, or changed or shaved.'

Periodic raids on the house, arrests and overnight stays in the cells, were the only variants in Perrett's otherwise routine immersion in drug time. With his wife Zena also addicted, and a parental responsibility to their two children, Perrett grew locked, partly out of guilt, into agoraphobic inertia. A succession of burglaries stripped the decaying house of its valuable antiques and carpets, with Perrett little able to discern in his drugged state whether the intruders were bailiffs or criminals. An abortive attempt to reunite with John Perry generated some brilliant unreleased studio demos in February and March 1990, but the volatile creative partnership quickly dissolved due to the usual hypersensitive modalities of drug abuse and rivalry between the two, their creative co-dependency feeding a proportionate mutual hostility. In their absence, the release of the band's highly productive Peel Sessions on the cult adulated Strange Fruit label, together with *Faster Than Lightning*, a compilation of live and TV appearance clips, invited critical re-evaluation of the kind that invariably attempts to rehabilitate a band long after the injustice of their demise through critical misunderstanding or indifference, as indispensable indie heroes. With the plug irreparably pulled on their disjointed firepower, it was now felt safe to acknowledge their seminal influence on most aspiring cutting edge bands.

It was, as always, too late for The Only Ones. Perrett's habit was as debilitating as it was seemingly irreversible, and while owning up to the fact that he would like to make music again, he admitted that he now lacked the strength to tour. The complete absence of physical exercise from his life, together with minimal nutrition and the radical slowing down effects of the drug, had left him chronically phobic and dysfunctional outside of the immediate confines of his basement lair. A brief return to creativity as The One signed to Demon Records in 1995, for their *Woke Up Sticky* venture, provoked a brief flurry of activity on Perrett's part, including a number of largely uninspired live performances, in which new songs as well as retreads of Only Ones classics, were given shape by a loosely assembled band auditioned through ads placed in Melody Maker.

Is there ever a bottom to the long way down? On the strength of a Vodafone ad campaign in 2006, featuring 'Another Girl Another Planet', The Only Ones briefly reformed in 2007 for a UK tour accompanied by festivals including Glastonbury, and began recording characteristically dystopian new material in the studio, before imploding again due to renewed and insoluble internal conflicts. Despite attempts at rehab, and moving location to Islington, Perrett's habits were little changed, the curtains permanently drawn on the day, the accumulated foils glinting like migraines in the semi-dark. And isn't addiction in part the attempt to free the user of social gravity, by which I mean not only a place in community; but the responsibility to the body to interact with the collective? That heroin induces passivity, and total bodily neglect, makes it the chosen drug of those who wish to arrest time and centre themselves almost exclusively in the dopamine chemistry of inner space. Ambition, impetus, competitive rivalry all disappear in the subtext of the drug's opiated vocabulary, to be replaced by an uncontested absorption into a timeless present.

Perrett's epitaph with The Only Ones may well be 'Don't Feel Too Good', the last song on *Remains*, a compilation of outtakes and alternative mixes put out by Closer in 1984, with Perry's guitar pursuing so fluent an interpretative line that it sounds like he is executing a sonic inscription for a gravestone. The song's story of addiction, arrest and being charged for possession in Georgia, together with Perrett's sense of total abdication from reality, finds him never sounding more desperate, more final. It's appropriate that the distinctly moribund number should end on the line, 'That's all I've got to say to you', and that the song's placing on *Remains*, as a closer, seems suitably terminal. It's the last word on an album with a title suggesting the songs have been bodybagged together for last rites over studio remains.

Legends never really die, because people hold on to them tenaciously in the attempt to reinvest them with life. Perrett's creative freeze and total withdrawal from the world are, of course, the kind of building blocks from which cult legends are made. It takes a combination of immense dignity, in his case tantric, and unshakable self-conviction to accept that work done is final, and even if The Only Ones' studio output was small, its legacy continues to live like an underground river in the collective indie consciousness. Perrett's seemingly irreversible disappearing act, until the surprise release of a solo album *How the West Was Won* in 2017, is in a way complementary to his music, and to songs that unremittingly gravitate towards individual decline into dissolution and death. Whatever the damage done, Perrett's surprisingly still there, reinvigorated by the fluently compressed guitar energies of his sons' accompaniment on an assumed valedictory album that refocuses his talent to confessionally document and distil aspects of self-ruin into transcendent lyric. Irrespective of this rogue solo return to music on Perrett's part,

The Only Ones have survived their wreckage as a band and live on through the enduring legacy of their ultimately despairing but unforgettably romantically infected strain of punk. Listen to Perrett's voice in the dark. It's a coercive instructor leading you to places you never expected to visit, but which are entirely familiar on arrival. It's the way of good writing to make fear habitable, and Perrett does that. He takes you down to the river, and has you journey with him on his voice to the other side. The Only Ones' story is about getting to that nocturnal place and reporting back right on the edge of the big sleep.

SISTER RAY AND CECIL'S NEW PIECE

Lyrically and musically there's no precedent in rock to 'Sister Ray', and if you're looking for sources or inspirational signposting that may have fed into Lou Reed's writing resource at the time, circa 1967, the strains can in part be found not only in William Burroughs' seminal *Naked Lunch* (1959), but also in cult underground classics like Alexander Trocchi's *Cain's Book* (1960), John Rechy's *City of the Night* (1963), Hubert Selby's *Last Exit To Brooklyn* (1964), and in the gossipy irreverent tone of Frank O'Hara's *Lunch Poems* (1964), a book that arguably, through its casual streetwise tone, brings poetry, and specifically New York city, coolly alive to the modern world.

'Sister Ray' is in the genre of rock music as epic narrative, compressed to 17 minutes studio time, or extended live to 24 or 48 minutes, an urban folk tale or blues shot through by sleaze and coloured by a cast of drag queens, pimps and dealers. Now a song isn't the words on the page, like a poem, it's an expression of feeling brought to those words, which helps to explain why song lyrics when they're printed always seem to lack the excitement of their sung equivalent. The absence of an authorised lyric for 'Sister Ray', together with its variant live readings – Reed was still admitting a stripped-down version of the song to his live solo set in 1977 – has given it an ambiguous, almost apocryphal place in VU recordings, an isolation that further increases the song's magnitude as the powerfully impacting legendary progenitor of heavy pharmaceutical rock.

The song's eminently quirky opening line, that I used as the title for a book of my poetry in 2004, is one of the oddest in rock – 'Duck and Sally inside', or as an alternative 'A drug hit Sally inside'. The two names Duck and Sally, so perfectly suit drag queens, 'ducky' being a commonly used word of endearment in gay terminology during the 1960s, and the two are unequivocally cooking up drugs with Miss Rayon who is busy staring at an apartment that resembles a pig pen. We're told nothing of Sister Ray other than that the song's narrator, who is busy searching for his mainline, presumably to shoot up crystal meth, agrees with her that you can't get the needle in sideways.

What is so flagrantly subversive here, and we're thinking 1968, is that no rock lyricist prior to Lou Reed had ever dared risk such deviated subject material or written so amorally and lawlessly about an underworld in which drugs, drag and fellatio are the accepted dominants. Almost all of Reed's subject matter on *The Velvet Underground and Nico* (1967) and *White Light White Heat* (1968) violated taboo, with Reed bleeding adult material better suited to the underground novel into songs radically at variance with the essentially lightweight gravity of most pop lyrics. Not even The Rolling Stones, despite their notoriety at the time, had ever conceived of converting their largely dissolute personal lifestyles into the confessional bite of their music.

Through the song's progressively menacing saturation of drone and dissonant feedback, we're introduced to Rosy, who together with Miss Rayon is waiting for a dealer who's just got back from Carolina, presumably on a drug run. Reed uses place names, Carolina and Alabama, to free the song up geographically from its druggy apartment ambience, as well as place space around a lyric constantly threatened by sonic extinction. Reed's characteristic monotonal drawl surfs noise to introduce Cecil and his new 'piece' or gun, as an addition to the cast; a new arrival who callously, pathologically proceeds to shoot the dealer dead on the floor. The even cooler response of the narrator to the incident is not aimed towards the shooting, but is simply the reproach, 'Aw you shouldn't do that/Don't you know you'll stain the carpet,'. It's the glacial freeze on emotions that stuns the listener into an abrupt jolt at this point in the narrative. The impact is like a condensed gun shot before the narrator lets loose the casual disclosure that he can't do anything anyhow because he's too busy getting his cock sucked – 'She's busy sucking on my dingdong.'

Even to have got this musically abrasive, lyrically subversive song through the censors at MGM/Verve was in itself an arthouse achievement, the album's commercial limitations – it reached 199/200 on Billboard – built into its total absence of radio-friendly appeal.

According to Lou, 'When we did "Sister Ray", we turned up to ten flat out, leakage all over the place. They asked us what we were going to do. We said, "We're going to start." They said, "'Who's playing the bass?"' We said, "There is no bass." They asked us when it ends. We didn't know. When it ends, that's when it ends. It did a lot to the music of the seventies. We were doing the whole heavy-metal trip back then. I mean if "Sister Ray" is not an example of heavy metal, then nothing is.'

For the VU completist, every live version of 'Sister Ray' expands the song's epic potential in a way individual to that performance. While the lyric is often improvised live, but remains essentially integral to the recorded version, the musical interpretation of the song develops an autonomy that can last for up to 38 minutes, as instanced at The Matrix, San Francisco, on 27th November 1969. Interviewed in the same year by Ramblin' Jim Martin for Open City 78, Reed spoke of the almost unstoppable momentum the song established live. 'Mainly the instruments are wrecked by the time we finish. We close out with it. You see, "Sister Ray" depends on whether we're playing part two, part three. "Sister Ray" in its entirety might run three days sometime, depending upon the energy level of the group, but, you know we have tapes of this, but we won't release them because it's more than an hour long already.'

The tapes to which Reed refers have never been officially released and the closest we can get to the assumed existence of the originals, in terms of raw live recordings, comes from the Robert Quine tapes issued as *The Velvet Underground Bootleg Series Volume 1* (2001). By listening to three disparate, aurally shape-shifting slabs of 'Sister Ray' recorded between May and December 1969 by Quine on a Sony cassette recorder with a hand-held microphone, we can hear approximately 90 minutes of 'Sister Ray' distorted by fuzz and the highly idiosyncratic methedrine-inflected figures Reed was able to create with his guitar playing against Moe Tucker's frantic pounding of the skins. There's no extensive re-working of the lyric on any of these three versions, but the aggressive instrumentation that is the band's metabolism on stage is so powerful that it threatens to swallow the audience into a black hole. Reed at the time compared the effects of his guitar playing to entering into an aural 'cloud' in which he alone could hear all sorts of effects that appeared to be happening independent of his making.

Robert Quine's suicide on May 31st, 2004 seems sadly to have terminated the official Velvet Underground Bootleg series, but on the three discs contained in the first box we get to hear the working constituents of the band far more productively and rewardingly than on their legitimate live releases, *The Velvet Underground Live* and *Live at Max's Kansas City*. That a 'Sister Ray' part two existed, using the refrain 'Sweet rock and roll, it'll cleanse your soul' as a preamble to the song, was confirmed by Sterling Morrison as performed live in 1968. 'It kind of just goes along [the preamble] and then hits the chords, which were very heavy . . . Cale played keyboard on "Sweet Rock and Roll" and that was really what carried it. Good keyboards.' Lester

Bangs remembered the threatening fusion being incorporated and gunned into a San Diego 1968 set, but again, apart from the initial refrain, the lyric appears to have stayed unaltered, and remained the spinal column to the song's variously mutating chord structures.

Perhaps what we're all hoping for with 'Sister Ray' is the existence of a recorded version with an alternative lyric as cutting edge, degrading, controversial and realistically focused as the original, something Reed was well capable of doing, given his extraordinary ability to spontaneously restructure VU songs like 'Sweet Jane' and 'Waiting for the Man' on his *Take No Prisoners* (1978) live set at the Bottom Line, New York, in which the revamps are in effect remade songs.

Raids on gay people were an endemic part of policing in America and Britain, pre-Stonewall and the Wolfenden Report in the late sixties, and it's not surprising that 'Sister Ray' as a song ends on a note of invasive menace, with the fear on the narrator's part that it's the police who are knocking on the apartment door with the intention of ramraiding and taking him and his friends for a ride. The defiant resistance on the narrator's part to open the door – he's too busy getting blown – is sustained right to the end, as the song's assertion of lawlessness over safe pop and conventional living.

It's a fact that the most creatively productive time of Reed's songwriting career – and it has formed to a large degree the basis for his live solo repertoire – was during his period of involvement with The Velvet Underground from the mid to the late sixties. Nothing in Reed's solo career has ever, to my mind, superseded the dynamic of the invasively poetic and realistic songs he wrote between 1965 and 1970, when he singularly crafted literate cutting edge songs that pushed rock music forward into a more serious recognition of its potential to have intellectual appeal. Reed's radical East Coast reaction to West Coast psychedelia and surf music and the breezy summer pop instigated by the British

Invasion was to write songs so relentlessly uncommercial that they appeared to bypass all established criteria that engineered manufactured hits.

The sheer industrial density of 'Sister Ray', its abnormal length and deviant subject matter, leave it isolated even today like a decommissioned plane pulled out of service, but to many VU fans the song continues to represent the band's most sustained achievement in terms of confrontational menace through lyric and dissonant noise. Duck, Sally, Rosy, Miss Rayon, Cecil and Sister Ray, the dealer from Carolina and the sailor from Alabama, they're all in it, only their characters can't be developed as in a short story or novel, rather they can only operate nominally and minimally within the record's duration – 17 minutes of unforgettably energised assault.

My sympathies are with Duck and Sally. For me, the song's opening line 'Duck and Sally inside' remains one of the oddest, most skewed and memorable intros in rock and never fails to alert me full on to its optimally pitched quirkiness. I first heard it as a student drinking red wine on the white-painted floor of my friend John Robinson's flat in Natal Road at the end of the Piccadilly line, and tonight I'm listening to the song come up on the black-painted boards of my underlit basement flat in Hampstead. As Lou's voice comes in as incorrigibly dismissive narrator, bored by every form of deviance, I'm aware of being older now in my listening, but everything within the song has remained exactly the same.

BIKER BOYS, ELIZABETHANS AND THOM GUNN'S COOL LINE

Backstage at the London Palladium on Soho's Great Marlborough Street, left of the toilets at the entrance to Carnaby Street's retro-focused tourist hoopla, there's Coffee Republic, a biker cafe, where leather-jacketed, pony-tailed couriers chill in interludes between jobs and fire up on double espressos. It's something to do with their speed-injected apparent sense of lawlessness, the fact that their sloganed jackets make outlaw statements in the traffic, and the risk entailed in gunning a Triumph, Honda, Suzuki or Harley across town that attracts me to the place as my chosen milieu in which to write about Thom Gunn. I expect, too, that this black-skinned biker cult, who always stay outside on the street, care as little for literature as I do, but may, through their interest in rock music and drugs, have the buried expectation that some sorts of poetry transmit a corresponding neural charge that is sympathetic to their lifestyle. I sit outside with them, as I always like to write directly on the street, and there's Liberty to the left hazed by CO_2 emissions, nitrogen dioxide level 40 ppb, and right up the street, media facades and the endless reconfiguration of Soho to accommodate predatory corporates. The air's so whiffily toxic I can feel carbon emissions carried in my blood.

Thom Gunn, who began writing poetry as a Cambridge undergraduate in the drape-coat, gelled-pompadour Teddy boy era of the early 50s, interests me in part because he was the first British poet to write about Elvis Presley, biker boys and cool at a time when nobody else did. James Dean, Marlon Brando and Elvis Presley were the cool icons spearheading emergent youth culture to Gunn's generation through a look inciting gender antagonism, in Presley's case a music that converted black blues into white exhibitionism, and in Dean and Brando through rebel film roles, primarily *Rebel Without a Cause* and *The Wild One*. Gunn was alert to the radical rip they had made in contemporary culture and, as a gay man, was attracted to their image, part greaser, part dandy, part Ted, part defiant rebel, and quickly integrated their look and influence as role models into his formative private mythology of heroes. That Gunn wrote about 1950s teenage rebellion employing the cool metaphysical constructs of those earlier prototypical punks the Elizabethans, wasn't so much a clash of cultures — Marlowe would have been happy to fuck Jimmy Dean — as a violent incompatibility of form chosen to express Ted-rock culture. Gunn's technical resources crunched biker boys into formal poetics, as the only way of sanctioning his subject matter to the refrigerated sensibilities of his contemporaries; the literary equivalent of fitting a Honda exhaust muffler to engine tone.

I've got my ear buds in as I write outside Coffee Republic, so that I can crank up my thoughts with surges of noise from a Rolling Stones classic *Let it Bleed* as a sonic boost to my neural network. Gunn's early successes like 'On the Move' are processed by the speed of intelligent questing. There's more curiosity than empathy on show, more of a need to find some sort of intellectual resolution in speed and rock music than there is in affirming its subjective importance in his life. The British Gunn is all attitude, he's frosty like a bottle pulled from the fridge, acutely defensive of his sexuality and understandably drenched in his Tudor influences, those reckless, hard-drinking hustlers who brawled, worked as operatives for MI5, cared nothing for literary reputation and lived directly in the moment as their only purchase on time. Gunn was their smart update in terms of metaphysics, that tricky little pasta twirl in the line that kinks with self-regarding intelligence, but was too humanely middle-class at the time to be their match in debasement and revelling with lowlife. If the taste was there in Gunn, then the socially repressed ethos of reactionary, burnt-out, post-war Britain, with its sexual restraint, hadn't as yet exploded into the dynamic of sixties pop and liberated youth. Gunn's sexuality was temporarily on hold as he negotiated a pretend heterosexuality in the neutral orientation expressed almost uniformly in his first five collections from *Fighting Terms* (1954) to *Moly* (1971).

The consequences of writing dishonestly about your life carry. If you don't do right the residue hangs round like a rod-shaped bacterial infection in the urinary tract. Gunn's early work is slick, objective, technically accomplished, but mechanistic, is in a very real sense a preparation for coming out, something he was to do in *Jack Straw's Castle* (1976), his first real presentation of himself to his reading public as a poet who could now write about every aspect of his life without inhibition.

Couriers live for the thrill of danger and speed. These guys at the adjoining stainless steel tables do coke before picking up so as to metabolically emulate the speed they'll get out of the bike as the physical extension of themselves. It's what I do when I write: burn, the opposite of Gunn's metaphysical cool. The Elizabethans drank themselves onto the floor, Marlowe, Shakespeare and Ben Johnson, all of whom refused to correct proofs even if they were offered them, were alcoholics who drank because death was in their face. Mostly they drank ale brewed from malted barley – Shakespeare's own father was an official ale taster in Stratford – and because of its potency there were 58 ale brewers to 32 beer brewers in London in 1574. Ale had altered-state hallucinogenic properties, was the colour of a county under rain and submerged the drinker in shape-shifting toxins.

Gunn's freeing-up process began with his experimentation with LSD at his Haight Ashbury home in California in the late sixties, and some of the poems in *Moly*, like 'The Fair in the Woods', 'The Messenger' and 'At the Centre', are attributed by the poet to the drug's insightful and powerful psychoactive properties. LSD, courtesy of pill-making mavericks like Charles Owsley, was freely available in San Francisco at the time, and the drug helped crack Gunn's literary kernel, and with it the implacable reserve he had shown up to this point in his choice of subject matter for his poetry. Gunn's earlier, more formal preoccupations with heroes, soldiers, history, elemental phenomena and impersonal human relations, all of which had given his poetry muscle, now appear contrived in view of the poet liberated by LSD into increasingly personal expression, a transition marked by coming out in the title poem of his 1976 collection *Jack Straw's Castle*. Gunn's tendency towards formal poetics, not helped by the fact that he taught literature for long stretches at Berkeley, needed this break with inherent reserve, and while he was never to avail himself of the more radical innovations of other West Coast practitioners and friends like Robert Duncan, Jack Spicer, Philip Lamantia and Gary Snyder, Gunn's best work, to my mind, was made in the second half of his life, as the hybrid mix of Anglo-American influences.

I'm looking, as I write on this rain-smudged Soho day, at the Robert Mapplethorpe photo (1980) of a leather-jacketed Thom Gunn that appears on the black and white dust jacket of the American FSG edition of his *Collected Poems*. I'm staring at Gunn at 50 in a studio freeze 28 years ago, his good looks tanned by the orange California sunshine, his black hair maintained in a 1950s Jimmy Dean style, his bushy eyebrows making the brown eyes appear quizzical, nose and ears symmetrically proportioned, the generic masculinity softened by the mouth's sensitivity (it's Gunn's weak point), the possible giveaway that he's gay, but the force of the man is directed by the look, inwardly philosophical and outwardly searching for the dissolve in consciousness between inner and outer realities. How a poet looks is important because you see Gunn's image before you start dipping into the book, and it's possible if you don't like him you won't bother to read. I show it to the bikers and they all agree Gunn looks good – he's a throwback to their Teddy boy archetype, gel, leather and grease. It's a questionable bonus that he's a poet. It's the look that counts.

The door opened for Gunn when he wrote 'Jack Straw's Castle', the title referencing a landmark white, weather-boarded pub he knew in his youth, at 12 North End Way, Hampstead, on the northern edge of Hampstead Heath, a densely wooded area cruised by gay men and territorial at night as a partly legitimised sexual arena. The Jack Straw of Gunn's poem, variously the folklore hero John Rackstraw of the Great Rising of 1381, the peasant's revolt, and, nearer in time and locale, Charlie Manson, the psychotic guru to the Family and Hell's Angels, dissolves through dream-imagery into a desirable sexual partner who Gunn endorses as his kind.

> So humid, we lie sheetless – bare and close
> Facing apart, but leaning ass to ass
> And that mere contact is sufficient touch,
> A hinge, it separates but not too much.
> An air moves over us, as calm and cool
> As the green water of a swimming pool.

Gunn was acutely aware that by affirming same-sex relations he risked losing critical support as well as a conventional readership, but that equally his gain lay in being able to write about his personal life explicitly as the firepower to his poetry. But things were still foggy at the edges, as though Gunn was only prepared to meet the light half way, and poems like 'Saturnalia', 'Fever', 'The Geysers', and 'The Corporal' all up the ratchet a notch on Gunn's characteristically masculine world, as though the denial of femininity in his world – Gunn rarely writes of women – endorsed same-sex relations as a male prerogative that excluded fags. The collection *Jack Straw's Castle* is full of what Gunn calls 'the sniff of the real' – the musty horse chestnut smell of his formative memories of sitting on Hampstead's Parliament Hill and getting to know the heath as a green map, tree by tree, path by coiling path like a snake extending over a radius of 3.2 km, 2, 791 acres, as part of the retrieval of his past as it came up proportionate to his life at 1216 Cole Street, an address I've pulled from the many letters he so generously sent me. 'Jack Straw's Castle', as a seminal piece of Gunn revisionism, is like a DJ remix of his London past with a sexually, chemically and re-modified lifestyle adapted to his Haight-Ashbury post-hippie existence as a user and gay man active on the scene. Gunn, it could be argued, was liberated from Britain, enjoyed the emotional support of a secure partner in Mike Kitaj, a relatively hedonistic and laid-back lifestyle, and could afford to facilitate the break with his literary past that would deepen with each of his three successive collections, *The Passages of Joy*, *The Man with Night Sweats* and *Boss Cupid*. Because Gunn was such a slow, meticulous writer, working more from the need to clarify intellectual resolution than spontaneous lyrical impulse, the intervals between his books ranged from five to ten years, meaning that considerable moving-on time had occurred in the interval between books, which, of course, reflect the deepening changes in his life. When he turns up again in book form it's like he's been away indefinitely, not just in his head but physically, unless as a collector you'd road-mapped his progress through the small limited editions he regularly put out of work in progress as signs along the way. But each time something of the inveterate cool, the apparent disinterest, the detachment in writing about human relations had started to give, and if *Jack Straw's Castle* was the first real evidence of Gunn finding a personal voice in his poetry, rather than a dodgy intellectual reserve, then by the time Gunn came to publish *The Passages of Joy* in 1982, an even more radical confessional tone was adopted to personalize same-sex relations. Gunn seems at 50 to have come out on the side of living, rather than caring for literary politics and reputation, and to have gone for it like grabbing a gun. Right from the first startling, blow-your-head-off poem in the book, 'Elegy', a piece that anticipates the endemic die-off of an Aids generation, there is, through the letting go of formal discipline, more natural protein than steroid in the verse, as Gunn debates olfactory logistics of this thin, tall guy's last taste of his own blood simultaneous with shooting himself in the head under a eucalyptus tree.

> Though I hardly knew him
> I rehearse it again and again
> Did he smell eucalyptus last?
> No it was his own blood
> as he choked on it

The prolonged moment of suspension the poem creates, written almost in the manner of Robert Creeley's natural speech rhythms, sets the tone for a book that is often casual, flat, voyeuristic about other people's lives – Gunn invariably filters others more through implication than empathy – but ultimately closer to getting under his skin than any previous collection. There's a sense of community, too, of Gunn belonging to a gay family threatened by plague, the still largely undiagnosed Aids virus already virulently policing the cells of his friends as a form of devastating cellular undercover. Aids had been discovered in blood as early as 1981, when five young men in Los Angeles were diagnosed with PCP – pneumocystis carinii pneumonia – without identifiable cause, and as a strain that proved resistant to the drug pentamine used to combat it. Aids transmission quickly became a major issue in San Francisco, its epicentre, where the Police Department equipped patrol officers with special gloves and masks for use when dealing with what the police called 'a suspected Aids patient'.

I'm back to the bikers on rainy Great Marlborough Street at the intersection of Carnaby Street and Liberty. I'm a speed freak who wants a book to be finished before it has begun, and dopamine rushes the propellant to my writing. Bikers want the same sort of Kamikaze implosion. Writing over any sustained period gets diffused. You lose the initial speed and impetus and connect with a different energy that's about going on. Today I'd rather write a poem than bother with Gunn, and look after the six red, pink and white poppies on crinkly osteoporotic stems that have made it up in a cracked terracotta pot on my back steps, but I'll get back to him.

The best poems for me in *The Passages of Joy* are the more controversial ones that challenge received notions of what is thought acceptable subject matter according to the reactionary conservatism of British poetry. Gunn writes about his attraction for a teen hustler in 'San Francisco Streets', sex with a stranger in a MacDonald's rest room on the way to the airport in 'The Miracle', Sid Vicious knifing Nancy in 'The Victim', Elvis Presley's habit in 'Painkillers', a dealer in 'Crystal', and his life as a nocturnal sexual outlaw in London in 1964–5 in the autobiographical 'Talbot Road'. All of these poems succeed in setting Gunn apart from his British contemporaries as much by attitude as the integrants of a gay lifestyle in which drugs and casual sex are the dominants. What suddenly pushed Gunn forward was that his subject matter couldn't be copied by the uninitiated into these practices – you couldn't pretend to be gay or doing drugs and write about it convincingly – and suddenly he began to occupy a special place in British poetry, that of the tolerated bad boy. The fact that his academic status gave him endorsement and that he never quite went far enough in terms of alienation, kept Gunn locked into acceptance by literary institutions as a tolerated antagonist to convention. While Gunn had too much respect for literature ever to break with it in the way of the radical poetics employed by William Burroughs, Allen Ginsberg, Robert Duncan, Frank O'Hara or John Wieners, to name a few of his American pioneering contemporaries, he remained in British terms the only rogue gene in the refrigerated Petri-dish of institutionalized British poetry. Gunn was still a bit cold climate, but he was warming and his sneer at times cut like wire. Something of the social contempt Gunn felt for accepted heterosexual standards is injected powerfully into the hotted-up tempo of 'The Miracle', a poem in which he succeeds in perfecting something of the punkish snarl and swagger of his lawless Elizabethan prototypes.

'Then suddenly he dropped down on one knee
Right by the urinal in his only suit
And let it fly, saying keep it there for me,
And smiling up. I can still see him shoot.
Look at that snail-track on the toe of my boot.'

– 'Snail-track?' – 'Yes, there.' – That was six months ago.
How can it still be there? – 'My friend, at night
I make it shine again, I love him so,
Like they renew a saint's blood out of sight.
But we're not Catholic, see, so it's all right.'

'The Miracle' is about the closest Gunn gets to crunching the bits of his Elizabethan influences into a metaphysically updated wit that is both irreverent and arguably offensive. It was an affirmative sign that he was headed in the right direction. British mainstream poetry in the 1980s was dead. Philip Larkin's residual grey smear stuck like polymer to his alumni,

Ted Hughes' shamanic savagery had burnt out, Seamus Heaney's matey inoffensive political correctness existed largely in denial of the present, and Gunn seemed the only poet of his generation to have plugged into counterculture as the indispensable energy needed to revitalize poetry. Gunn extracted from the catastrophic debacle of the Sex Pistols' chaotically short-lived career, the tragic but inevitable postscript to the split, the murder of Nancy Spungen, 20, by the band's heroin-addicted bassist Sid Vicious with a blade in a room at New York's legendary Chelsea Hotel, on Twenty-third street between Seventh and Eighth. What exactly happened on the night of 12th October 1978, and if in fact a methadone-dosed Sid delusionally pulled a knife on Nancy, or she was murdered by a dealer in the process of robbing their room, has never been properly ascertained, largely due to Sid's heroin OD months after the killing, on Feb 2nd, 1979. In Sid's confused account to the photographer Joe Stevens of what happened, he reconstructed events as disconnected incidents, as though the whole thing had been done in such a dissociated state that it could have been him, or not. '. . . she stuck her belly right in front of my knife. She didn't know. I didn't know we had done anything really bad. She crashed out on the bed. I crashed out on the other. I woke up first and decided to get some methadone. Took a forty-five minute taxi-ride.'

Gunn pretty much sticks to Sid's confused account in the storyline of his poem and stays with the notion that Sid knifed Nancy in a drug-induced deluded state. Gunn's attitude is full on unsparing. Addressing the poem to Nancy as the victim – there's no least compassion in Gunn's ruthlessly objective tone.

Now it was with sharp things he played:

Needles, and you, not with the band,
Till something greater than you planned
Opened erect within his hand.

You smiled. He pushed it through your shirt
Deep in your belly, where it hurt.
You turned – and ate the carpet's dirt.

And then not understanding why
He watched out with a heavy eye
The several hours you took to die.

You could argue that this is reportage put into verse, but it's done with a precisional skill that typifies imperturbable Gunn cool. The writing is cold as Sid's putative blade, and there's an edge suggesting that Gunn feels Nancy got what she deserved and that his sympathies come out on the side of the Tuinal-zombified Sid as another of rock's habituated, self-destructing zombies. Gunn's at his most inimitably brilliant writing about psychopathy; he was later to eulogize the Jeffrey Dahmer serial killings in a sequence of poems initially published by Enitharmon Press called *In the Twilight Slot* and included in Gunn's final collection *Boss Cupid* (2000). An engaging cold is how I feel Gunn's intellectual energy, but one that fires up controversy by a choice of subject matter calculated to alienate. Gunn, while creating dialogue with his imaginative findings, invariably attempts to subordinate them to a processing intellect, a refinement by which each becomes the metaphysical coefficient of the other.

I'm writing this slumped out on the fissured concrete back steps of where I live, drinking wine and reminded that apart from Gunn and the Elizabethans I have no other British poetry books on my shelves, which are made up totally of the Americans, from the New York school John Ashbery, Frank O'Hara, Ted Berrigan and Jimmy Schuyler, to Black Mountain, Robert Duncan, Ed Dorn, Robert Creeley and John Wieners, through to whoever and whatever interests me today for energized, vitaminized fizz. My problem is that I look for the contagious energy of rock music in poetry, come down hard on rock's often scrambled lyrics, get depressed by British poetry's lack of engagement with the new (it's still largely an academic sideline), and come out unanimously on the side of rock. I'd rather die, if I had the choice, listening to the Rolling Stones' 'Gimme Shelter' than reading a poem, because I'm addicted to high octane energy input. Most poetry moves too slow for my liking, unless it's written by the likes of prose stylists like William Gibson, whose smart, neuroscientistic attachment to detail creates the sort of imagery in prose that poetry lacks.

Ten years after *The Passages of Joy*, having remained partially blocked for much of the eighties, Gunn got it nearer right with the publication of *The Man with Night Sweats* in 1992, his book of elegies for the sick and the dead in his life. The author photo of Gunn on the back of the dust jacket of the American edition, taken by his brother Ander, finds a surprisingly youthful Gunn, hair shot through by grey, in relaxed style, his left hand supporting his left cheek, a white dress shirt with two-button cuffs concealed beneath a fitted check jacket, a thin leather watch strap on a thin left wrist, and the look, the antithesis of his biker image, asserting compassionate well being. And even if the photo is posed, Gunn appears right side up on compassion, and in the process of meeting a particular point in his life with a corresponding awareness of its needs from him as a person. It's not that the poetry has changed, there's still the persistently unreconciled conflict in attempting to apply formal technique to dodgy subject matter, it's more that feeling has come to replace attitude in the elegies and honesty restraint. In 'In Time of Plague', he writes:

> My thoughts are crowded with death
> and it draws so oddly on the sexual
> that I am confused
> confused to be attracted

> by, in effect, my own annihilation.
> Who are these two, these fiercely attractive men
> who want me to stick their needle in my arm?

There's no tactical messing here, no attempt at concealment. These two men, Brad and John, are the sort of company Gunn keeps in his private life, and the book made him into a sort of hero to straight poetry readers, whose lives, by contrast, appeared so predictably safe. That poets like John Wieners had been writing about a druggy gay underworld for two decades was a fact lost on most British readers, so that Gunn's take on doing drugs and men appeared startlingly fresh. If there had ever been the suspicion that Gunn lived a purely academic life, then the confessions in *The Man with Night Sweats* blew any such preconceptions apart. In 'Lament' and 'Sacred Heart', both treated with the formal technique of rhyming couplets, Gunn, in writing of nursing and watching over dying friends, succeeded in finding a sufficiently elevated humane tone to match the gravity of his catastrophic subjects as to mark him out as the great elegist of his generation. There's little doubt that 'Lament', in particular, a courageously harrowing excursion into a friend Allan Noseworthy's death from excruciating PCP-related symptoms, must rate as one of the superb elegies in British poetry, an unflinching journey accompanying a friend stage by stage towards the radical emaciated shaking off of his bones into death. The compression of Gunn's dynamic bleeds into the symptoms, the spinal tap, the unstoppably virulent viral attack, the racked nailing of this flesh to bone, the kamikaze breakdown of immune defences; the proliferation of sarcomas.

> But then the spinal tap.
> It brought a hard headache, and when night came
> I heard you wake up from the same bad dream
> Every half hour with the same short cry

> Of mild outrage, before immediately
> Slipping into the nightmare once again
> Empty of content but the drip of pain.

The writing, dead level in its concentrated focus, is lean as the poem's dying subject, Allan, and his name, given by Gunn in Acknowledgements and Notes, is important, as his life was individually significant and slipping away. Writing a poem doesn't save anyone's life or help them in the least when they're dead, but it notes and celebrates the individual's unique characteristics as they were once and once only and unrepeatable in that state. Watching someone die also entails anticipating one's own death, and much of Gunn's thoughts at the time of writing 'Lament' must have been preoccupied with the possibilities that he too had contracted the virus, or at any rate the fact that he would come one day to die. What's present in the writing of these great elegies is the man's biochemistry, his amino acids and proteins, nucleic acids and DNA, lipids, fats, cellular respiration, neural networks, metabolic pathways, the whole push of the human confronting illness and tragedy with the little help he can give and receive, and words that often don't do anything but make the pain worse. But humanly this was Gunn's moment, and it's reflected powerfully in verse that becomes an extension of his body, the hard physical act of writing out of loss about devastating pain. It takes strength, resolution, and real poetic facility to do this, all of which Gunn possessed in abundance. He got to the work with heroic application at a time when no other poet seemed aware of or even concerned about the pandemic. If Gunn had got lost for ten years because his subject matter had run thin, he now returned on the frontline as a poet elegizing a generation threatened with liquidation by plague. What he brought to his poetry was compassion and muscle, humanitarianism, rationale and masculinity rather than his earlier calculated cool. Gunn wasn't so much running scared; he was helping out and learning to cope with appalling loss. The dignity Gunn's poetry affords his dying friends is the other quality that shines through his unflinching line, and again it's something of the Elizabethan in his tone, and cooking in his genes, that has him lift human degradation into an elevated state absent of any rhetoric. Of Allan Noseworthy's last moments, Gunn observes the little note of resignation on which his life ends.

> Nothing was said, everything was understood,
> At least by us. Your own concerns were not
> Long-term, precisely, when they gave the shot
> – You made local arrangements to the bed
> And pulled a pillow round beside your head.
> And so you slept and died, your skin gone grey,
> Achieving your completeness, in a way.

Gunn's immediate response on being liberated from a long time of waiting and watching in a white hospital room, and on re-entering real time, with all the busy demands made by the day, is to feel confusion and guilt at being alive, but at the same time instinctually absorbed by its process. While we're alive we can't escape immediate involvement in living; our blood, our thought processes, move us on autonomously and independently of ourselves, regardless of loss, break ups, the deaths of those we love, financial ruin, whatever. We go on because there's nothing else to do. Gunn goes back into life as a reminder that he too will die. Gunn's eloquence is similarly sustained in poems like 'Sacred Heart', 'Courtesies of the Interregnum', 'The J Car' and 'The Missing', in all of which he carries the true responsibility of the poet to speak for the oppressed, the marginalized, the disenfranchised, the disaffected, the dispossessed and, of course, the sick. Gunn created a first in Anglo-American poetry by writing about Aids, an entirely new subject for poetry and not one the careerists were going to leech. Aids as a topic was considered taboo and Gunn was cool for making a singularly defiant purchase on legitimizing it or not as a subject for poetry. In the poem 'The J Car', written for Charlie Hinkle, Gunn again links himself as co-journeyer to a friend's death, the advantage of his own health appearing like a betrayal to his virally nuked friend. Of Charlie's promise as a poet Gunn writes,

> 'Of course. It tears me still that he should die
> As only an apprentice to his trade,
> The ultimate engagements not yet made.'

Gunn's tone here is given characteristic gravity by the use of rhyming couplets, and it's the form that tightens the expression, the hard won craft that takes it home. There's a long-haul feel, too, to some of Gunn's poetry, in that although California had been his adopted home since 1956, his primary readership was always British and the poetry, in crossing the Atlantic, kept its indigenous roots with only minor concessions to Americanization. West Coast America had been on red alert to the devastating escalation of Aids casualties for a decade by the time Gunn published his seminal *The Man with Night Sweats*, while the death-count from the illness, although significant, was substantially less in the UK. And perhaps what Gunn pointed to, for the brief time his book came into critical awareness, was that there still is a place in life for poetry to assume public importance by bringing imaginative intellect to focus on issues that are a common concern.

I'm still writing this in discontinuous surges, in Soho, like a biker locked into a choked tailback and segueing round hot impatient metal. Today I met with Johnny at Starbucks and gave him the poem I'd written about him called 'Thieves Like Us (Baby Love)' as he lives by shoplifting from the high-end department stores, Liberty, Harrods, Harvey Nichols etc., largely for the powered-up adrenalin boosts he gets from the danger. He's sweating, and I laugh at him laughing at the poem I've given him. I always write about friends and give them the poems, and that too is an act of theft. I lift aspects of their character and recreate it through mine, but in the process I've stolen. Johnny will doubtless throw the poem away, but that's all right, too.

After the publication of *The Man with Night Sweats* (1992), Gunn again disappeared for almost a decade before returning with his final book *Boss Cupid* (2000). *Boss Cupid*, a more relaxed affair than its predecessor, still picks up on Aids as a central issue, and mixes formal craft with free verse, but is often refreshingly and openly autobiographical, as though Gunn had at last found a personal voice that could speak directly of his life, past and present. It is as though he had finally perfected a way to cut the apple clean. Gunn writes in *Boss Cupid* of his mother's suicide by gas, in Hampstead, when he was still a boy, dying and dead friends, his health issues like blood pressure, his use of speed, and, significantly, the new love in his life, 'American Boy', finding in ordinary things the needs of poetry. The tone is most often downbeat, confessional, at worst cynical, at best shaved to an unapologetic, almost throwaway blues. There's no loss of Gunn's paradigmatic cool, his warmth is always moderated by rationale, but the autobiographical give allows us to feel more reader-friendly to Gunn simply by knowing him a bit better on his own terms. Growing older stripped Gunn's reserves, and to a large degree his zipped-up literary self-consciousness, and helped open him out to tell, or die with, his secrets. In 'Blues for the New Year, 1997' Gunn writes:

> My dealer left town
> (sounds like a song).
> Had a date with
> a certain man, but
> he got pneumonia.
> I guess it's off.

There's nothing fired up or elevated in these lines, it's just Gunn blue and moping about the house and peeled honest, as though the poem comprises consoling notes for being end-of-the-year at a loose low end. Drugs, a cancelled date, Aids-related pneumonia, these are part of Gunn's day to day life, concerns that may be alien to some of his readers but normal to his private life. Gunn in 1971 had bought a two-flat Victorian on upper Cole Street with a $3,300 down payment and combined the two units, sharing the house with Mike Kitay, Bill Schuessler and an assortment of friends and companions – refusing always to exploit the property for profit and only ever renting to friends, and it was there, in his later years, that he heavily abused methamphetamine – crystal meth and alcohol – in the attempt to maintain optimal libido and whack his inveterately sluggish lyric inspiration back into action. Gunn's last book is predominantly chemicalised by crystal meth, a drug common on the gay club scene, and the bathtub substance accounts in part both for the book's sharp-edged and dull-edged perceptions – its ups and downs. It's the two affectionately moving poems, finely crafted as anything Gunn ever wrote, for his newest young lover the 'American Boy', that to my mind stand out in his last collection as superlative for their metrical dexterity and resigned feeling of loss as integral to happiness. While admitting that when young he hated the sexual attention of older men, Gunn's gratitude now in having a youth's demands in his later years leads to a note of constrained affirmation.

> Affectionate young man,
> Your wisdom feeds
> My dried up impulses, my needs,
> With energy and juice.
> Expertly you know how to maintain me
> At the exact degree
> Of hunger without starving. We produce
> What warmth we can.

Gunn calls the attraction a 'bicoastal romance', a coolly maintained balance of mutual attraction in which he is surprised to find himself needed in proportion to his need. The sexual liaison – and he doesn't admit personal details – puts Gunn back into the role of affirmative cool observer, his intellectual control in writing acting as a red traffic light on the heat he refused to describe, dragging the energy down to 'warmth'. No matter how much Gunn rocks, reticence ultimately pulls him back, a plus for the formal institutions of British poetry, a minus to those who always longed for Gunn to down defences, totally plug in and let rip. But there's fineness, a delicacy at work here that shows Gunn the fine-tuned craftsman to advantage. He maintains form to the last as the inner architecture out of which he builds poetry. It's hard to know if the control asserted by both people in this relationship is the product of Gunn's philosophic detachment in measuring intellect against passion, or an actual reality. The same relationship is revisited in a second poem, 'In Trust', clearly intended as a companion piece to 'American Boy', in which Gunn adopts a similarly dissociated tone – a concern that has take-it-or-leave-it themed as a subtext to whatever's happening between them. The boy who has travelled east on vacation to help his relatives is replaceable, Gunn admits ('I go out with a new boyfriend'), but is constantly in his mind, despite the flexibility of an open relationship.

> As you began
> You'll end the year with me.
> We'll hug each other while we can,
> Work or stray while we must.
> Nothing is, or will ever be,
> Mine, I suppose. No one can hold a heart,
> But what we hold in trust
> We do hold, even apart.

This is Gunn the Elizabethan stylist pulling off the difficult in deceptively casual tones. There is no concession to loss, no note of jealousy as the older partner, and there are no reproaches as to separation, just the sense of being resigned to the fact that we can't really lay claim to anyone in life, other than imaginatively, and in a kind of unconditional trust. I find the line 'No one can hold a heart' nakedly compelling in its existential truth, and sad in that it's a realisation that came near to the end of Thom Gunn's life, as a fact that couldn't be redeemed or reversed. You just learn it one day, standing in the sunny kitchen, that you're ultimately alone in your personal space now and forever, in a relationship or out.

Gunn's *Boss Cupid* comes as close to us ever knowing the man through his poetry as we will. Local issues like having coffee on Cole Street, looking over boys in the post office, online dating, nurturing his garden sunflowers, all take their place as part of the poet's day and the stuff of poetry. The fact that nobody really wants poetry and that poets, when they die, usually go down, are the limitations we have to accept as part of the activity, and it's usually the acceptance that prevents disappointment, the awareness of the maintained boundaries that permits freedom to push hard into inevitable disillusionment. Gunn seemed to have reached that point of acceptance in the tired, but always dignified strains that inform the writing in *Boss Cupid*.

I'm finishing this piece at Coffee Republic, the September light smudgy like a girl's gold eye shadow, the bikers convened in a sprawl that's all attitude – boots up on chairs – mobiles in hand like guns. If I look to my right there's Aquascutum, Beyond Retro, Le Pain Quotidien, The Original Pharmacy, Starbucks and the London College of Beauty Therapy, and left, Wild At Heart Liberty, where tall-stemmed purple anemones contend for attention with dark red scrolled roses and ultramarine hydrangeas looking like umbels of blue coral. I feel I've got to know Gunn a bit deeper by looking at possibilities of meaning in some of his poems that are my tried favourites.

Thom Gunn died on April 25th, 2004, in circumstances as mysterious as those surrounding Elvis Presley's death, of a heart attack induced by 'acute polysubstance abuse' – a cocktail of recreational drugs that included crystal meth, heroin and Viagra. His friends Mike Kitay, Bill Schuessler and Bob Bair were all in the house on Cole Street that Saturday night, with the usual note pinned on the door, 'Please do not ring the doorbell before 9 a.m. or after 9 p.m.', which was house rules. At 6 a.m. on Sunday morning, the gym-toned septuagenarian Gunn had a visitor, most clearly a dealer. According to his friend Billy Lux, Gunn 'kept his freak on in a big, big way, doing three-day speed and sex binges when he was in his seventies. PNP, or party and play, it's called. I think one of these party-and-play episodes might have killed him. Although I wasn't part of that whole scene, I did, in a way, admire his aggressive pursuit of sensual pleasure. I just wish he was still around to relay his latest sexcapade in a letter or a poem or over lunch at Zazie's.' And according to Mike Kitay, his lifelong partner, Gunn was in a desperate state, 'It was terrible to watch. He would stay awake and Thom would just be out of it. Out of it.' People on crystal meth can stay up for days, and Gunn, who had retired from teaching and wasn't writing much, had lost the plot, and was also drinking heavily. Whether Gunn died by accident, intentionally overdosed, or was supplied bad drugs, we don't know, only that at 8 p.m. on the Sunday, after Gunn hadn't shown all day, Bob Bair, suspecting something was wrong, went into Gunn's flat and found him fully clothed dead on the bed. Bill Schuessler, who came running to Bob's call, gave Gunn immediate mouth to mouth resuscitation while a doctor was called. Gunn was pronounced dead at 8.58 with the cause of death given as 'acute polysubstance abuse'. Maybe the timing was right. Gunn was irremediably attached to his youthful image and didn't want to lose out on sex or the energy count by which he remained a consistent irritant to the poetry establishment.

There's a Suzuki bike that roars off into the late dusty bronze afternoon, its leather-jacketed rider sloganed in red with 'Born to Lose'. He's forty-something, hair pulled back in a ponytail, skinny, wired, and although he's going to pick up you could imagine he's an outlaw. Like me, he doesn't like convention, that's why he's drugged and burning speed, and stays out on the street, even in rain, rather than go inside into our café. I'm the same, I won't go inside – I want to write directly into the hydrocarbon blanket choking the city – and think of Gunn as I once read with him at the London Lighthouse, slim, black faded T-shirt, tight blue jeans, and, of course, lived-in black biker boots with pointed toes.

AND THE STARS WERE SHINING: THE GLITTER AND MENTHOL COOL OF JOHN ASHBERY'S POETRY

If, like me, you're obsessed with big city people-spotting and cloud-spotting, the Nero on the corner of Earlham Street and Monmouth at Seven Dials, fronting the obelisk, provides a continuous hub of urban potentialities for accidental meetings with strangers, rather like the randomised subject matter that comes up in a John Ashbery poem, in a free-floating context that effortlessly remains non-specific in its meaning. Sit outside on the circular plinth to the obelisk and you're looking over to Renzo Piano's urban village, Central St Giles, its psychedelically coloured lime, orange, yellow floating island of office space and top-end apartments as the gentrification of a quarter that polarised the homeless – junkies who collected packets of hypodermics dispensed by a white van parked on the High Street outside First Out Café, a degraded barrio characterised by what was a local resistance to developmental change.

You can't get to John Ashbery directly, so I'm coming at him tangentially, writing both inside and outside on a showery November afternoon, the lavender sky deepening over High Holborn to solid slabs of indigo. John Ashbery's books have always been first day of release purchases for me – the only poetry I go out and buy or pull off Amazon simultaneous with its publication. I'm an Ashbery addict, and that doesn't mean I necessarily read whole poems, I may just dip into colour blocks of imagery, incongruously weird associations, free-floaters, or chop the thing up like DNA in the lab into 10–25 trillion pieces, a process called library construction. The thrill of reading Ashbery is that you can approach the work from so many different angles and always locate something that excites response, without even being aware you're reading poetry. It's more that once you've smashed the space-time window into Ashbery, you have the feeling you're attached to his thought-patterns as they're shaped by his preferred directional flow. Now thought, like light, is essentially weightless, it's only words that make it stick like fingerprints. Words are to poetry like lube on a micro-thin condom.

Ashbery tells me – and it's 1974 at the time of his writing 'Grand Galop', one of the poems in his seminal breakthrough volume *Self-Portrait in a Convex Mirror* (1975) – something I stick *with* and *to* that's excerpted like film.

> And I still have a sweater and one or two other things
> I had then.
> It seems only yesterday we saw
> The movie with the cow in it
> And turned to one at your side, who burped
> As morning saw a new garnet-and-pea-green order
>   propose
> Itself out of the endless bathos, like science-fiction lumps.
> Impossible not to be moved by the tiny number
> Those people wore, indicating they should be raised to
>   this or that power.
> But now we are at Cape Fear and the overland trail
> Is impassable, and a dense curtain of mist hangs over the
>   sea.

I can relate to this stuff: a sweater – only, disappointingly, I have to imagine the colour, the movie with the cow in it, and the sudden colour-coding of a new saturated morning coming up like a sci-fi concept, the people looking future-forward and the whole landscape terminating in a sea hung over by dense, smoky mist. A lot of Ashbery's seventies poems push their imaginative content to the sea's edge as vanishing point, like a clean ambiguous dissolve into the big blue pond.

I like prolific poets, rather than the overly self-regarding careerists who give you a forensically workshopped sixty pages every four years, and Ashbery offers not only size, but continuous reinvention, a slab of work in which you map the reconstructions as part of the block. And part of his greatness is to liberate the reader from the preconceptions locked into what's expected of poetry, and, in doing this, to discover a new place for its potential, accidentally, in the course of writing his way there. It seems to me that poetry, like Ashbery's, becomes interesting when the poet integrates into the plot, rather than eliminates, his peripheral vision. While I'm writing this I'm as much involved in my visual distractions as the text. I'm sighting the skinny jeans' logos on two auburn-haired Korean girls sitting down in the café, one carrying a National Portrait Gallery black canvas bag, the other a green Daunts Bookshop. A poem should do that, too, by running time backwards and forwards, while still remaining in the present. Ashbery as good as tells us this in the same poem, 'Grand Galop'. This is how accidentals come to cohere in the randomised contemporary moment of writing. Ashbery's talking in the poem of waiting for things to fill in time, like I'm face-spotting out the window.

> The wait is built into the things just coming into their own.
> Nothing is partially incomplete, but the wait
> Invests everything like a climate.
> What time of day is it?

Does anything matter?
Yes, for you must wait to see what it is really like,
This event rounding the corner
Which will be unlike anything else and really
Cause no surprise: it's too ample.'

It's this sense of continuous surprise as to what checks in next that makes an Ashbery poem autonomously new, impersonal in that emotions are frozen out, and alien for lacking any motivating subject matter other than the imperative to connect one perception directly to the next. Ashbery doesn't write personalised poems for dead friends, messed up ones, emotional dumps, or specifically themed things; he just works like he's in on whatever's autonomously cool. Ashbery doesn't come at you telling you his blood pressure, medications, alcohol intake (huge), sexual tourism or habits; there aren't any admissions of fears, phobias, regrets, rejections, disappointments; rather there's this off-message unstoppable flowchart of immediacy. It's always the present in Ashbery's poetry, with refreshingly no reference to growing older, or the past as curative – a rare trait for a poet not to concede to the throat-gripping physical reality of age.

Concentration on anything I write goes in and out. I'm quickly diversified into reading Keith Richards' recently published *Life* when I should be doing Ashbery. Keith writes so quirkily you feel he's frozen incidents from his past, cryopreserved them, and returned to retrieve them with all their original high-octane colouring, like cans left behind in someone's fridge in Mississippi. I'm also sighting a Japanese boy who has stepped outside, black leather zipper aviator jacket and pre-faded jeans – to smoke a cigarette, each measured drag creating its own dusty lexicon of smoky exhalations.

Ashbery's collection *And the Stars Were Shining* appeared in 1994, his sixteenth collection, so it's well into his development, and as near right in tone as he gets since *Houseboat Days*

(1977), in many ways his breeziest, bluest and most concisely perfected book. But it's the compacted allusiveness of the poems in *And the Stars Were Shining* that gives them an edgy 6 p.m. feel, like waiting for your first drink to arrive at the bar; and also a pronounced sexual ambiguity, like Ashbery's right on the edge of coming out, but leaves you to guess. Like their title, the poems have a cold, brilliant mineral glitter to their feel, a sparkle chased into the lyric like tonic into gin. In 'Local Time' Ashbery's sexual coding, apparently one of picking up without bonding, gets talked up the right side of indifference, but with just a downside of disappointment coming in to add flavour to the experience.

> Tight boy,
> you reminded me of dragonflies skulking,
> of aromatic fires peaking,
> and neither of us gets to know the other.
> Next thing you know it's winter.
> The skylight, now aproned with white,
> is our bare harvest.
> But there is good in reappearing:
> the flame's roar, beaker of scotch, the old way
> things were probably supposed to be all along anyway.

It's the time-slip from casual acquaintance or sex to 'Next thing you know it's winter,' putting a whiteout on the whole affair that I so like, that quantum timeline that's really life, rather than linear fake, and that Ashbery pulls off so naturally. In the compacted unit of a poem you need to treat time as quantum, otherwise you end up provincial by trying to manipulate parallel world experience into linear narrative, something that gives a lot of mainstream poetry a village pond effect, like think local and stay there, rather than get radically off-world.

Poetry is to me about recreating as its intended imaginative equivalent the experience I target. It's like dying your hair in the process a different colour, black to blonde, or whatever. A poem needs to have a convincing look; and Ashbery's all about style; the jacket suits the knitwear and shirt. When I saw Ashbery talking at the ICA in 1990, he was wearing a perfectly chosen mint green V-neck jumper over an air-miles blue shirt, as casuals with aesthetic, like one of his poems.

'Works on Paper 1', from the same collection, pushes me all senses alert into the full-on Ashbery method of using bitty fragments of narrative to get a compelling mix, in the way that Ray Davies of the Kinks remembered 'an old trick – find a hook in the song that isn't the melody and repeat it,' as the winning formula for his infectious 1970 smash hit 'Lola'.

The poem also provides a hint of Ashbery's drink problem, quickly dispersed into impersonal discursive narrative.

> I never get hangovers until late afternoon
> and then it's like a souvenir, an arrangement.
> An old Dutch taxi takes us down to the sea
> where other passengers are trying to change their
>   reservations
> but the great flummoxed geodesic dome won't let them.

I didn't tell you that in the course of writing this I've walked diagonally across Oxford Street to meet my friend Bill Franks at Selfridge's, the concessionary high-end retail stack where Saudi black gold strips the rails, because Bill's looking for what he can't find, three-ply cashmere in pink, charcoal, teal or French blue. So now I'm at Selfridge's post-Bill sitting in their second floor Lab café, the Marble Arch crunch under my feet, the manual assault of foot traffic almost percussive, returned to 'Works on Paper 1.'

> I tell particularly a thousand pounds of dust I saw
> interspersed between the benign mountain-shapes on the
>   outskirts,
> and how everyone was reasonably free to change. After all
> we make no effort to distinguish ourselves.
> Those who wish to remain naked are coaxed out of
>   laughter
> with tea and nobody's nose is to the grindstone
> anymore, I bet, and you can figure out these shivering
>   trees.
> But the owner of the bookstore knew that the flea was
>   blown out of all proportion,
> with September steps to go down in passing
> before the tremendous dogs are unleashed.

This is an odd mix from a thousand pounds of dust to the ordinariness of being ourselves, to the enigmatic owner of a bookstore, chunky September beach steps to go down, and finally and menacingly and arrestingly, 'before the tremendous dogs are unleashed.' It's the random, almost cut-up method here, the sort of booze-freed-up associations that belong to each other and don't that accelerate the rush forwards. I don't personally care what it means, but to me it's what I identify as poetry, whatever that is, other than something that programs my neural networks to fire responsively to what charged language is doing with images.

Of the writing process itself, Ashbery, in a 1988 interview with John Tranter, said, 'I postpone it as long as possible, which is probably why I write in the late afternoon. I also think that my mind in the morning – though it might be fresher and have more ideas in it – is not as critical as it is later on in the day . . . I also used to think that I had to wait until I was "inspired" before I could write, and then I realised that I hardly ever *was* inspired, so that I'd have to come up with something . . . something else.

So usually my poems, when I write, I'm just in a sort of . . . everyday frame of mind. Which is all I know, really, I suppose.'

The reason for writing poetry, at least mine, is that the doing of it, like a drug, alters reality into an alternative and more exciting state, and I'd guess that's part of Ashbery's underlying incentive. People write poems because being in control they can adjust the universe to their own terms, rather than erroneously attempting to blame it for any injustices they experience. You can do anything in a poem, slash the sky with hot raspberry, come out on top against the system, bash corporates and governments, infiltrate underworlds, win love back from loss, imagine yourself where you shouldn't be, reveal things you've totally repressed, share obsessions and submerged secrets, admit to things you'd never usually dare, and generally be free to do and say what you like because it's poetry.

Ashbery's tone is invariably quiet, self-referential, non-specific, and while his personality fills the poem centre-stage, the person is largely bleached out: Ashbery himself remains virtual. What he asks of the reader, and it's never an imperative, is that you take up with him wherever he's at, that you zone into the characteristic weird that's usually the poem's starting point. In the poem 'Tower of Darkness' from the collection *Can You Hear, Bird* (1995), he hits on alienation, for once, in an alarmingly personal way.

> I cannot remain outside any longer
> in the cold and persuasive rain.
> I grab my crotch wishing for a ball of light
> in the shaggy interior other people have.
> I shall go away without fetching a grain
> from the earth,
> compact with the climbing design
> we knew and hated so well, and when it was our turn
> to die we just gave up, mumbling some excuse.

The admission, hangover-flat, dejected and offering no optimal alternative within the poem, gives you a feeling of Ashbery's morning-after blues, the Alka Seltzer glass fizzing, the day slicing the window and the incredible ordinariness that depression brings to things excited into overdrive by alcohol.

Ashbery's a poet to read in bed for some stimulating space tourism. I never find myself reading him outdoors, but more in a comfort zone, 11–12 p.m., and for me his work will always belong by association to Compendium Books at Camden Loch, who, as a pioneering counterculture outlet, were pre-Ashbery's institutionalisation, the only London source importing his books at a time when he didn't have a UK publisher, and most probably didn't care. He existed excitingly by word of mouth and in the pages of small magazines.

As a process of transitioning, Bill phoned later, after I'd returned to Seven Dials, to say he wasn't on getting home, and looking at it more closely, was very impressed by the quality of the cashmere sweater he'd bought. On my way back to my chosen Nero I'd encountered somebody homeless and cold needing drug money or tea money, and that little recognition of sharing hurt in the corners of our eyes alerts me to the recognition of the ubiquitous indifference and meanness of crowds and how my contact of giving is the starting point of a poem I'll catch up with tomorrow; and leaving him on Wardour Street I'm still thinking of Ashbery somewhere in the Soho mix, like a shocking pink stripe I saw on a jumper in Selfridge's.

Nero's busy now and I like writing directly into noise. The thirteen-part title poem 'And the Stars Were Shining', from the book of the same name, hints at transient stabs at rent or male prostitutes, and the edginess attendant on offering care often where it's not wanted. The luminous late year cold frosting the sequence gives it a starlit glow, and Ashbery, in performing his usual trick of dispersing each new subject into a dissolve, stays long enough with the crystallized bits to offer oblique clues. The sadness always compressed into Ashbery's writing comes up strong in this sequence, like it does when you realise life's running out without your getting what you imagined you wanted, usually love, sex, money or recognition.

> I let so many people go by me
> I sort of long for one of them, any
> one, to turn back toward me,
> forget these tears. As children we played at being grownups.
> Now there's trouble brewing on the horizon.

Somebody's in trouble here, a homeless boy picked up as the sequence alludes, hungry, desperate, and presumably selling sex. 'You get hungry/you eat hot.' Ashbery won't give him a name, Johnny, Jimmy, whoever, and with his life important to him as yours or mine at this moment in time. When the heartbreak comes up, it's Ashbery's, realising, as you do in a big city, all the missed chances that come of making eye contact with strangers in the crowd, and it's always the one who got away, knowing you'd never connect again, that so painfully, memorably hurts. In London you get so scarred by it if you're tuned into the emotional possibilities that, like Ashbery in this elegiac sequence, you could cry city-coloured tears.

Elsewhere in this charged-up suite of winter poems you get bits of personalised Ashbery versus his renowned abstraction. What he teaches me, the reader, is constantly what I wouldn't expect poetry to do, and that's to cut short the beautiful moment the instant it's realised. Reading Ashbery you can feel like a voyeur blacked out at the critical moment by a venetian blind run up in an apartment. You're almost there, and he changes the subject. You move with Ashbery, or rather follow him to places you didn't expect to go. I'm compelled by this place in part VII from the sequence and I'm clueless as to its physicals.

> The bug-black German
> heels and black areas, the long tilted
> cloaks for sale, the others – yes,
> they're still here?
> Something must be done about it
> before it does itself. You know
> what that will be like. The white tables with their
> roses are so beautiful. It doesn't matter if the corn is
>   faded.

Where are we? In a department store, or restaurant, with roses grouped on white tablecloths? I don't know where it is, but I want to stay there a bit, and also view 'the long tilted cloaks for sale.' Ashbery suggests throughout his work that there are other places for poetry than the obviously recognisable ones that tend to endlessly repeat, nature, the domestic and the provincially compressed milieu, and worse, incestuously sticky workshops. I'd personally rather hang with his odd than be in the overworked familiar. Ashbery's so refreshingly free of poetic self-consciousness and of ticking all the right prize-winning boxes that he's a hero to anyone who thinks outside these things into odd. I don't tend to know many poets, and one of the reasons I write is because there isn't any poetry like mine around, a poetry that feeds off immediate sensation, so that everything that happens in the specifically London day gets metabolised into juice for poetry, whether it's a pink stripe in a charcoal jumper, the barcode on a Corona bottle, the inventive logo on a Camper shoes carrier, or, for neon red alert on lips, a swipe of MAC Russian Red. And because I'm obsessive, I'll make a poem magnifying that singular detail, rather than integrate it into a more general theme, because I want instantaneous retrieval, whether it's a two-tone nail transfer a girl is wearing, or a guy's unrepeatable look coming up the stairs of the Broadwick Street toilets into the aqua winter light of my immediate now.

I don't eat when I'm writing, only drink, but Govinda's Vegetarian Restaurant in Soho Square offers (I have their list): Nachos Mexicana, Spinach and Mushroom Lasagne, Falafel, Spinach and Red Pepper Tortilla and Mezze with Baba Ganoush, houmous, spicy chick peas, broad bean paté, black olives and warm pita bread. You notice how, listing food, it becomes like poetry, because the senses go on overdrive imagining taste. It's actually far more exciting than a lot of poetry in its linguistic provocation, colour and nose. Ashbery also tells me of throwaway accidental menu choices in his poem 'Grand Galop.'

> And today is Monday. Today's lunch is: Spanish omelette,
> lettuce and tomato salad.
> Jello, milk and cookies. Tomorrow's: sloppy joe on bun,
> Scalloped corn, stewed tomatoes, rice pudding and milk.
> The names we stole don't remove us:
> We have moved on a little ahead of them
> And now it is time to wait again.

It's the incredible sense of transience here, we've moved on ahead of the menu choices just by reading them, and that's a typical Ashbery trick to get ahead and quickly delete the topic. Once Ashbery has mentioned something in a poem he makes it very clear that it's now past its sell-by date in terms of personal interest, and that he won't be going back there again. It's the sort of risk that people who lack the facility for reinvention can't afford to make, but which he achieves so weirdly, laconically, as a slice of domestic news, take it or leave it.

That poetry continues to survive suggests it has become in time coded into synaptic genes as an encrypted resource, an expression that connects with those responsive to its frequency. Part of the disappointment that underlies Ashbery's writing is the realisation that poetry is so marginalised, something that seems all the more incongruous when you live in big cities like

New York or London, where the speed of transient sensory experience would seem ideally better suited to the compact minimal unit the poem offers, rather than the long-haul process of reading a novel, but it doesn't. But poetry was always essentially intended to stay underground, whether it was the Elizabethans Daniel, Drayton and Constable, circulating their manuscripts for decades without thought of publication, or the aggressively prolific small press scene in the 1960s and 1970s that coincided with Ashbery's beginnings in poetry, when small, stapled chapbooks and inconsistently inked mimeo magazines, printed on confetti-coloured papers, usually with A4 silkscreened covers, appeared like money laundering to disrupt the mainstream. Ashbery was initially part of that piratical circulation – 200 copies largely given away to interested friends.

It was the publication of *Houseboat Days* (1977) that really set Ashbery up in force, following on from his award-winning *Self-Portrait in a Convex Mirror* (1975), as possibly the most accessibly lyrical of his abstrusely postmodern books, and certainly the most reader-friendly. It's in poems like 'Loving Mad Tom' that Ashbery sounds so exhilaratingly modern – the affair's alluded to and submerged in a poetry that deliberately cuts dream with reality. Resignation and loss are all written into the poem – things never work out – which is why we write poems, but Ashbery colours up the end dramatically so you exit where you never expected, and you don't know what became of Tom.

> A spear of fire, a horse of air,
> and the rest is done for you, to go with the rest,
> to match up with everything accomplished until now.
> And always one stream is pointing north
> To reeds and leaves, and the stunned land
> Flowers in dejection. This station in the woods,
> How was it built? This place
> Of communicating back along the way, all the way back?

> And in an orgy of minutes the waiting
> Seeks to continue, to begin again,
> Amid bugs, the harking of dogs, all the
> Maddening irregularities of trees, and night falls anyway.

The reader just goes with the accumulative build, you can't turn loss back, but it can take you to interesting places, like across America, all the way back to fractured memories Ashbery recalls, like a station in the woods somewhere, and the fact that in the end night falls anyway, the big dumbed-down block of indifference that leaves you done in and alone and writing a poem because nothing else attempts to make sense of it all.

That's one way of looking at it, because I don't suspect Ashbery intends meanings to his poems, but more possibilities of interpretation. The idea a poem has to *mean* is the product of criticism and not of poetry.

I'm getting all this into a West End writing day, and to distract myself I've accidentally lucked on the perfect found poem on a Duckie club flyer giving essential dress code for what seems to read like the amalgamated subjects of a typically compressed book of my poetry.

> effeminate dilly boys
> dusty dykes & divers
> modest mods & retrosexual rockers
> sister George and closet cases toffs and spivs
> Belgravia brasses and married men
> Jamaican sailors and ladies in tweed
> & the criminal underworld

I've personally known the lot, and the typographical layout looks like a poem, and what's more it's rush hour 5 p.m., that first drinks hour I've been waiting for all day to do something about my shot-down nerves. Ashbery's probably been at the gin all day, and some of his later work, particularly the epic *Flow Chart* (1991) reacts drunk, something that in turn gives the work that blank no-colour no-time feel you get in the anodyne amnesia of a Boeing cabin when disconnect takes over.

Flow Chart, 216 pages of apparently autonomous epic blocked into unrelieved abstraction, breaks every rule in signposting the existence of poetry as something like repurposed architecture slung up in the big city sky, where buildings and clouds adopt the same off-white off-grey colours in a spatialized architectural dissolve. There's a passage on p. 134, and I don't know who's captivated Ashbery, but it has tearjerker sustenance.

> I saw your face on some bookjacket. It looked beautiful.
>   May I write to you?
> I wouldn't really swallow poison if I was you. Meanwhile
>   I have the rain
> to experience with the others, each of us finding it un
>   comfortable though seldom
> talking about it, as there are more important subjects.
>   Fishing, for example.
> I have to get home before the music disappears. I love
>   you.
> I thought I said never to come in this café?

I don't need to know where that fits, or what it's about, it just appeals on the level of falling in love with someone's photo on a bookjacket, most likely flashy autumn rains drumming down for weeks in the rainy season, and the fear of personal rejection triggering the offensive, 'I thought I said never to come in this café?'

Inside the rear flap of the Trevor Winkfield designed jacket to *Flow Chart*, there's a superb black and white author's photo of Ashbery by Anna Tomzcat, he's on the beach, tanned and wearing shades, linen jacket carried over his shoulder, but it's the patterned tie and button-down collar shirt open at the neck that attract, the pastel-coloured shirt has deep barrel cuffs – it's really the look, casually maintained, but impeccably aesthetic, even on the beach. It's that look that's built into *Flow Chart*; the inescapable likeness of being a poet. Ashbery, rather in the manner that I'm writing this, tells us in a 1982 interview of all sorts of random things that intrude on his writing. He'll write listening to a music station and when there are announcements or commercials, bits might get sucked into the poem, 'as do all kinds of things in my immediate environment: papers that happen to be on my desk at the time, or letters, stray books, magazines. I always answer the phone when I'm writing and frequently find it has helped me to forget an unprofitable line of thinking, or that whoever I'm talking to will say something that gives me an idea. These things are very important. They're the environment that we live in and there's no point in trying to pretend that it's different or should be different.'

The process is all part of the poem, absorbing its immediate environment rather than excluding it, like picking up the accidental signals in a recording studio – the stuff that shouldn't be there – and sampling it into the sound. *Flow Chart*'s full of such accidents, the long lines engage in stories that are always incomplete, a continuously fragmented narrative, because life's like that; you remember excerpted bits and rarely the whole. Even trying to think back to last week's like a hundred years ago. People mostly tell you things about your life that you've forgotten, or only partly remember in a re-contextualized way. For Ashbery, everything's so inclusive that it's got down almost before conversion into lyric. I take, for instance, a passage of *Flow Chart* p. 49 I particularly like, and return to, and yes, it's about clothes.

> I thought I should
> sharpen my appearance, for that way lies light, lies life,
>   and yes I am
> talking about new clothes as well. He wore a black suit –
> that's what image those threads project? Arts& leisure –
>   80 bucks!

Deceptively casual, Ashbery's exploitative diagram takes in the lot – the makeover a sharp black suit affords, the telling, 'It's what you can do that matters more than the whole picture,' as the clue to his method of writing, and lastly the unacceptable idea of dying, more acute as we grow older and expand into life, than when we're nineteen and attracted to the idea of being a teen suicide to leave a perverse impacting mark on future generations.

Flow Chart's a book you can't ever really begin or end; you can't tell the bottom from the top; it's more that it sucks you into its weird, undemanding undertow of self-reflection, so that Ashbery's preoccupations push the poem forward like a river, not to an assumed end, but to a persistent solipsistic flow. Reading it's sometimes as fluent as face-spotting out of the window. *Flow Chart* just takes you there without the need to qualify its subjective layering and without belonging to any time but the contemporary moment in which it's written.

It's impossible for me to imagine a world in which John Ashbery isn't writing, anymore than I can think of Oxford Street without the monumental art nouveau Selfridge's front, because his poetry always seems so much a part of the times, like the light-polluted sky, or pop, or the compacted surge of energy that hits you somewhere mid-city, like an iridescent boot in the brain centre, kicking the pineal gland. Odd things happen in cities, like making poems, and what I saw a few days ago in Soho, in a yard off Marshall Street, where a group of students had created pop-up cinema using an old projector and a sheet and were watching *She-Devils on Wheels*, a 1968 B-movie about a female motorbike gang, rapacious for studs, and had inventively turned a disused space into cinema in the raw shivery cold.

That's city life for you; the air smashed with diamonds and the poet watching light fill with time, or are the two the same? They're both in your cells and you can't do anything about it, only stare off into the big blue indifferent sky window as a gateway into space. The other day when I was writing a poem called 'Russian Tea', I cut it thematically by wondering at the time of writing what John Ashbery would be eating for lunch, and speculating on possible choices as a sub-theme to the poem's liberated field.

But I want to tell you something. The boy I gave the tea or drug money to, I saw him again against all of the improbabilities in a city choice of 12 million, in a doorway of course, in repurposed St Anne's Court, behind Wardour Street, a smudgy drizzle coming on, and he said to me – 'You're a poet aint you,' and I said, 'How'd you know that?' and he said 'Coz you look like it.' I gave him ten pounds and said, 'Nobody else would ever say that to me, thanks, you've really made my day,' and hurried off towards Tottenham Court Road to catch a 24 bus back home still thinking of Ashbery.

PINK CADILLACS AND SUBURBAN PSYCHOPATHS: ELVIS PRESLEY AND J.G. BALLARD

Almost contemporaneous with the arrival in fiction of J.G. Ballard, who was then working full-time as a research assistant on a technical journal, publishing his first story in *New Worlds* in 1956, the world was changed forever when a young, sulky kid from Memphis, with a cool, deliberately deconstructed quiff, and drop-dead gorgeous looks, called Elvis Presley, created endemic teenage hysteria through his electrifying performances on stage, with a series of sell-out shows at the Louisana Hayride, the Oprey, and in Tupelo at the Mississippi-Alabama between the years 1954–56.

However striking the contrast between Ballard as literary recluse, living in the sleepy Heathrow catchment suburb of Shepperton, and Presley as the pouty, androgynous exhibitionist, dressed in a blue velvet shirt, black pants and blue suede boots, and rotating his hips on stage like an accelerated tumble-dryer, both men in their own acutely individual ways were responsible for opening pioneering gateways into the radical social and sexual revolutions generated by youth in the last half of the 20th century. If Elvis was singularly responsible for endorsing black music to a white audience, then Ballard in his own way subverted the literary genre of science fiction into a novel that situated the possibilities for the future directly in the present. What Ballard realised before any of his contemporaries was that the technological advances of his century had made science fiction into a tech reality, a working tool he would appropriate for scientific language, while transposing the genre from planet conquest into exploring the unlimited frontiers of inner space. Ballard's early novels like *The Drowned World*, *The Drought* and *The Crystal World*, all written in the 1960s and mapping out hallucinated ecological collapses, were the beginnings of a momentum that was to explode in the early 1970s into the creation of a series of controversially cult-acclaimed novels like *The Atrocity Exhibition* (1970) *Crash* (1973) and *Concrete Island* (1974) written with such filmic clarity that it appears as if Ballard is, in the course of writing, also directing his own shoot of the novel in progress.

Ballard's assimilation by the underground as an unlikely counterculture icon began with the publication of *The Atrocity Exhibition* in 1970, at a time when the similarly reclusive and by now increasingly obese Elvis Presley, had no option but to return to the live circuit after a decade's absence from touring, in order to reaffirm his presence as the King in the face of the British pop invasion of America that had led in turn to a dramatic downturn in his record sales. If Ballard was, by then, a literary outlaw, then Presley, in his thirties, was already burdened with an image that appeared increasingly obsolete to an American youth influenced by the infectiously energised rock of The Doors, The Rolling Stones, Dylan, The Byrds, Jimi Hendrix, and the broad LSD spectrum of West Coast psychedelic music.

Ballard's first high in the morning, during this period of optimal creativity, was an 11 a.m. slug of scotch, as the necessary trigger to getting his brain fired-up to begin writing. His quota of a thousand words a day, either handwritten or punched out on an old black Olivetti typewriter, is a routine that held good for over forty years of continuously recreating the visionary present through the imaginative possibilities provided by his neuroscientific take on fiction. 'Imagination,' always his creative instructor, Ballard states, 'is the shortest route between any two conceivable points, and more than equal to any physical rearrangement of the brain's functions.' Presley doubtless would have conceived of the pop song as the fastest way to get from A to B in 2 minutes 50 seconds of high-octane emotionally charged hooky energy. But while Ballard was slugging scotch as the juice necessary to stimulate his creative energies, Elvis was self-medicating with downers and uppers as a form of regimented polypharmacy aimed at cushioning him from components of reality and mental suffering he found intolerable. His continuing grief over the loss of his mother, the divorce initiated by his teenage bride Priscilla, the manipulation of his career by dodgy management, the bad Hollywood movies he was contracted to fulfil for money, and the inability on his part as a singer to come up with songs that in any way lived up to the extraordinary range of his voice had all in part contributed to his increasing sense of decline as an artist.

Ballard, however, was by the early 1970s starting to come into his own, and, using William Burroughs as a role-model for shocking the reader into an amoral parallel universe, in which technological resources are downloaded into the human genes, was responsible, through the writing of *Crash*, for placing the British novel 100 years ahead of his constrained mainstream contemporaries. Ballard's definition of a car crash as a moment of extreme erotic crisis could arguably be construed as the verbal equivalent of the sort of sonic distortion Jimi Hendrix had attained in the late 60s when detonating his amps. At the time of writing *Crash*, Ballard, in interview, had spoken of the erotic potentials of being involved in a head-on collision. 'The car crash,' he conjectured, 'is the most dramatic event in most people's lives, apart from their own deaths, and in many cases the two coincide. I think there's something about the automobile crash that taps all kinds of barely recognised impulses in people's minds and imaginations. It's a mistake to adopt a purely rational attitude towards events like the car crash; one can't simply say that this is a meaningless and horrific tragedy. It is that, but it's other things as well, and in *Crash* I've tried to find out exactly what that is…It's a massive collision of the central nervous system, a total explosion of the senses.'

Presley, with his love of big American cars, finned pink Cadillacs, chromed Lincolns and alloyed Chevrolets, viewed cars not as symbols of auto-destruction, but more as symptomatic of wealth surrounding his privileged status, their bodywork representing the expansive American twentieth-century dream of optimal power and global capitalisation. And while backseat limo sex was part of every American teenager's liberating experience, nobody before Ballard had ever thought to fetishise the car as an erotically constructed object that on impact distorted itself into a supra-orgasmic sexual geometry, exciting to the spectator of the accident as well as to the car's impacted occupants. Nor had any novelist before Ballard employed so specifically clinical a scientific vocabulary to describe events of interiorised reality. Ballard's two years as a medical student at Cambridge had provided him with a medical terminology he rapidly saw as essential to any novelist living in the technology-saturated urban landscapes of the late 20th century.

By mid-afternoon in the 1970s, Ballard's bottle of Merlot had diminished to a red, neck-choker's width of dark red wine, which, on top of the whisky, had by the late day shifted his consciousness directly into the altered landscape about which he was writing. When the imagination is optimally stretched it gets beyond the present and bootstraps its findings into the future. It's this shift out of time that creates the visionary: the artist who jumps one step ahead of the present to situate himself in the future. For Ballard no apology was needed. 'Given that external reality is a fiction the writer's role is almost superfluous. He does not need to invent the fiction because it is already there.'

Eleven hours behind Ballard's time it was 6 a.m. in Memphis, and Elvis, distressed by a variety of sleep disorders, was waiting for a sealed envelope of downers he and his aides called a 'drug attack' to knock him out. Natural sleep hadn't formed part of Elvis' daily life since his mother's death, and the cocktail of brain-numbing tranquillisers on which he was dependent was calculated to induce artificial sleep for a maximum of five or six hours. On waking each day, Elvis was given a dose of amphetamines to help jump-start him into the day. As he grew older, and progressively more disillusioned by the serious challenge of the likes of The Beatles and The Stones to his uncontested celebrity, Elvis conscripted almost every known prescribed pharmaceutical into his chemical regime. He used Dexies, Dilaudid, Codeine, Amytal, Carbrital, Nembutal, Seconal, Placidyl, Quaalude, and Valium on a regular basis, the chemicals daily churned over in his gut like the impacted tyre-treads on an American highway.

Ballard, despite drinking regularly as a compensation for his solitary writing life, was dependent on no other drug but imagination as the source of his creativity. By contrast, Presley couldn't, try as he did, get his head round fame as the trigger to personal stimulus. He couldn't get to left or right of a fixed image he believed was Elvis Presley; the persona he felt forced to maintain, lacquered quiff intact, in order to continue being a manufactured star. Ballard, on the other hand, had performed the perfect disappearing trick. He was invisible to his readers, and while he may have empathised in his work with iconic archetypes like James Dean, Jayne Mansfield, JF Kennedy, Marilyn Monroe and the astronaut heroes of the Apollo 11 mission, he was free, without the need for a pronounced personal image, to infiltrate the collective psyche and, through his gifts as a novelist, tweak the violent psychopathology of his times into an art every bit as valid to youth as the urgent and continually mutating expressions of rock music. Ballard was as much up there at his creative peak in fiction as his contemporaries in music like

Pink Floyd, The Rolling Stones or The Who, in interpreting the disruptive social ethos that ushered in the transitional period between the late 1960s and early 70s. In an interview with *New Musical Express* in 1985, Ballard, as much cult hero as any subject of the music press, commented significantly that, 'Music is the carrier wave and on it is modulated all this fascinating stuff – what I call the real news.'

Back, however, to Presley. Elvis wasn't really at home in the 1970s. He lacked good songs, and the hits had dried up. It was becoming progressively necessary to dye his hair and eyebrows black, to eliminate grey, and his weight had escalated to dangerous obesity on account of excessive comfort eating. Elvis was addicted to junk food, namely doorstep-thick cheeseburgers, peanut butter quadrangles, French fries, mashed potatoes, bacon fry-ups, pork chops, steaks, high-rise omelettes and ice cream and crème caramel. His preferred customised car was by now less ostentatious, and scaled-down to a speedy black Stutz Blackhawk. He refused ever to repair the cracked glass at Graceland, which his mother, Gladys, fell through on the day before she was taken to the Methodist Hospital in Memphis, where she died, and he allowed loss and grief to keep pushing him back into the past at the expense of the present. On top of it all, Elvis had grown obsessed with guns, and was starting quite unpredictably to shoot holes in his television screen and bedroom ceiling, almost like one of the delusional psychopaths ranging across the mental landscapes of Ballard's fiction. And while Presley was clogging his arteries with cholesterol-rich junk food, Ballard's main calorie intake was alcohol and his home cooking simple, and improvised from his reading of Elizabeth David's cookbooks. Parma ham for lunch sprinkled with drops of truffle oil, and something simple like a mushroom omelette for dinner.

Forced out to work the Las Vegas circuit of casino ballrooms in the early 70s for 200,000 dollars a week, at a time when

Ballard was reliant on selling work to largely US cult sci-fi magazines, Presley found himself on the defensive, telling audiences, 'I've sold over 200,000,000 records, and I've got fifty-six gold records. That's a record and I'm proud of it! That is more than The Beatles, Stones, and Tom Jones put together.' Ballard, however, was on the offensive; the publication of *The Disaster Area* in 1969 had precipitated in the author a collection of rogue sci-fi short stories, full of urban poetry, scientifically correct, rejecting naturalism as redundant, and streamlining the prose like a silver-bullet Ferrari exploding out of the present into the incalculable moment in which we read the writing now. 'Everything is becoming science fiction,' Ballard wrote. 'From the margins of an almost invisible literature has sprung the intact reality of the 20th century.'

At the same time, Elvis' physical body was turning perversely science fictional, as his dependency on prescription drugs like Demerol increased and illnesses like hepatitis, pleurisy, pneumonia, fluid retention and a twisted colon took hold of his body, and his deteriorating sight proved to be 50:50 lesioned, with the very real underlying threat of glaucoma and possible blindness. Dressed in gladiatorial rhinestone-studded jumpsuits and, because of his weight and balance problems, sometimes transported to the dressing room in a golf-cart, Elvis had become the embodiment of the rock legend living out on stage the excesses that had destroyed him. Injected with amphetamines to go on, and sedated backstage after the show by his private doctor, Elvis was still adulated by the unstoppable loyalty of his fans, who refused to separate the youthful image of the moody Beale Street King from the physically degenerating icon who was often forced to abandon shows after the first set for reasons of ill health. Back home at Graceland, sheltered from the public by his image, Elvis was confined to bed for weeks at a time, morbidly reflecting on his youth and consoling himself with sticky hamburger buns, grizzled meat and repeated requests for homemade banana-splits. He was immobile to the point of having televisions installed in the ceiling of his bedroom, so that he could view them lying down.

Ballard's uncompromising prose burnt on as symptomatic of the turbulence of his age, his assimilation of the psychopath as central to his fiction, sanctioned in his mind by the fact that twentieth-century war crimes were so atrocious that we as a species had, to his mind, evolved into a pathologically criminal society. 'I think,' Ballard commented in 1973, 'we're living at a transfer point, we're moving from one economy of the imagination and the body to a future economy of the imagination and the body. And during this unhappy transfer period it's sadly true that, for all kinds of reasons, people seem to be generating more cruelty than love. I deplore this, but as a writer I've got to face it.'

The publication of *Crash* led by extension to a dystopian themed trilogy, continued through *Concrete Island* (1973) and *High-Rise* (1975), novels in which the urban outlaw as hero has no option but to turn intransigently pathological as a necessary part of a modern survival-kit. The potential for a high-rise or corporate tower to become an isolated ecosphere, subject to its own internal politics and anarchic disruption, vandalism, blackouts, dead dogs eaten or piled up in the elevators, was the premise of a novel triggered into imaginative existence by an incident experienced by the author while on holiday in 1974. 'Before starting *High-Rise*, I was staying one summer in a beach high-rise at Rosas on the Costa Brava, not far from Dali's home at Port Lligat, and I noticed that one of the French ground-floor tenants, driven to a fury by cigarette butts thrown down from the upper floors, began to patrol the beach and photograph the offenders with a zoom lens. He then pinned the photos to a notice board in the foyer of the block. A very curious exhibition, that I took to be another green light to my imagination.'

Ballard's green light had the novel's central character, Dr Robert Laing, cast as an extremist psycho, eating his dead

Alsatian on the balcony of his marooned apartment on the 30th floor, in the book's opening lines; the extremity of the act made to appear natural in the course of Ballard's vision of a high-rise community imploding into a strictly internalised violence, like a warring planet governed by its own entropy. As always in predicting social and ecological upheavals, Ballard had made a typically quantum leap in time, anticipating, in the course of writing the novel, inner-city violence, the necessity for gated communities, hoodies armed with kitchen knives, suicide-bombers, and the whole demographic of random terrorist acts initiated into a media-saturated 21st century.

Presley, too, in 1975, when he wasn't working the road for income his record sales no longer provided, had insulated himself at Graceland in a domestic scenario as weird as anything in Ballard's fiction. Hospitalised in January for liver problems, treated in June for possible glaucoma, Elvis had on July 28th blazed a gun at the TV set, hitting Dr Nichopoulos, his personal physician, in the chest, and had also narrowly missed shooting his girlfriend, Ginger Alden, in the shower, after impulsively blasting a shot through his bedroom ceiling. Even the 'Memphis Mafia', as they were called – the male entourage composed of Memphis friends that Elvis so generously payrolled to act as minders – were starting to leave Graceland on account of the disordered personality changes Elvis showed when abusing prescription drugs. Elvis's natural generosity of character now alternated with detonating bouts of megalomaniacal rage, as he faced the unwelcome realities of declining income, divorce, his father's death from heart disease and the exhausting physical demands made on his body by live touring.

Ballard, on the contrary, was moving rapidly towards the creation of another seminal, loosely connected trilogy of books importing apocalyptic potentialities hot with the radical social tensions of the times into the significantly altered present. The raw subversion of Thatcher politics by punk, space-travel, air crashes, missing time, the imagined downfall of America as a global power, all of these themes were worked out in the course of writing *Low-Flying Aircraft*, *The Unlimited Dream Company* and *Hello America*. Ballard's concern with mapping lost places, deserts, suburban oases waiting to explode into revolution, deserted swimming pools, vacant atriums, interzones, airport departure lounges, motorway cafes, car parks, etc., is all part of his work of imaginatively retrieving wastelands and marginalised cultures and restoring them to the remit of a fiction occupying, in his own words, 'the visionary present.'

Largely disconnected from reality at the time of his death from suspected cardiac arrest on August 16th, 1977, in a scarlet-carpeted bathroom, sitting on the leopard-print seat of a black toilet, faced by a purple sink built into a marble counter, Elvis, in bringing about a premature closure to his life, also succeeded in creating for himself the post-human legacy of a legend; and in doing so joined the roster of those icons who, like James Dean, Marilyn Monroe, Janis Joplin, Brian Jones, Jim Morrison and Jimi Hendrix, have become, due to the reluctance of fans to let them go, the subjects of conspiracy theories calculated to keep them continuously alive in apparently contactable parallel worlds.

Viewing Elvis and Ballard as contemporaries who succeeded unintentionally in changing the world through their respective visions, we see Elvis lives on like a sun that refuses to set over Graceland, guided tours of his house, merchandise, downloads, DVD and music reissues all contributing to the financial management of his estate, while Ballard continued to live in the domestic chaos of his rundown Shepperton house, driving his indefatigable fiction on through books like *Cocaine Nights*, *Super-Cannes*, *Millennium People* and *Kingdom Come*, into the ongoing twenty-first century. Ballard, who died in 2009, of his own admission enjoyed cholesterol-rich lobster at the Maquis in West London, or quails, or, his favourite, grouse, eaten with a good, flinty red wine from the St Emilion region. It's unlikely that he and Elvis would have found much to talk about if they had met, except a mutual love of cars, and, as a symptom of 1950s cool, black shades; but both are inexorably linked by the maximum impact each brought to his individual art at a time when the modern world accelerated into the socially disruptive revolution that we are still, as a species, experiencing so forcibly now. Elvis had his name painted in black on his customised, strawberry-pink Cadillac, and wore a pink sapphire ring to match. Ballard, in appearance, could have been mistaken for one of the largely featureless doctors or psychiatrists who are often the protagonists of his novels. Whether or not we recognise it, both men have infiltrated our cultural genes and affect the way we look, act and think. I would go so far as to argue that the unlikely partnership of Presley/Ballard is still a solvent 21st century one. Both men continue to shape the reality in which we live – the science fiction that America has become, the psychopathic oligarchs who rule and contend for world leadership, the commonplace event that space travel has become, the planet starting to act as a whole like reality television, and the feeling that anything is possible as a terrorist reprisal, at any given moment, is all indirectly a part of their artistic legacy. If Elvis personified the idea of the American Dream, the poor boy who got rich despite his socially deprived beginnings, and who went on to become the most flamboyantly spectacular rock performer of his generation, then Ballard has made a fiction out of the modern world Elvis helped create, and in the process touched on and anticipated every significant futuristic component of the past 50 years, that we have watched become reality and lived through in the world of tyrannically militant politics. Elvis and Ballard plugged into the mains of their times and let rip. Both men, by the nature of their art, overtook themselves, like fast cars burning down the highway. In terms of the future, we're still inquisitive spectators, waiting for them to arrive.

ORANGE SUNSHINE IN ROBERT DUNCAN'S POETRY

For a physical location to write about Robert Duncan, as I prefer to work in public places, I chose Yauatcha in Soho's Broadwick Street as my transient workroom in which to convene on fuzzy October afternoons with my imaginatively virtualised subject, who died in 1988, of chronic kidney failure.

Yauatcha, with its ultramarine glass frontage, a postmodern update of an oriental tearoom, and with generic Asian waitresses wearing white, bare at the midriff uniforms, designed by Tom Yip (I've done my research), is my chosen site to work on individual ways of contacting my subject. It's like writing inside a blue fish tank, with Broadwick Street outside, the locale of my novel *The Grid*, and today the sky's no-colour Smirnoff blue is rumbled by Boeing fins.

My brain weighs three pounds in terms of grey matter, but I can't calculate the weight of thought, and the zero resting mass of each thought I shape about Robert Duncan, in between the 60,000 thoughts we ideate each day, together with the thousands of bits of information we process as a result of external stimulus. I can't track Robert Duncan's micrograms transmitted through my neural networks, but I feel if I could project them as footage, the substance of each would be surrounded by a luminous halo of orange sunshine. Robert Duncan lived a lot of his time in saturated orange Californian sunshine, and I've never seen a picture of him in shades. Light fills the empty spaces on the page he structured with his inimitable typographic dance, as the organic soundtrack of how he heard words register in inner space. I'm sure Duncan heard orange as a sound, while looking into its interface between red and yellow in the visible spectrum at a wavelength of about 585–620 nm, and as a tone numerically half way between red and yellow in a gamma-compressed RGB colour space.

In a letter dated September 11th, 1960, written to the poet H.D., who Duncan was so influential in rehabilitating to reader awareness in the sixties, after she suffered decades of literary neglect spent in Klinik Hirslanden in Zurich, he talks of the analogy between the bee's waggle dance and its sugar-fix target, the rose.

'The bee and the rose – the bee-dance, the sky map and the food-source – is one figure of the command. And let the bee-dance and the sky-map give hint of what we too are calld to to be poets (with some sure instinct that the line must be sweet and also rough, must flow and yet be cut in stone) the signatures and the way; the hive, the poem was only home. In the rose we'll read Elysium.'

Robert Duncan, who was born in Oakland, California, on January 7th, 1919, was a visionary. A poet of gay domesticity, he lived with his partner, the exceptional collagist Jess Collins, for over thirty years, and with a Burmese cat called Pumpkin, and lived so much immersed in poetic energy that poetry became as much a part of him as the epidermal mapping of his skin. If he called his art 'manipulative magic', then he was the prankster who morphed images as hoodoo in the poem's altered physics, rather like bending light as a shortcut to reaching a different reality.

Orange again. Orange occurs in human perception when two sets of eye cones are firing together with red a primary colour and yellow a secondary, combining to be seen as orange, a tertiary colour.

In his poem 'Upon Taking Hold', Duncan comes up with amazingly lyrical orange.

> This is the bunch of ranunculus,
> rose, butter, orange crowfoot
> profuse bouquet in its white china pitcher;
> this is the hookd rug worked in rich color
> the red, blue, ochre,
> violet, emerald, azure,
> the black, pink, rose,
> oyster white, the orange…
> this is the orange measurement of the lines
> as I design them.
> The joys of the household are fates that command us.

What Duncan gets out of his colour-drenched, twinkling bunch of ranunculus grouped randomly in a white pot, is what he calls, 'the orange measurement of the lines as I design them,' the I being central to the poet assuming power through the subjective interpretation of what he sees. Duncan believed, 'responsibility is to keep the ability to respond.' And poetry is all about response to sensory input, by which I mean the reorganisation of things into their imaginative equivalent. You could say that Duncan looked at things to imagine with them.

I'm drinking a dark Yunnan tea called Puer Ya Jian that has a smoky twist in its complex leaf, as I touch the nerve of Robert Duncan's hard-grafted virtuoso poetry that is so self-consciously schemed that it always comes back on the poet observing himself writing, like having sex reflected by a mirrored ceiling. When I go for a leak downstairs, the toilet's like an obsidian slab, black on black, like a subterranean cell, unlike the public one in the middle of the street, where men diligently pick up in an under-the-street tiled interior, that's optimistically Mediterranean blue. It's a transitional, transient thing, but it helps shift my mind, so that I return to Duncan refreshed by having made a journey down to come back. The sexy waitress with a black bob tells me her name is Yuka, the 'a' pronounced like rattling dice in the larynx.

What's so clear in reading Duncan is the transparency of his poetic figures. In his poem 'The Question' he asks, taking sensitivity to shivering point:

> Have you a gold cup
> dedicated to thought
> that is like clear water
> held in a flower?

Duncan answers his own question affirmatively, by suggesting the concept; his line is always like light in clarity. Light, too, like thought, in that a photon's energy content has no rest mass, and travels at 186,000 miles per second. The poet's neural speed is much faster than light in linking one perception directly to another – as Duncan demonstrates – clicking on through one trillion cells, with one hundred trillion connections, at a thought-speed of approximately 750 milliseconds, to direct the image. Duncan's fast, and his look, in the way his left eye is differently focused to the right, like David Bowie's compelling mismatch of pupils, gives him a quality that's alien, like he's seeing as natural what you can't see.

I'm thinking orange again, and how engagement with Duncan's line is a privilege on this grainy Soho day, a verbal nutrient, a piggyback across free space, that islands me to Duncan's poem 'The Structure of Rime III', so that I'm in close to it, with that rare concentration that excludes most peripheral distraction. Orange pigments, I remind myself, are largely in the cadmium families and absorb mostly blue light. 'The Structure of Rime III', from *The Opening of the Field* (1969) is a poem poured like orange juice.

> Twice he saw an orange snake that reard up and
> spread his hood, cobra-wise.
> The orange color does not hold
> When the skin is workd. Summer advances
> preparing new orange.
>
> The human hood spread orange in time
> fixation of relentless color
> – character, scaly-feathered presumption.
> After a shower, the mirror
> shows the body spreading, orange in time,
> reveals accumulations
> of my uses, beyond all earliness,
> that I bring to my time,
> whatever the pretense,
> to this
> rearing up
> this
> snake stance.

The poem I've chanced on as an orange event, has Duncan, with his predisposition to esoteric archetypes, link snake-dance to word-dance, stitching the two into an orange skin, with 'the human hood spread orange in time' as though, he, Duncan, has been morphed into the orange snake he visualises in imaginative reality. The fusion radiates orange energies in the poem's electromagnetic field, it provides us with an assured diagram of the poet's fine-tuned nervous system, an RD mapping.

Robert Duncan's sensibility-type was romantic idealist, gay activist, his pioneering essay 'The Homosexual in Society', published in Dwight Macdonald's journal *Politics* in 1944, was a seminal treatise, comparing anti-gay discrimination to that suffered by African Americans and Jews. Duncan spent time in the late fifties teaching at Black Mountain College, was a committed pacifist, and a dynamic mover in the San Francisco poetry renaissance, together with his friends Jack Spicer and Robin Blaser. Duncan was genetically, organically so much a poet, that he lived poetry as his cellular respiration, and if his work was marginalised by mainstream careerists, that is, poets who network to substitute for creative originality, then living the edge taught him to centre himself totally in his inexhaustible recreation of living as inalienable from poetry. Duncan didn't so much live for poetry, as live it as his total immersive identity. In 'The Performance We Wait For', from the collection *The Opening of the Field*, he casts the poet in the role of central legislator for organising bits in the universal pattern.

> A King – the one we call Poet
> under the crown of an Idea
> seeks quiet of a garden
> even if it be a single plant,
> tended in the evening. Prosper
> O green friend! for I have seen
> signature that is ground of all delight
> in the sight of you, that from seed
> has given stem, leaves, flower
> of your nature

I come back to Yauatcha another day to relocate Duncan. I'm an inveterate multitasker, so I've been working at poetry and fiction, and doing what I do, soak in my real interest, my sounds library of rock and pop. This time Yuka, the waitress I know, has one inch more of magnolia midriff visible, and she's clearly zapped from work, her eyes have dropped a tone in shine, and she's probably overdosed on serving dim sum. This time I go for a jade orchid tea. I don't eat when I write, because I'm firing up too much adrenalin, and like the Rolling Stones I keep a 28" waist. Poetry and fat don't tango in my vocabulary.

Why are poets so confederated to loneliness? Duncan was so lonely in language that he had to keep filling in empty space that he might otherwise fall through as a black hole into death. I'm singularly lonely as I review his loneliness. If you're a poet by profession you're so odd as to be an alien mind virus, an off-worlder, a romantic humanoid, whatever the alienated designation. It's an addiction using words as chemicals, and Duncan was terminal. I read his loneliness in 'The Structure of Rime XI', and it rains outside in sheeting flurries of see-through polka dots, all over Soho like a hissy soundtrack to loss. What'd Robert write?

> Of my first lover there is a boat drifting. The
> oars have been cast down into a shell. As if
> this were no water but a wall, there is a
> repeated knock as of hollow against hollow, wood
> against wood. Stopping to knock on wood against
> the traps of the nightfishers, I hear before my
> knocking the sound of a knock drifting…
> All night a boat swings as if to sink. Weight
> returning to weight in the cold water. A hotel room
> returns from Wilmington into morning. A boat
> sets out without boatmen into twenty years of
> snow returning.

Walking by water amplifies loneliness, and you can hear how Duncan heard the acoustics of his memory in these want-to-give-up-on-life lines, like those you write to try and reconcile yourself to a loss when you know it won't make it better. That's what the blues are for, giving song to a mood that's like frozen cyan pigment. Duncan can't shake it off, nor could Bob Dylan in 'Tangled Up in Blue,' his post-Sara emotional destitution that took him out on the road on a tour that has never ended. Art doesn't heal anything; the making of it simply expresses the shape of the pain, not its closure.

The thing is, Duncan knew the problems of poetry too presciently to ever delude himself into the belief he could get outside or beyond them. Understanding limitations was his compensation for total disillusionment as to how few people poetry ever really affected.

'The problems in poetry,' he wrote, 'which have interested me most are... how to increase the complexity of interpenetration of parts; how to make the poem go on as long as possible – that is to contain the maximum quantity of moving parts so that the final performance of choreography and design will keep me intrigued intellectually and emotionally; all this posed against the endurance of the ideal audience – the ideal audience being one that can take precisely as much as I could take myself.'

Everyone can only take so much of poetry, like Yuka serving dim sum under moody cove lighting, Chilean sea bass mooli rolls, baked venison puffs, hand-pulled noodles and Shanghai siew long buns, roast duck and pumpkin dumplings, and pear and taro croquette, as well as a sensual anthology of subtle gastro-patisserie.

She's probably thinking of her day off, while I'm thinking of Robert Duncan's poetry looking typographically like the molecular formula of a drug, diazepam for instance, $C_{16}H_{13}ClN_2O$ as it's synthesised, in his case through spatial imagination. And while Duncan's poems are, in their stanza-patterns, partly influenced by the 17th century metaphysical poets, like Donne and Herbert, with their snowflake or acid-drop shapes, his are dominated by how breath organically dictates the poem's figure on the page. It often appears he's engaged in transposing his DNA sequences into poetry. In 'Proofs', he writes, playfully but seriously, of the printing errors in his work, because Duncan so often makes a poetry out of telling you how he is writing the poem, in the way I'm lifting Yauatcha, with its fish-tank like ergonomics, and arranged red hydrangea feature today, on the slim-line bar, into my writing on Robert Duncan.

Insert "need" after
"mine is a first song"
For "wrong" read "wring."

I am tired of the images
That follow me. Delete them.
Don't desert me. You are so far away,
 dear Printer, in another
part, puzzling over my intention
with cold fingers. Don't

lose the word R O S E

isolated on the page.
It is not a flower, but put there
for an old rising.

Duncan's obsessive saturation in language often gives the impression that he was locked into converting all personal happenings into words given the music of poetry, and that there wasn't the time or accountability to know experience in any other way. Duncan overdosed on his poetic facility to the point of imploding, and his friend, the pioneeringly innovative poet, Michael Palmer, in his essay 'Ground Work on Robert Duncan', tells us of Duncan's checking his unstoppable output arbitrarily after the publication of *Bending the Bow* (1968).

'The story is well-known,' Palmer writes, 'in poetry circles: around 1968, disgusted by his difficulties with publishers and what he perceived as the careerist strategies of many poets, Duncan vowed not to publish a new collection for fifteen years. He felt that this decision would free him to listen to the demands of his (supremely demanding) poetics and would liberate the architecture of his work from all compromised considerations.'

Duncan's experiences growing up as a homosexual in pre-Stonewall America, as a pacifist, visionary idealist, with what amounted to a criminalised sexuality, made him naturally intolerant of authority, a characteristic that was to find superb eloquence in his indictment of the Vietnam War as an obscene, illegal catastrophe. In the early 1940s, and living in New York, Duncan had supported himself by salaried prostitution, working the all night cafeteria near Central Park and 6th Avenue. He told his biographer Ekbert Faas: 'I wore paint on my face and eye shadow. I wore clothes that went much further than people in that period went, outside of ones that were in drag. I liked to go to dance halls and I would dress in the dyke end of it, like lumber jackets, but with my hair cut in bangs, and earrings, and my face painted. And I got successfully tossed out of a bar and told not to bring my trade in there.'

There's a strong link between the criminal and the poet, and it isn't only that they both steal, it's that they can't let go of what they see and so lay claim to it by possession. The poet attempts to recreate the present in the past, by a process of visual retrieval, and the shoplifter is motivated similarly, in that he or she can't be separated from the object appropriated, almost as an expression of separation anxiety. Writing and stealing are arguably linked to feelings of grief and the need to compensate in some way for loss. The poet usually doesn't want the poem once it's written, and the shoplifter, losing the dopamine rush triggering of theft, often quickly sells or disposes of the stolen item.

Anyhow, Robert Duncan lived most of his life outside the law, and poetry was his compensation. Like most non-careerist poets, he probably had, in his own estimate, 50 readers, but his overriding conviction sustained his untiring creativity. The person at the table next to me is squirting a capsule of sake into the sponge, chocolate and cream tiered into a glass of Japanese tea, a layered affair shaped like a confectionary gherkin, while I'm thinking orange in terms of Robert Duncan, and wondering if I'll break here to write a poem I want to call 'It Takes Two Baby', or keep on with Robert.

More than Ginsberg's often journalistic anti-war polemic, Duncan's protest extends to naming his antagonists as perpetrators of genocidal crimes he the poet reckons to be up there with Hitler. *Of the War* remains one of the most powerful protest thrusts to ever be phrased in poetry.

> Now Johnson would go up to join the great simulacra of men
> Hitler and Stalin, to work his fame
> with planes roaring out from Guam over Asia,
> all America become a sea of toiling men
> stirrd at his will, which would be a bloated thing,
> drawing from the underbelly of the nation
> such blood and dreams as swell the idiot psyche
> out of its courses into an elemental thing
> until his name stinks with burning meat and heapt honors

Having named Lyndon Johnson as autocratic warlord, as British poets should name the oligarchal jackal, Tony Blair, Duncan ups the volume of his anger to global proportions.

> the all-American boy in the cockpit
>   loosing his flow of napalm, below in the jungles
>   "any sign at all or sign of life" his target, drawing now
>   not with crayons in his secret room
>   the burning of homes and the torture of mothers and
>   fathers and children,
>   their hair a-flame, screaming in agony, but
>   in the line of duty, for the might and enduring fame
>   of Johnson . . .

Readers who think of Duncan as primarily motivated by aesthetics, and providing metre with spatial dance steps, will be jolted by a lyrical invective as powerful as Pound's tormented hostility in *The Pisan Cantos*, in that Duncan, too, goes public, as out-of-the-closet agitprop, all his outlawed years of persecution finding empathetic resonance with the physical and psychological torture inflicted on a nation with napalm and the scorching defoliant Agent Orange, employed by a totalitarian power against pockets of guerrilla resistance. All of Duncan's experience of oppression, and his opposition to this through the liberating forces of imagination, came together in his lacerating condemnation of Johnson's chemical terrorism of a country with little defence, its victims licked into genetic travesties by hawkish despotism and militantly imposed regime change.

Duncan's political voice, previously confined largely to issues of gay liberation, is levelled with sustained political rage at Johnson's US liquidation of the Viet Cong. Using Whitman's and Ginsberg's long line as a poetic highway down which to traffic invective, Duncan declares war on war. What horrifies Duncan is the lie; the deceit of apparently democratic civilians transformed into willing mass-murderers.

> – Back of the scene the atomic stockpile; the vials of
>   synthesized
> diseases eager biologists have developed over half a
>   century dreaming
> of the bodies of mothers and fathers and children and
>   hated rivals
> swollen with new plagues, measles grown enormous,
>   influenzas
> perfected; and the grasses of despair, confusion of the
> senses, mania
>   inducing terror of the universe, coma, existential
> wounds,
>   that

> chemists we have met at cocktail parties, passt daily and with a
> happy "Good day" on the way to classes or work, have workt to
> make war too terrible for men to wage –

Duncan's disillusionment, so courageously elevated into poetic condemnation, is his positive anti-war effort, the consolidation of his energies as a poet against the unstoppable military. It's his singular push against military tech, in criminalising Johnson on the line that is so heroic, even if poetry is powerless to change external events, but necessary as a creative act that takes issue with history.

The peculiarly orange sunshine I feel at play in Duncan's work is a Californian orange, and it's also the title of my 250-page book-length poem on 1960s rock music, as well as the brand name of over ten million hits of LSD, synthesised in 1969 on the West Coast by the illegal tableters Sand and Scully. I quote orange from Martin A. Lee and Bruce Shlain's book *Acid Dreams* that documents a time when Duncan was at his creative peak.

'At a rock concert in Anaheim, it suddenly began to rain orange pills. A man in black leather trousers wearing a T-shirt that read "Orange Sunshine Express" was scattering LSD into the air, his long hair flowing behind him.'

The tablets, cut with a pinch of methedrine, created an internal orange neural aura for the user, and were in effect designer drugs tinted psychedelic orange. Orange sunshine as a hallucinogenic pill went global, reaching outposts like Goa Beach in India, the mountains of Nepal, Indonesia, Australia, Japan, South Vietnam, Costa Rica, Israel, and the ancient Muslim shrine of Mecca; but its origin of illegal and ingenious manufacture in a chemical lab was West Coast CA.

Duncan didn't need chemically induced altered states, but he lived through the sixties on a coast where Orange Sunshine was used virally as a counterculture incentive to drug-induced psychedelic hits. Duncan's orange sunshine, an external phenomenon as much as internal, spatialized light surrounding the poem, was his constant that came on to shine whenever he wrote of aspects in which light is the dominant.

It's another day in my life in writing this essay and on my way to Yauatcha I stop at Let's Fill The Town With Artists to buy some orange pigment so that I've got my own orange while I concentrate on Robert Duncan. I go for Risk Reactor PF38 Fluorescent Tropical Sunlight Orange UV Pigment, specific gravity 1.37, particle size 3.5 to 4.5 microns. I like detail and brands, both of which fill my own poetry, and I'm glad of this sachet of pigment, like an artificial sun I place in my pocket.

I'm struck today – it's a Wednesday with a cool Viagra-blue sky sighting over Soho – by an early poem of Duncan's, 'An African Elegy', that pushes into the visionary zone and brings together incongruously, but rightly, the figure of the African shaman with that of Virginia Woolf wading out into the foggy Thames at Richmond to drown, her coat pockets weighted with stones.

> Death is the dog-headed man zebra striped
> and surrounded by silence who walks with a lion,
> who is black. It was his voice crying come back,
> that Virginia Woolf heard, turnd
> her fine skull, hounded and haunted, stopt,
> pointed into the scent where
> I see her in willows, in fog, at the river of sound
> in the trees. I see her prepare there
> to enter Death's mountains
> like a white Afghan hound pass into the forest,

As a poetic conception of death, the empathetic imagination at work here takes some beating, particularly in the contrasting black and white imagery and the voices in Woolf's head calling her back, trying to turn her around before she enters death's gateway, in the remarkable image, appearing out of Duncan's fluency, of a white Afghan hound slipping into a dark forest.

I personally find these lines in Duncan's 'An African Elegy' one of the most stunningly imagined evocations of death in poetry, a sustained compression of originality that has you think that this is exactly what Woolf encountered as she dragged slowly out into the cold green current at Richmond to go under.

Duncan continues the image as a tranquil dissolve, imagining the transition into death as fluent as the body's passage through fog, or, in Woolf's case, submission to water. He writes on the tail of Woolf's recreated last moments.

> And I see
> all our tortures absolved in the fog,
> dispersed in Death's forests, forgotten. I see
> all this gentleness like a hound in the water
> float upward and outward beyond my dark hand.

The letting go into death imagined in these lines is also a dispersal of pain, so that the accumulative negative drag we all collect inwardly gets wiped like river fog in the transitional process of dying and we become easy with gentleness, in Duncan's figure, 'like a hound in the water.'

Robert Duncan's 'An African Elegy', written in the forties, attempts shamanic identification with black resources by way of empathy and is a return to blues a decade before the San Francisco Poetry Renaissance and the emergence of the North Beach scene during the 50s and 60s, in which Duncan (with Jack Spicer and Robin Blaser) was to play such a central role.

For Duncan, the negro became the symbol for the oppressed gay outlaw he felt himself to be in a materially homogenised American society, and his getting under black skin through a process of conducive empathy allowed him further to identify with the primal, the disaffected, and the dissident. Duncan saw in black blues, too, the inalienable rhythm of poetry; a rhythmic source the white poet draws on through a generic sensibility type.

In a 1969 interview given to George Bowering at the Ritz-Carlton Hotel in Montreal, Duncan spoke of the strong emphasis on the individual in his poetry, and of the affirmative qualities of unique difference in each person amounting to freedom. He commented, 'And you will find throughout my poetry the idea of an individuality that has absolute freedom and a law to itself, that has its being in a larger being, but of course for me that's not just the state, that's the cosmos finally. And there I would be like Charles Olson I think, although my cosmos is different very clearly, by having a being in the cosmos; and certainly like Charles in that I'm interested in the divine. You find in me a cosmos that's perennial and that's destroyed – the law constantly destroys the law, which is not a dogma but a thing devouring itself and undoing itself, and you will find that in my poetry, I undo my propositions.'

Robert Duncan's poetry, in its continuous experimentation, is rather like decoding the human genome, in the attempt to sequence the chemical base pairs that map the approximately 20–25,000 genes of the human genome, with each human cell containing 3 million pairs of base DNA. The analogy here with the biological instructions of genes is that Duncan self-analytically references words in their formation so that there is potentially no closure to a poem, only what he calls the opening of the field. A Duncan poem can be like remixing a song 12 times, and it's a matter of choice as to whether a remix or rewrite ever improves the original or is simply different. Duncan's discourse with language appears to entertain orange and blue scattered sunlight, and the fascination for me is in the scattered pattern always searching to coalesce. He articulates the contradictions inherent in his work in the poem 'Metamorphosis'.

> Three men seated around a table talking
> of words, of tones, of colors, – of one, one art
> a poetry – at odds each one,
> emerging as if from an enlightened singleness
> into all contradictions realer upon the real

It's tempting to think that the three guys in this passage are Duncan, Jack Spicer and Robin Blaser, the North Beach coterie of instructive poets committed to their craft like a jeweller cutting a blue diamond. And it's often discourse about poetry, words, tones, colours, that become Duncan's subject matter like a Chinese box, a puzzle he couldn't escape as he writes writing into possibilities that are inevitably unresolved lyrical suggestions.

In 'A Poem Beginning with a Line by Pindar', essentially a reflective poem on male Grecian beauty that converts midway into ideological disgust with American war policies, naming Roosevelt and Johnson as criminal perpetrators of negative capability, Duncan leads in with lines so light that they travel like photons.

> The light foot hears you and the brightness begins
> god-step at the margins of thought,
> quick adulterous tread at the heart.
> Who is it that goes there?

What begins there, in my association, is the orange sunshine that floods Duncan's poetry as his inwardly choreographed dance-steps take up balletic motion. I read my version of the poem in the UK edition published by Jonathan Cape, because I like to find distraction in Leigh Taylor's lipstick-red and black dust jacket design with stars raining, a revamped Flammarion engraving, but it's the stars that dominate like they're being beamed up in a red sky in which an alchemical human-faced sun and moon are in conjunction. Nobody can read poetry for sustained periods, so the jacket design is a necessary complementary visual that brings some entertainment to the eye.

Duncan's Pindar poem is a weird one, taking as its starting point Goya's canvas *Cupid and Psyche* for homoerotic appraisal of physique, before making a dissolve into disdain for presidents Hoover, Roosevelt, Truman, Eisenhower, and Johnson the White House rats Duncan opposes on humanitarian grounds as the systematic oppressors of individual liberty.

> There is no continuity then. Only a few
> posts of the good remain. I too
> that am a nation sustain the damage
> where smokes of continual ravage
> obscure the flame.

Duncan routes the poem back to myth as a liberating Olsonian energy, and to the hero or journeyer moving through different states towards something like pure information, and to the figure of the poet responsible for directing the journey. Duncan catches himself out late at night—

> A line of Pindar
> moves from the area of my lamp
> towards morning.

That's his work, late at night in the conical, planetary glow of a lamp, the galactic sky up there over the Pacific roofed with hot and cool space rocks.

Chan, today's waitress, tells me she's going back to Burma next week; the drizzled-diamond London rain isn't part of her essentially sunshiney personality. I tell her when I write I'm a space tourist in neural galaxies as she moves onto dim sum, amazed at the clarity of my handwriting directed by a black Pentel Sign pen. October's starting to dampen the atmosphere and I listen at nights to the edgy music of Babyshambles, with their dark, punkish disdain, layered with fuck-you three-chord guitar aimed at the gutter.

Of himself and his poetic method, Duncan wrote, 'I am dramatic and romantic . . . in my general attitude – namely: the poem as ritual, projecting a poetic life. I do not write poetry in reference to a literature but to an immediate excitement which has noticeable effect in a sign-centred mental and emotional existence.'

Duncan occupies his poetry so fully that the commitment is total. He metabolises poetry like a drug, the metabolites converted into the preferred direction of words. In the poem 'Words Open out upon Grief', he literally opens words out of life.

> like windows in that house high
> showd distances clear to the horizon
> upon grandeur,
> time-vistas for the eye, clear –
> as far as the Hudson –
> three imaginary states we saw.

It's not only the space opened up here that's the movement of the poem, it's the visual retrieval looking out as far as the Hudson of 'three imaginary states', that gives the poem a spatial dimension that shocks. You go with Duncan in his seeing and sense of discovery, knowing that Jimmy and Blanche, his friends, are looking at different city views to the poet's 'three imaginary states'.

My reading of poetry over the years takes in little that is British, due to lack of subversive or visionary stimulus in the British canon, and looks mostly to America for the sort of risk, experimentation, explosively uninhibited subject matter, and update of language that I personally need in order to engage with poetry. The British do rock music best, but the Americans always lead in poetry.

The Soho light's cold gold today, like a cornflower-blue postmodern light-box on Broadwick Street, as I leave Yauatcha and head off in the direction of Newburgh Street and Marshall, my thoughts still busy with all the exciting ways Robert Duncan makes poetry happen, and for me his work is always associated with orange sunshine, like the poem turned orange in the process of reading. Francis Bacon said in an interview, 'Some paint comes across directly onto the nervous system and other paint tells you the story in a long diatribe through the brain.' Robert Duncan affects both these tonal methods in the fusion of his private and public poetry, his domestic lyric and his political invective. I'm glad for what he's given me in the process of my afternoons at Yauatcha. Chan's back in Burma now, Yuka's probably serving venison puffs and pumpkin dumplings to suits in the place's moody lighting, and I'm off to meet the only friend I have in this city who sometimes reads Robert Duncan.

KIT MARLOWE, BRAWLING AND THE PARISH OF ST GILES

To warm myself to Kit Marlowe's majestically brawlish poetry, in which his elevated line never loses sight of the street, I'm listening to Pete Doherty's debut solo album *Grace/Wastelands*, which finds the romantically bruised punk troubadour mining familiar themes of ruin and addiction, including the beautiful lurchy 'Last of the English Roses', a classic tilt at indie pop with a superior lyric. Pete Doherty's musical duration is so far relatively short, and Christopher Marlowe's legacy one of five hundred years, but somehow in my private mythology they meet as intransigent sensibility types. Kit Marlowe, Marlow, Morley, Marly, whatever his name, died at the age of 29 on 30th May 1593, in a suspected contract killing at Eleanor Bull's closed house at Deptford Creek, murdered reportedly by Ingram Frizer who savagely pointed a knife blade through the superior orbital fissure at the back of the eye socket of Marlowe's right eye, the blade slicing through major blood vessels, the cavernous sinus, the internal carotid artery, to a depth of two inches and killing him almost immediately.

Marlowe was in deep trouble at the time; a warrant was issued for his arrest on 18th May 1593, and on the 20th May he was brought to court and bailed on condition he report to the Privy Council every day until formally charged or acquitted. Allegations of his punkish disdain for the state, money-laundering, openly declared homosexuality, his dodginess as a suspected double agent, and his contempt for religious dogma, together with his love of lowlife, had won him a reputation as a binge-drinking urban trouble-maker.

It's Kit's irremediable bad boy image, I suspect, that has helped sustain his reputation over the centuries as a literary outlaw; a hoodlum playwright who subverted class, because as a spy he was paid on both sides for inside knowledge of government spin and corruption, by both Walsingham and Burleigh, as heads of intelligence. Kit's unstoppable twist of self-destruction worked in his favour, rather like Sid Vicious' heroin-drenched OD has helped fuel the Sex Pistols' continuing legacy despite their only recording one studio album, *Never Mind The Bollocks* (1976). Sid regularly carved into his own body to self-harm, a destructive streak ending with him plunging a blade into his junky partner Nancy Spurgeon to figuratively write the Pistols' legacy in infected blood.

You need to understand my difficulties. I'm trying on a gold-dusted Soho September afternoon in 2015, sitting outside on the chilled stone steps to the Chinese pagoda, where they're playing mah-jong in Soho's Newport Place, opposite fast food Canton and China Buffet, to access coded events in 1593 without any proper signposting but only roaming speculation. I come here not only for the sizzling Soho charge, but because Cindy who massages my right forefinger straight with extraordinary adept Chinese neural navigation of the persistent distress given the joint by the barrel of my Pentel Sign Pen does it weekly for me. Today her navy tee, worn with white skinny jeans, accentuates her ivory skin tone, sensitive as a magnolia petal, and a black topknot that's black on black on black. She's so intuitively attentive to my finger that after each session it appears weightless and like it's floating in weak gravity. I tell her it turns gold.

But it's Kit who needs posthumous attention. How do I get back to him or fuck him into physical awareness of who he was in the 1580s/90s?

I've been Kit's way before and situated him as a modified copy in my 2008 novel *The Grid*, in which, alive in the 21st century, he recollects aspects of his past in the dystopian capital in which Tony Blair as a warlord is run into a bunker, the novel ending with a flameout terrorist kamikaze, in which Shakespeare fucks Marlowe on a rooftop while a Boeing's rogue pilot points the impacted nose cone through the Treasury.

Unlike Shakespeare, Marlowe's essentially off-message, lugubrious sensibility has resisted conversion into academic industry. Marlowe is altogether too disreputable, controversial and underground to have his DNA stretched like Shakespeare's into a global brand of chewing gum in the redundant search for meaning in what is, after all, highly communicable poetry.

Marlowe, or a vivid historic snapshot of him, time-slips into the re-creatable present between 2 and 3 p.m. on 18th September 1589 on Hog Lane, a dirt road running west from Shoreditch to Finsbury Fields, and what is now Worship Lane leading west from Curtain Street towards Finsbury Square. Hog Lane was generic outlaw territory, outside the city's jurisdiction, like the quarter called Norton Folgate where Marlowe lived, just a few blocks from Bishopsgate's Heron Tower – essentially a lowlife complex where criminals, outlaws, highwaymen and poor poets like Marlowe lived.

On Hog Lane, and presumably already drunk and vicious in the hazy autumn afternoon, Kit and his friend Thomas Watson, also most likely a spy, were brawling with a barman called William Bradley, who may have evicted the two from his father's pub. Bradley, a dodgy 26-year-old pub owner from Bishopsgate, had defaulted that summer over payment of a debt of £14 to John Alleyn, a friend of Watson's, so, even without the eviction, there was already a contentious undertow to what began as a street fight between Bradley and Marlowe, and attracted the usual crowd of spectators. It's not clear to what extent Marlowe was injured before Watson launched in with a drawn sword to defend his friend, rushing at Bradley, who quickly had the better of him, ripping him with a knife. Watson was driven back by his opponent, with repeated sword cuts from the heavier man, as far as the ditch that ran along the roadside. About to be slammed back into the polluted ditch, the adept Watson, who had up to this point only defended himself, drove his sword six inches deep into Bradley's chest, killing his attacker instantly.

Drenched in blood, the two friends were arrested by the constable of the precinct, Stephen Wyld, a tailor, and marched off to Sir Owen Hopton, Lieutenant of the tower of London, whose home was at Norton Folgate, before being manacled and deposited in Newgate Prison in a black rat-infested cavernous space called Limbo, lit by a single candle, where the sick, hallucinating and semi-starved inmates were left without medical help or hygiene to rot. Marlowe, as a spy, however, who lived from selling sensitive information, used his time in Newgate to his advantage, getting to know the money-laundering John Poole, incarcerated for counterfeiting in 1587. Poole seems to have been a formative influence on Marlowe and Richard Baines' later scheme to seriously tamper with currency.

Two weeks later, on 1st October 1589, a demoralised, dried-out Marlowe was released from Newgate on bail of £40, provided by Richard Kitchen, attorney of Clifford's Inn, and Humphrey Rowland, horner. We don't know the place of these individuals in Marlowe's life and they probably didn't know or care he was a poet, anymore than he would have told them. Tom Watson waited two agonizing months in Newgate to be reprieved by the Queen and freed on the grounds he had killed Bradley in self-defence. We'll never know the true cause of the brawl and subsequent killing, but the circumstances of Marlowe's bandit life in what was a tenement in London's underbelly suggests that unlike his contemporary, Shakespeare, he was mostly broke, worked as a sleazy operative for money and drank what came his way. Kit, unlike Shakespeare, was a singularly committed poet, because arguably he never took it seriously, just wrote it as a Canterbury shoemaker's son, and probably had the best line of his generation, sufficient, I believe, to have Shakespeare's hit men or Tudor hoodies, via the Earl of Southampton, murder him out of rivalry. Basically, Marlowe annoyed his contemporaries with his total disrespect for convention, his celebration of the male body as homoerotic ideal, his vehement put-down of religion and the moral majority, none of which did him any favours outside of his own compressed circle. In his unfinished epic *Hero and Leander*, later worked on to completion by George Chapman, and first published by Adam Islip London for Edward Blunt in 1598, and arguably one of the most beautiful pieces of writing in English poetry, Marlowe's descriptions of Hero are almost unparalleled in male idealisation.

> His most kind sister all his secrets knew.
> And to her singing, like a shower, he flew,
> Sprinkling the earth, that to their tombs took in
> Streams dead for love, to leave his ivory skin,
> Which yet a snowy foam did leave above
> As soul to the dead water that did love;
> And from hence did the first white roses spring
> (For love is sweet and fair in every thing,)
> And all the sweeten'd shore, as he did go,
> Was crown'd with od'rous roses, white as snow.

The flip-side of this was that Queen Elizabeth I renewed the Law Against Buggery in her second parliament in 1563 on the same grounds as its first instatement, that 'divers ill-disposed persons have been the more bold to commit this most horrible detestable vice' – perhaps a pointer to some of Marlowe's gay implicated circle, Francis Bacon, Henry Wriothesley, Earl of Southampton, Henry Howard, Thomas Walsingham (Marlowe's patron), and the queen's cousin Lord Munsdon, under mercury treatment for a cocktail of STDs, who rented out his properties at Paris Gardens, Hoxton to Francis Langley and others as male brothels. That Marlowe alternated between lowlife acquaintances and diffident aristos was undoubtedly because of his sexuality; it also raises the question as to how, as a shoemaker's son, he went to Cambridge with no adequate resources to fund his studies, presumably other than his body. It's been suggested that Marlowe's social mobility was patronised by Sir Roger Manwood, Chief Baron of the Exchequer, who owned a mansion at St Stephen's, Canterbury. In fact, on the back of the title page of a copy of *Hero and Leander*, 1629 ed., a book lover found a manuscript epitaph for Roger Manwood, who died one year before Marlowe in 1592, inscribed with Marlowe's name, strengthening the case for some sort of dubious connection between the two.

Restless to move on, and needing a drink, I leave Newport Place and walk over to The Angel, 61 St Giles High Street (Marlowe's territory) – a Samuel Smith pub with a 1930s throwback look and an interlocking Chinese-box assemblage of three rooms, including one with a red Chesterfield – to wait for Stu who deals me white Indian valium as anti-anxiety stabilisers. £1 per tablet: little dusty white moons.

In Marlowe's time, St Giles' Field extended to the Uxbridge Road (now Oxford Street) and bordered on the west Colman Hedge Lane (now Wardour Street) and on the east Hog Lane (now integrated into Charing Cross Road). Most of the 30 acres, including stinking plague pits, the Burton Lazar Lands of St Giles' Hospital and the Abingdon Lands, was owned by James Bristow in 1585 and comprised a rundown sprawl of cheap cottages and tenements attracting the sort of criminally degenerate seditionaries to which Marlowe as a punk gravitated.

Stu, with his two smartphones in simultaneous use is characteristically late, so, having called Marlowe one, I go back to Johnny Rotten's definition of punk. 'It's an American word for a male prostitute in prison. I don't want to be no king of that! You can shove that one. There was something about the Pistols the record companies could not grasp. They didn't know what the threat was. They wanted the poncey little tarts that most groups are made up of. They were disturbed with the real McCoy.'

People were equally disturbed by Kit Marlowe's apparently effortless gifts as a poet, because mainstream literature was and still is in Britain associated with class and privilege, and Marlowe, as a rogue gene in the system, had neither. William Burroughs grew acutely alcoholic and junk-depressed during his London years in the late sixties precisely because of the exclusion principle, nobody literary wanted to know the gay, junky author of the gun-toting cut-up dystopian *Naked Lunch*, partly due to his manslaughter conviction, smack habit and fascination with Piccadilly rent boys.

To my mind the only real purpose in writing is to annoy people by rocking their limitations and pushing it. Marlowe's reputation at the time of his death earned him one dismissive line in the St Nicholas parish church register, in which even his murderer's name is given incorrectly. 'Christopher Marlowe, slain by Francis Frezer, the 1 June 1593.' In fact, his murdered body had been dumped without funeral rites in the Deptford churchyard, as though he'd never existed.

The Agas Map of 1570 shows St Giles as a wooded community, a disaffected tenement, a bit like Marlowe's cheap rent in Norton Folgate: a place where thieves, prostitutes, foreigners come in off the river, blacks, sailors, Chinese shared a common subversive alienation from society. London was dark, stinking and minimally policed, all aspects that suited Kit. But it's important to remember that his singular apprehension of beauty lived like gold dust molecularised in his veins; nobody ever got it to ring that sensually perfect. You could call Kit a beauty addict.

It was Marlowe's first play, *Tamburlaine*, that broke him, with the part of Tamburlaine played by the pioneering entrepreneur Edward Alleyn, who came on in red velvet trousers and a knee-length copper-coloured coat to the kind of applause, from every class of society including its rampant underbelly, as would greet a rock band. In fact, Elizabethan theatre, and Marlowe played the popular auditoria, was also a common place of business for trade in sex, and Lord Strange, Marlowe's patron and Lord Pembroke's Men were to be found playing at the Rose Theatre, behind which lay Rose Alley and Gilde Alley, both popular brothel streets. Marlowe's Tamburlaine, Edward Alleyn, the son of a Gray's Inn Road landlord, was in disrepute for prostituting his wife Joan Woodward, and together with his equally acquisitive father-in-law, Philip Henslowe, expanded his business rapidly through speculating and money-lending; together they bought up many of the Bankside brothels like The Barge, The Bell and The Cock as a trade-off from theatre. The Elizabethan underworld in which Kit Marlowe was an insidious operative was tricky, sticky gangland, and as a double-agent, Kit, perhaps more than any of his contemporaries, put his stunningly violent and beautiful poetry at risk of a blade, finally being set-up and murdered in what was quite clearly a secret service-planned homophobic killing, in a closed house in Deptford Creek.

Renzo Piano's fabulous reconstruction of Central Saint Giles into a psychedelically coloured futures workspace comprising 408,000 square feet of office space, retail, restaurants, cafes, residential space and outdoor public piazza, with multi-storey planes of orange, lemon, red, turquoise and lime, resembling mutant chewy sweets, and winter gardens incorporated into the design, has projected Marlowe's piss-tangy hangout into a £450 million brightly coloured, glazed terracotta blingmeister; a Lego-type assemblage of floating architecture that I personally go for as a sci-fi microcosmic implant into central London's urban fabric.

After picking up my silver foil-backed blister packs of white Indian Diazepam 10 mgs from Stu, I make tracks down Flitcroft Street, an alley behind St Giles' church, to meet John under the street at the Phoenix Theatre Bar; our low-lit, chicly camp rendezvous each Wednesday, presided over until his death in 2011 by Maurice Huggett, a viperfish recipient of pink gossip with a chain-smoker's exaggerated drawl, hoarsely furred and baritone as William Burroughs, and kind in a way that is eloquent of vulnerable hurt sensitivity. The Phoenix is always dark, in a way of which Marlowe would doubtless have approved; you search out your table under blue, green and red drizzled lights like you're stepping parallel.

Anyhow, I tell John my particular angle on Marlowe, and the weird thrust is just what he'd expect of me and hope of Marlowe: it takes two. Over the years John has seen most of my books thrown back at me by the poetry police on account of their liberal lawless imagination and their subversion of Marlowe's obstacles: class and privilege.

Marlowe's criminal record was extended in 1591, when he was ignominiously arrested at the seaport, Flushing, in Holland, a town under English occupation, together with another spy, Richard Baines, and Clifford Gilbert, a goldsmith, on charges of counterfeiting. With the inside knowledge Marlowe had gained from John Poole while incarcerated at Newgate, and taking advantage of Gilbert's expertise as a goldsmith, this highly dodgy trio of individuals set about counterfeiting Dutch shillings and a variety of other currencies including French, Spanish and English. Counterfeiting was a serious crime, and the report sent to Lord Burghley in London, naming Marlowe as Christofer Marly, suggests he was the instigator of a scheme that reeked of treasonable fraud. Pushed for money, the contraband mint in Flushing offered Marlowe a way out of financial anxiety through the criminal activity of profiteering.

Marlowe, who may well have been in Flushing on a secret service job, was duly escorted back to London by David Lloyd, where lord Burghley had the authority to hang him for counterfeiting English currency, an offence accountable as treason.

That Burghley released Marlowe without charges suggests he may have been a spy in his service, or provided Burghley with sensitive information, or even been sexually implicated with the Lord Treasurer. What we do know was that Marlowe was back on the London streets, brawling again, on May 9th, this time on Holywell Street in Shoreditch, when he was arrested for attacking and threatening two constables, Allen Nicholls and Nicholas Helliott, and taken before Justice Owen Hopton and bound to appear at the next General Sessions of the Middlesex County Court in October. Marlowe was now a noted criminal, as well as a popular playwright in competition with Shakespeare, both of whom were agented by Lord Strange's Men, as well as the Earl of Pembroke's, lived in and around Shoreditch, but apparently never met.

If Marlowe constantly challenged the limits of acceptable public behaviour, then he was, of course, most of the time drunk and on edge in case he was sprung by a contract killer paid for the job. In addition to this, the works of popular playwrights were considered literary trash, in the same way as bubblegum pop in the 50s and 60s wasn't considered an art form. *Tamburlaine*, Marlowe's one big hit, was conceived as a desperado's pitch for quick cash – £6: the play's poetic contents taking time to saturate like dying hair. In fact, Marlowe's name wasn't directly attributed to the play until 1609, fifteen years after his death. Marlowe would probably have been amused by his contemporary Thomas Nash's denigration of his work as 'the swelling bombast of braggart blank verse'. Marlowe's style was an uncompromising mixture of beauty and violence. When you don't fit in you often accelerate your extreme characteristics to auto-destruction, like ramming a car against a wall.

I've gone back to Soho's Newport Place, with its black and red bilingual English/Chinese street sign, and it's as busy as you'll get. Jen Café on the corner is painted peppermint green and I fixate on the menthol colour. When Colin, who I know from my days at Red Snapper Books, raps by in a sixties-style gangster's velvet-collared Crombie, he spots me and stops to sing, arms thrown up, a hammed-up pitch-perfect version of Sinatra's trademark 'My Way', his gesturally improvised street coloratura personalising the song as something we share accidentally, on the spot, as two come together in the capital's nameless 15 million. Colin walks and talks like he's got a gun in his hand, no messing, like he did in the seventies. It's a kind of Marlowe interface: the poet and the criminal morphing into one.

Marlowe was probably pro-Jacobean, his support of King James partly based on James' overt homosexuality, and both Kit and his friend the poet Matthew Roydon had a Scottish espionage mission planned shortly before Marlowe's murder, the operation instanced by Thomas Kyd who wrote of Kit, 'He would persuade men of quality to go unto the K of Scots, whither I hear Roydon is gone, and where if he had lived, he told me when I saw him last, he meant to be.' Beefing up the sensitive area of the succession took a serious edge-walker's attraction to risk, inviting assassination, and, together with his generally scandalous criminal portfolio, this undoubtedly contributed to the plot surrounding his death.

Today, mainstream writers are so acutely self-conscious of reputation, rewrites, social networking, agenting and criticism directed at their work, that they've lost the spontaneous risk of sometimes fucking up in pursuit of the one-off, the optimally charged moment that's either right or wrong, like a Bob Dylan song, one take and one only. The Elizabethans didn't have time, only urgency, and the awareness that if you didn't do it now you might be dead tomorrow, and that realisation is impacted into the velocity and neural surge of Marlowe's writing. The excitement is in the line and not in its bleached rewrite: the impact of its arrival in its original frequency and colour vibrations, and not in its revision.

Marlowe's homosexuality, itself an affront to the marital alliances that maintained class, was an interloper's angle on disrupting continuity. Marlowe was dangerous not only for the potential of trading sex for reward, but also as a subverter of straight convention, through an illicit, destructive mode of sexuality. Male prostitutes hung out at Blackfriars Theatre, and were described by the playwright Thomas Middleton as 'a nest of boys able to ravish a man.' What Marlowe gets in his 1592 play *Edward II* is the perfect homoerotic recreation of androgyny through the idealization of Gaveston transformed into a girl.

> With hair that gilds the water as it glides,
> Crownets of pearls about his naked arms,
> And in his sportful hands an olive tree
> To hide those parts that men delight to see,
> Shall bathe him in a spring; and there, hard by,
> One like Actaeon, peeping through the grove,
> Shall by the angry goddess be transformed,
> And, running in the likeness of a hart,
> By yelping hounds brought down and seem to die.

Marlowe must have known the intrinsic value of his work in those self-questioning moments of awareness that come up when writing and you're conscious of an autonomy independent of you that's driving language as its physical signature. It's a distractive window on what you're doing – you might be sitting in a Starbucks, out walking, or shopping in M&S, and this affirmative click comes on telling you that you're connected to your creative resources and it means something. Marlowe must have experienced affirmative insights that he was special, in a process of seal-realisation, in and around Norton Folgate, as a basis from which to continue his art in between bouts of binge drinking and the constant dangers of espionage.

It's important to understand that outside of a small group of booking agents and bitchy, incestuous writers, including Shakespeare. Kyd and Nash, Marlowe wasn't known; the pretence of calling himself a writer cut no ice, except with friends like Thomas Kyd and Matthew Roydon; and the mirage of posthumous fame that has become integrated into the modern writing sensibility was altogether alien to Kit's daily survival tactics as a spy and poet.

Marlowe's last patron, Thomas Walsingham, was incarcerated in Fleet Prison in 1590 for defaulting on debts, but became solvent on his brother Edmund's death in 1589, when he proceeded from prison to the family's ancestral manor house at Scadbury in north Kent. The nature of Kit's relations with Thomas are unclear, other than that he bought Marlowe time to work at Scadbury on his incomplete epic *Hero and Leander*, and sheltered him in the weeks preceding his murder when he was wanted by conflicting factions for allegedly personal and state crimes. What we do know is that Edward Blount, the printer of the first edition of *Hero and Leander* in 1598, dedicated the book to Walsingham, adding, of Marlowe's relations to his patron, 'knowing that in his lifetime you bestowed many kind favours, entertaining the parts of reckoning and worth which you found in him, with good countenance and liberal affection.'

Blount makes Thomas Walsingham sound kind, cultured, cool, and most possibly gay. Marlowe was being virally attacked on every side. A raging plague pandemic accelerated by the complete absence of sanitation in the capital, together with the Privy Council's decision in June 1592 to close the playhouses on account of the pimps, lowlife and prostitutes they attracted, effectively deprived Marlowe of income. That the theatres were attracting riots, disorder and orgies, left the Mayor of London, William Roe, morally outraged. He complained that playwrights like Marlowe and Ben Jonson were attracting crowds of undesirables to the Shoreditch theatres. The Mayor designated these types as 'great numbers of light and lewd-disposed persons [including] whores, pickpockets, pilferers, and such like, who under the cover of resort to those places to hear the plays devise diverse and evil matches, confederacies and conspiracies.' In other words, people like Colin, who I've just met on a drug delivery in Newport Place, went to the theatre to fuck, do dodgy deals, pick pockets, form rings, act yobbishly like streetwise hooligans and by their sheer numbers subvert the law. Elizabethan theatre was blamed for inciting social disruption, in the same way as rock festivals in their formative years invited media outrage at the cocktail of sex, drugs and youthful rebellion incorporated into the music's defiant cultural expression. Marlowe and his gang were the precursors of rock terrorism – the sort of androgynous banditry done in stadiums by the likes of Bob Dylan, The Rolling Stones, Led Zeppelin, The Who, Pink Floyd, and, of course, the lacerating, socially engaged punks.

Now, Thomas Walsingham, who recruited Kit into Secretary Francis Walsingham's sticky network as an operative, was also an intermediary between his cousin Francis and field agents like Robert Poley, one of the trio implicated in Marlowe's murder, and so the mesh locks intelligence into an asphyxiating loop. I'll come back to that.

I'm a vegan; people eat what they do, and Colin was on his way to Exmouth Market for pie and mash, an old river dish served with the owner's customised green sauce known as liquor.

What did Marlowe eat and drink? Kit would have drunk strong beer with names like Huffcap, the Mad Dog, Father Whoresonne and Dragon's Milk, potent brews maxxed up with with herbs and spices such as sage, betony, mace and nutmeg into hallucinatory toxins. Beer came in three strengths – single, double, Marlowe's strength. Kit would also have drunk Spanish wine, considered the strongest, and sack, a dry amber wine imported from Shiraz. Marlowe got blind drunk and would have eaten pub food like baked stuffed fish, chicken pie, capon in orange sauce, mincemeat pie, stuffed veal scallops, oyster, lamb casserole, etc.

Back to Thomas Walsingham, Marlowe's Chislehurst patron and cousin to the head of espionage Francis Walsingham, because Ingram Frizer, the property speculator, commodity broker, and owner of the Angel Inn in Basingstoke, who murdered Marlowe, was linked to Walsingham as a slippery spy at the time of Marlowe's set-up. The plot is like trying to untangle a plate of spaghetti or decode a DNA strand. Did Frizer know what he was severing when he viciously dug into Marlowe's right eye, the connection he slashed for money or out of ferocious homophobia – the neural micro-circuitry that sustained Marlowe's inimitable poetry? Frizer, like Marlowe, belonged to the semi-legitimate underbelly; he remains famous for murdering poetry.

It should be remembered that a government messenger despatched to find Kit Marlowe on 18th May was directed 'to repair to the house of Mr Tho: Walsingham in Kent.'

Walsingham would have known there was a man tracking the wooded highway carrying a warrant for Marlowe's arrest, closing in on Scadbury, and told Kit to go, clear out and stay undercover. As Marlowe's patron and assumed gay lover, it's unlikely that Walsingham was instrumental to Marlowe's death, but operatives in intelligence would have certainly leaked information to him that Kit's time was running out. That Marlowe remained at liberty after having a warrant served on him for the two weeks preceding his death suggests Walsingham's possible intervention for sensitive reasons in the Elizabethan intelligence service.

What was Ingram Frizer's right hand like, the one that struck Marlowe with a knife as impacted dynamic? It was probably dirty from lack of personal hygiene, the bumped up indigo veins standing out like pasta twirls, a hand that no one held, a criminal one used to grabbing money and smelling of its residual traces, together with food and bacteria collected from contact with polluted surfaces.

Disturbance enters my writing here, as I'm told by the Phoenix staff today that Maurice has had a stroke, but navigated his way through initially, only he is resistant to modifying his 50-a-day smoking habit that squeezes his cardiovascular system and furs his voice to a camp gunslinger's drawl. My attempt to visualise Ingram Frizer's hand gets disrupted by anxiety-waves as I reflect on Maurice's inimitable style and his irreplaceable personality. And on his apparent vulnerability: how is he making out now in his cramped apartment at Cecil Court – a slab of high-end real estate still in the ownership of the Cecil family – Marlowe's old associate in spying, Robert Cecil, making the link between Maurice and Marlowe. And that's how I write, by clicking on imaginatively to accidentals that appear in quantum terms to coalesce.

Four men in a small, closed room at Eleanor Bull's in Deptford Creek, all with police records, and three of them possibly ignorant of the fact that Kit Marlowe's poetic line could stop a train with its attitude. It was a recipe for trouble and because the facts were whitewashed at the time we'll never really know what happened, other than that an audaciously brilliant poet was butchered by a cheap lowlife contract killer. Robert Poley, Nicholas Skeres and Ingram Frizer, they deserve to be named and tried posthumously as the sticky trio of operatives who did for Kit. As we know it, the three were as loan sharks working insidiously to defraud a young man, Drew Woodleff of Aylesbury, of his inheritance. According to the coroner's spin on events Marlowe was apparently invited to dinner by his murderer, Ingram Frizer, and his two henchmen. No reason is given for this invitation, nor why Marlowe should have travelled to Deptford Creek, the site of a Royal Navy dock, a place that we assume was alien to his daily life spent in and around the dissolute scummy world of Shoreditch. There's no reason to connect Marlowe with the Woodleff scam – he was already suspected of the Dutch church libel, an anti-immigrant graffiti slash signed 'Tamburlaine' that had him viewed as an inciter to sedition: a punk. Marlowe's friend, the playwright Thomas Kyd was arrested on May 11th and brutally tortured into confessing that a three-page manuscript found amongst his papers promoting extreme atheist views was in fact written by Marlowe. The State, outraged by Marlowe's subversive intellectual propaganda was however reluctant to hang him on account of his carrying knowledge as virally dangerous as today's HIV virus.

So Marlowe was set-up by pathologically homophobic lowlife who were also extortionists – one theory – by Shakespeare's party – my theory – Marlowe was a serious rival to Shakespeare and his agents and was murdered, amongst other things, as a rival. 'It strikes a man more dead than a great reckoning in a little room' was Shakespeare's compressed allusion to the homicide in *As You Like It*. Was he part of the ring that conspired to liquidate Kit Marlowe? I maintain an affirmative yes.

Back to the killing that happened soon after 6 p.m. Backgammon had been played, tobacco smoked, no mention is made of it, but there was doubtless booze inciting temper, and apparently the men had walked together in the garden. We're told the room contained a bed, a table and a bench. According to the official story an altercation broke out between Frizer and Marlowe, an escalating dispute over payment of the bill that had them drawing knives; but why a contention when Marlowe was Frizer's guest? According to coroner Danby's flawed and doubtlessly fabricated report, 'And so it befell, in that affray, that the said Ingram, in defence of his life, with the dagger aforesaid of the value of twelve pence, gave the said Christopher a mortal wound above his right eye, of the depth of two inches and of the width of one inch.'

I've got Pete Doherty on download and go back to St Giles and the Phoenix. There's a Denmark Street crowd there – indie aspirers talking music and garage bands, and frothy with beer, and I do parallel moon-walking in the submerged dark to my table in the corner under a fixture of red, green and blue globe lights. Maurice has been back in again, post-stroke, and the bar staff tell me he was drunk, skewed on Bombay Sapphires, and his condition has worsened. I worry; it's not just a matter of how do these friends of mine get into Kit Marlowe's narrative, but how do they get out? We're all somehow locked into this incongruous circuit together. It's like Kit's murder: however hard we try to smash the official whitewash, the pieces never fit.

I'm still fascinated by Ingram Frizer's hand. What was his heart rate and blood pressure when he stabbed Kit and did it lower later that night? We're told he made no attempt to escape, but he didn't need to, as he'd just carried out a contract killing for which he'd be formally acquitted the next day. The visual recreation of stabbing Marlowe probably didn't even disturb his sleep, that blinding red flash of plasma that had never before been exposed in Kit Marlowe until Frizer's hand slashed it open.

Shirley Bassey's singing the epic Bond soundtrack 'Goldfinger', only it's a live update, the voice indomitably expensive as blue rocks and mink, a soprano extravaganza so torchy, the phrasing so optimal, you die into the saturated coloratura. It's like what I tell Cindy after massage: my worked-on finger turns gold. Goldfinger. It maker her laugh in a way that frames her mouth into a red lipsticked oval. She says, 'You're a poet,' and I'm glad she's in with Marlowe, along with John, Colin, Stu and Maurice, because that's how organic writing's done with the inclusion of those close to you, and all the little physical distractions arising from Soho integrated into the time-slip of rehabilitating the subversive outlaw Kit Marlowe to the always discontinuous present.

Maurice Huggett died on 16th December 2011.

ALL OR NOTHING

The best definition of a poet is that of someone who has the time purposefully to hang around and live directly in the contemporary moment. Future policies don't work if you want to write. The capitalist idea that the present should be deferred in the interests of future gain, and that material security is preferable to creative risk is a non-starter if you're serious about your art. You can't pursue poetry honestly by claiming a different identity during the day and arguing the compromise as necessary. The two colours don't mix with any credible authenticity.

When I left school, with no intention of to do anything but write, the system argued that what I needed was psychiatry and social rehabilitation. I didn't fit; I had too much imagination and kept stepping back into inner space. I had read Leonard Cohen's novel *Beautiful Losers* and Jean Genet's *Our Lady of the Flowers*. I hung out in cafés by the docks, took solitary walks in the pouring rain, was clothes-fixated, obsessed by pop and its image and resented conformity. My interests were in creating possible realities through poetic imagery, and right from the start I felt connected to an image resource that seemed archetypally inexhaustible. There was too much and I wrote with the urgent attack of someone canning a BMW with acrylic paint. It was my instinctual way of recreating the world, reclaiming it from the largely visionless targets of corporate execs and restoring it to the facilities created by imagination. My learning curve was aimed at making the sky bluer, the vision brighter, and, through my reading and life, to establishing sympathies primarily with the disaffected. I spent the years before I went to university mixing with men who wore berets, were often shoplifters, knew about makeup and labels and were refreshingly uncompromised. Living outside the system, they had created alternative realities for themselves in which poetry could be accommodated, and, what's more, stolen.

The distinction between those who live outright as poets and those who filter their art through conventional employment, was put perfectly by the Elizabethan John Daw, whose thesis written in 1580 was part of Christopher Marlowe's required reading at Cambridge. With rare insight Daw writes: 'Every man that writes in verse, is not a poet; you have of the wits that write verses, and yet are no poets: they are poets that live by it, the poor fellows that live by it.'

The idea of the poet as a flâneur, a loiterer, a fugitive who infiltrates the city's underground begins with Baudelaire's largely despondent and aimless excursions into the Paris suburbs at twilight in the 1850s. Obsessed with his nervous disintegration, his rejection by the literary world, his opium habit and the poverty to which poetry had reduced him, Baudelaire looked to the socially disdained for some sort of consolation. He took to hanging around as a displacement activity, writing, 'And as a crowning absurdity, IT IS VITAL – in the middle of all this unbearable commotion that's wearing me out – that I write poetry, for me the most exhausting activity of all.'

When I was starting to write, the only British poet who seemed to possess attitude and to hang out was Thom Gunn. With his rocker hairdo, stovepipe jeans and black leather biker boots, Gunn's bad boy image inherited in part from Jimmy Dean's fifties cool and from his adulation of the Elizabethans, like Christopher Marlowe, set him radically apart from his more restrained contemporaries. Gunn had relocated to California as a means of freeing up energies that were otherwise repressed by the narrow remit of British poetry. Initially writing about bikers, rock stars like Elvis Presley, and ambiguous sexuality with a blend of inherited metaphysical ingenuity, the American Gunn cultivated a defiance that returned the role of the poet to cutting-edge prospector. Gunn not only came out, but in addition confessed to having written a lot of the poems collected in *Moly* (1971) on LSD. What Gunn seemed to be implying was that his body was the experimental chemistry for his work, and that poetry wasn't a desk occupation, but something demanding risk and a repertoire of experience at odds with the notion of the poet as appointed academic or systemised civilian. Apart from Thom Gunn and the poetry of David Gascoyne, whose shattered life and visionary ideal appealed to me – Gascoyne had in the late fifties, as a delusional chiliastic mission, broken into Buckingham Palace, by slipping security, intending to announce the imminent apocalypse to the Queen – my reading was all American. John Ashbery, Frank O'Hara, James Schuyler and John Wieners were the modernist cocktail I took up with as influences that left a permanent mark. British poetry, with the exception of its American influenced defectors like Lee Harwood and Tom Raworth, offered nowhere constructive to go. The reactionary influence of Philip Larkin with his provincial resistance to all foreign voices had effectively sterilised romantic imagination in mainstream British poetry, and a poet who confessed to writing at most 2 or 3 poems a year as a sideline to being a university librarian, seemed to me to personify the antithesis of risk.

On first coming to live in London in 1980, I, like so many other troubled journeyers in pursuit of a vision, found myself invited to Kathleen Raine's house at 47 Paulton's Square, Chelsea. Kathleen's redoubtable reputation as a Blake scholar, a poet and the impassioned advocate of those who recklessly and singularly gave their lives to poetry, preceded her as I nervously stood in front of the tumble of white star-jasmine trailing dreadlocks over her front door, with its lion-faced knocker set into charcoal paint.

The dark suited, vibrantly energised woman of seventy who invited me in and listened so attentively to my poems displayed none of the redoubtable scholarship I had anticipated, but on the contrary a total naturalness in talking about life and its meaning through poetry. Domestic, she had baked a currant-popping, rum-dowsed fruitcake for my visit, her extraordinary kindness and personable compassion learnt from deep personal suffering, put me immediately at ease. We became friends before we were even acquainted, which is so often the way real friendships and relationships are formed.

Over the next 20 years my friendship with Kathleen was also to be my education. Lack of money hadn't in the least deterred her from the pursuit of what she called the learning of imagination, and giving away most of the little she earned from writing to those she felt in greater need was not only a part of her innate generosity, but also her way of dissociating from the materialist world. Kathleen was extravagant without means, pulling out notes from her handbag whenever she intuitively sensed I needed help and always with the proviso that the money should be spent on luxuries and not necessities.

This, we agreed, was how poets should live, and principally by honouring the necessity for freedom. I'm not advocating that this is a journey for everyone, for the commitment demands a courage and singularity of purpose given to few. Living as a poet is very different to writing poetry in the attempt to make sense of one's life, for it entails meeting experience in a way that Francis Bacon called an assault on the nervous system. Any true commitment to an art is neurologically shamanic, and will usually involve breakdowns as a deepening process, leading in turn to another form of initiation, that of Jungian or archetypal therapy as the means of evaluating the turbulent inner shake-up.

What I personally so valued in Kathleen Raine as a teacher was her unfailing support for those driven by an inner vision and unwilling to compromise their gift by conceding to the dictates of material living as a fake identity. Walking down the jeepy Kings Road from Sloane Square in the early eighties, the quarter still occupied by punks with lurid Mohicans, in the direction of the broody, urban sky filling in over World's End – the direction I inevitably took when visiting her at Paulton's Square – I was always aware of how privileged I was to be crossing the city specifically to visit Kathleen Raine. Our friendship disdained academic knowledge as a basis in favour of celebrating the real thing – the gift of poetry as it exists generically in the singularly driven individual whose imagination helps change the way people see the universe.

Those with subversive imagination, Kathleen's gang, invariably encounter hostility from the literary mainstream for being rogue genes infiltrating the organism. That there's a bonding, a shared genealogy of poets working within a particular alternative framework, and often encountering neglect for their work, was something addressed by Proust, who, struggling with his own lack of recognition, wrote, 'These still unrecognized masters, and those of the past, practice the same art, to the extent that the former remain the best critics of the latter.'

My take on writing is in part existential. It's something inspired that I do each day – mostly in cafes – and has about it something of the conception of work as redemption as its source. Bob Dylan once described his art as pursuing a trade, meaning that if you do something well you keep working at it, because it's who you are. In my poetry and prose it's the impact of sensational imagery that thrills me, as constituting the poem's core energy. Imagery is to poetry what hydrogen and kerosene is to a Boeing. If it wasn't for the rushed dopamine hit it provides me, as a way of transforming everything I see, I would have little interest in writing. It follows that I can only read a literature in which the protein building blocks are its visually transformative imagery. To me the rest is filler, like polymer. It's interesting that two of the most poetic novelists, J.G. Ballard and Edmund White, both of whom score by the dynamic thrust of their imagery, have admitted to generally finding more poetic content in the novel than in poetry. The argument is justifiable in that so much poetry reads like prose cut up for typographical effect. Edmund White's observation that prefaces his superb essay on the poet James Schuyler is worth taking into account.

'Here's an admission: I sometimes wonder why people bother with poetry. After all, the best novelists (Proust and Nabokov, to name just two) offer the reader page after page of language as precise, as unpredictable and as ravishing as the language of any poet – and the novelists simultaneously make their local delights serve larger structural or thematic ambitions (the generation of suspense, the play of ideas, the revelation of character, the depiction of society, the weaving of a thick, tragic sense of duration). In great fiction the language is not only satisfying in itself, but it also fulfils larger purposes of design: it is sculptural, in the round, gestural. Fiction makes a world, dense and social.'

I would argue that good poetry does the same, but is the exception. When it comes out right in a poem by John Ashbery, Thom Gunn or James Schuyler, in my repertoire of chosen reading, then it opens a dramatic colour moment in my day. But to be suitably fired up with the sort of energy I demand from poetry I read prose. The novels of J.G. Ballard with their accent on neuroscientific imagery and urban apocalypse, those of the cyberpunk prose stylist William Gibson, William Burroughs' pharmacologically excerpted narratives, Edmund White's densely poetical mapping of a resistant post-Aids community, Paul McAuley's verbal pyrotechnics as a postmodern fiction guerrilla, and the novels of Proust, Jean Genet and Anna Kavan all provide the acceleration into the poetic when I need inspirational oomph. They feed me a language excitement that poetry often doesn't. It's the difference between the taste of Coke and Pepsi, and while both target the brain's reward system, the tang that goes with the logo is zingier in its behavioural effect than the blue, at least to my response.

Poetry is a pursuit for which almost nobody pays, and yet its enduringly stimulating dynamic succeeds, for what it's worth, in maintaining a place in public consciousness. Writing is, after all, a radically anti-social act: it excludes you as the participant from involvement with community. It's a predominantly solitary act, it burns up time, and most people, in going about their lives, are intolerant of being around someone who is evidently not sharing the same reality. It's spooky to observe that person doing traffic in their head to the exclusion of others. It's a given that poets have not only to live with their gift, but must also learn how to defend it, almost as a subtle form of martial art. No age has ever been conducive to the writing of poetry, and it's necessary that the poet, in pursuit of his art, adjusts to the present and works with it, rather than idealize a past that never really existed. My poetry owes much of its intensely compressed focus to the unremitting speed of a big city living in my veins. That relentless stimulus is the glucose with which I work. I like to write on buses gridlocked in West End traffic, at wonky tables outside cafes, in places that demand adaptability and resilience, as well as in the relative quiet of home. The interaction between writer and place is an important survival tactic. It's all part of a necessary resilient defence.

When I first came to London I would sometimes write poems sitting at the top of the subway stairs at Piccadilly Circus, not only to witness the shocked surprise of strangers streaming up the steps into Regent Street or Shaftesbury Avenue, but for the challenge of being able to write anywhere. If the business of poetry is to radically morph our received notions of reality, then it follows that part of a poet's work is the facility to adapt, and to cultivate the ability to write about anything. It's not necessarily deliberate, but I've always written about subjects in poetry that are considered outside its remit: science fiction, cyber, pop, fashion, neuroscientific update, tech, gay subcultures and whatever hits my eye in the street and excites. Discovering Frank O'Hara's facility to write wacky poems about every aspect of his personal engagement with New York, as the city in which he lived and worked in the 1960s, right down to brand names, the colour coding of clothes, the investment of detailing personal obsessions, the naming of friends, and, above all, his adoption of Rimbaud's dictum 'we must be absolutely modern', provided me with something of an optimally constructive baseline from which to work. Frank was modern; his British contemporaries, with the exception of rogue influences like J.H. Prynne and Lee Harwood, appeared to be reactionaries, throwbacks from a debilitated past. It was John Ashbery who provided me with another link as to how poetry could assimilate almost anything into its metabolic function providing the poet was alive to the potentialities. Reading Ashbery changed my gateway into poetry forever, and had me realise that the odd, the singular and the weird were traits as interesting in poetry as they are in people. I can never read poetry as a bland affirmation of the normal, as for me the purpose of poetry is through roaming imagination to radically refocus the world. Normal people, suits, slickers, politicians, technocrats, academics, members of the board, all seem to possess a collective fear of the individual that has them sell the system as its substitute. Surely, poetry should be pushing somewhere else, somewhere in the interests of reclaiming different realities as its incomparable instructor.

Poetry is what? A method of phrasing, an ability to invest words with music, a means of compressing experience into charged language, a loop that links the first line to the last like head and tail, an emotional clarifier, a form of telepathic broadband, a nervous beat with a hooky rhythm; the definitions point to, but never quite fit their subject. Poetry is arguably the most extreme form of idealism, a pursuit in which the poet continually recreates the world in ways that quite literally make nothing happen outwardly. Jean Genet said that he became a poet through begging his way across Europe. Poor and humiliated, he felt himself unworthy of observing the extraordinary beauty of the Andalusian countryside he was crossing on foot. The only way he could look at it was by closing his eyes and, in doing so, reinventing the landscape through imagination. This was Genet's initiation into the power of the image as reconstructive currency. He could now, for the first time, see things inwardly as they really were, and what's more, write about them.

The power involved in morphing reality into an altered state equivalent is perhaps the quality that makes poetry addictive to the poet. The ability to dissolve reality in the process of writing is a fundamentally subversive act that outlaws the poet. That the right-brain hemisphere can suddenly sight the world in 3D and make of its object of perception a fractal reality is to me all part of the faculty of rehabilitating imagination. One could argue that the chemical chain set up by the writing of visionary poetry is psychotomimetic, that is, it imitates the effects of psychosis in the way of hallucinogens like LSD and DMT. Because of the richness of my imagery people have often asked me if I owe that aspect of my poetry and fiction to doing LSD. It's hard to convince people that imagination is its own chemical and one of the most toxic. At the same time, psychedelics can open a gateway to seeing. Daniel Pinchbeck's book *Breaking Open the Head*, his amazing firsthand account of experimenting with psychoactive substances, not as an ethnobotanist, but as a chemical adventurer disillusioned by the meaninglessness of capitalist life, should be required reading for all serious poets. Towards the end of a series of risk-taking experiments with chemicals that had the author journey to Africa, Mexico and the Amazon, Pinchbeck remarks: 'Psychedelics are catalysts for transformation, and when you take them you have to be ready to transform. Our society seems to be changing rapidly, but the psychedelic realms move with a tremendous velocity. They make the achievements of our present day technology seem tragically antique. While these chemicals should not be demonized or trivialized, they also cannot be reduced to therapeutic tools. They are more powerful than our categories. Someday, they may help us establish a science of the spirit.'

It's sad that poets don't write of their inner discoveries with the same excitement, an omission I put down to their being too busy doing other things to risk the level of the sort of encounters described by Daniel Pinchbeck or the equally pioneering Terence McKenna. It's cynicism that's so often the problem; it poisons the spontaneity needed to create. Cynical poetry always reminds me of dirty fingerprints. The attempt to undermine and flatten experience, so common in the poetry of those influenced detrimentally by Philip Larkin, invariably points to lack of originality. You know it when a poem sticks tackily like blackened chewing gum to your heel.

Writing a poem sometimes strikes me as the equivalent of what you might like to do on the last day of your life. It's about compressing everything that's meaningful at that given moment into a synthesis that condenses light and dark, beauty and sadness, up and down into one rush. Think of what you'd like to do before you die and you have the menu for a poem. The writing of it, though, demands the commitment of having reached a state in which you can utilize the experience. The more you write the better maintained your mechanism. Poetry is an art like dying and both require preparation and the willingness to risk the adventure.

I began with the image of the poet hanging around as the only way in which to learn what you might be able to steal of use to a poem. Almost everything that has gone into my writing comes from this selective faculty of being acutely on to what is there, which in my case means people and things which attract by being different. I'm somebody who notes obsessively each colour change in the sky, hour by hour, each detail of dress right to the stitching on a shirt collar or the logo on a bag, each flower's seasonal appearance, the mood atmospherics of a place, the hurt written into a stranger's eyes in the street, the trapped sunlight contained in a smile, the lexicon of messaged graffiti slashed across the underpass; my individual mind-set feeds on the particular. It's a way of life, a means of reading the world as intensified sensation.

My sympathies are nearly always channelled into subcultures, those who psychologically, sexually or emotionally don't fit into a PC society. Writing for the disaffected, the disenfranchised and the dispossessed has been a part of my journey. Writing poetry is one way of resisting the relentless drive towards conformity that technocratic commodification demands. Quite early in my life I realised that the fugitive, the criminalised and the emotionally damaged were very often the carriers of what I call poetry. It's my theory that difference or damage, particularly in the case of mental illness, is simply heightened sensitivity broken by its opposite: institutional intolerance. Poets see things all the time in terms of imagined phenomena, but they're usually only part-time madmen.

The café where I write most mornings is also a refuge for psychiatric outpatients visiting the Royal Free Hospital, or patients whose rehab programme permits them the privilege of leaving incarceration on a ward for time out with a minder. Most of these people gravitate immediately to the fact that I am writing poetry or prose from the resource of inner space, and will talk to me of their need, most often unrealised, to give creative expression to their inner states, which invariably have been pathologized as manic, psychotic, schizophrenic, whatever the diagnostic label. I think that what they recognize is that poetry imposes some sort of form and clarity on the contents they are unable to manage. It channels an energy that might otherwise be disruptively hallucinated or send out the wrong chemical messages to the brain. They're fascinated by the fact that I seem in control of my material, instead of blown into a corner by its biochemical impact. Again, I'm talking of mostly what appears to be incurable no-hopers here, people who have been broken, medicated and often additionally damaged by the side effects of toxic psychiatry, but who are nonetheless in contact with a disordered imagination. They very often relate to distressed visual imagery and constellated archetypes as their natural vocabulary of expression in a way that suggests potential without access to the means.

So what is the gateway to being a poet who doesn't crash and has the innate resilience to survive? I would say it's the ability to successfully integrate life and art. Once the two aren't separated, the conflict between creativity and careerism disappears, together with the misconceived notion of having to succeed in society. Poets don't occupy any place in the social register other than that of being an anomalous phenomenon. The 17th century poet Thomas Randolph raised highly credible questions about the difficulties of financing his art in his poem 'A Parley with his Empty Purse,' not that the dilemmas expressed ever stopped him writing.

> How shall my debts be paid? or can my scores
> Be clear'd with verses to my creditors?
> Hexameter's no sterling, and I feare
> What the brain coins goes scarce for current there
> Can metre cancel bonds? is there a time
> Ever to hope to wipe out chalk with rhyme?
> Or if I now were hurrying to the jaile
> Are the nine Muses held sufficient baile?

Thomas Randolph's questions have remained serious issues to any poet audacious enough to attempt to live solely by his art. It's one reason I'm attracted to poets of the 16th and 17th centuries, with their punkish disdain for mortality, the intensely short-lived burn-out of their tempestuous lives, their awareness, in between bouts of drinking, that it really was all or nothing. Shakespeare, we're told, didn't even bother to correct his proofs, and it's this apparent social disdain that lends these poets an air of heroic intransigence. Constantly alert to the imminent possibilities of death, their work vibrates with optimal living.

In reviewing the American poet Ted Berrigan's highly experimental, loosely cut-up book *The Sonnets* (1967), John Ashbery, in a memorable phrase, says of Berrigan's poems: 'They feel like what tomorrow is going to be like.' That to me is as good a definition as exists of the necessary criterion that a poem should fulfil. Poetry should be anticipating the flavour of the future, and in doing so be moving away from the past. Of course it's much easier to write backwards in an inherited literary language and this largely is what derivative poets do. But writing to anticipate 'what tomorrow is going to be like' is where the risk and excitement lie. But while American poetry commissioned the same zeitgeist as Andy Warhol's concept of pop in getting modern, Britain's revolution came by way of ripping up ideological convention through rock music. The street energy of the early Rolling Stones, for instance, connected with youth culture in a way that British poetry had radically failed to do and succeeded, in the process, in cooking up the bluesy poetry and primal rhythms needed to shock Britain awake.

W.H. Auden once said that poems are not written by intellectuals but by 'the man who likes to hang around words, trying to figure out what they mean.'

I'm back to the notion of hanging around, not this time on street corners, but on the page. Auden has the poet situated hanging around for words, an exemplary image in its casualness for the poet's necessary fascination with words and what they mean when they're charged up in a poetic context. Language wears out fast like last year's cars. Words can't be upgraded when a poet's dead and often as writers grow older their early work appears dated. 'For last year's words belong to last year's language,' T.S. Eliot tells us with a practitioner's acute sensitivity to their oxidised degradation.

Part of being a poet means working with a prescient facility to find a new, partially durable language. I look for language upgrade by reading science journals, books on time travel and neuroscience, sci-fi, pharmacology, medicine, psychology and get more excited about those variant terminologies than I do the largely exhausted attempts to rehabilitate tired literary language. There's such a wealth of language that poets resist, and yet novelists like William Burroughs, J.G. Ballard and William Gibson have compounded a brilliant poetry out of incorporating technological update into their work. Poets who still get mileage out of lived-in adjectival inaccuracies like 'pale', 'strange', 'pallid' etc., and who attempt to describe technology without a specific vocabulary aren't going very far in terms of the future. In writing a poem, the search is as much for originality of language as it is the sighting of individual subject matter. In British poetry the marginalised Cambridge poet J.H. Prynne is an example of someone making the language new, which means working with the potentialities of what's there in other sciences, risky to use, but not rejected like a donor organ by the language system.

Hanging around is part of the preparation for writing. Francis Bacon used to say that if he really wanted to know how a person looked as a preconceived configuration for a painting then he would ask his gay friends, because he considered straight people didn't pay sufficient attention to significant detail. I would say that if you want to know if a poem has the right attitude test the result on people who aren't poets, for they're the ones likely to be in the know. Literary people, like straight people in Bacon's analogy, are very often afraid of active imagination because it threatens the formulaic constraint under which they work.

Most people in the West begin their day with the sole objective of converting time into money, as though acquisitive capital was the only currency by which to live. I begin mine by sharpening the faculty to write through inner disciplines like a mantra combined with a window opened by meditation. I come to my art hoping perhaps to see things in ways that haven't been expressed before and yet that we all instantly recognize. When a poem comes right it re-sets the senses. It establishes an altered state, a way of seeing so charged with intensity that we can't any of us necessarily stay in there long. We read poetry because we know that it's the state in which we'd like to live all the time, but can't.

But my argument is that the more you stay on that frequency the better adapted you are to write. It's also an addictive place to be. The chemical high that comes from writing is busy with a neural network of endorphins. In the absence of such stimulus writers often turn to drugs or alcohol to compensate, like Coleridge and Baudelaire opium, Anna Kavan and William Burroughs heroin, Allen Ginsberg and Thom Gunn LSD. The need to keep going back there is what habitually drives me to write each day.

Marginalised, economically unjustifiable, impracticable and of little social value, poetry, for all its disadvantages, still maintains a signature profile in our times. There's a sense that everybody writes poetry, but that there are very few poets. People often confuse the therapeutic aspect of self-confession with poetry, thinking that because something is significant to them it is of corresponding importance to others. There's more to writing poetry than that and that 'more' constitutes the work done in order to arrive in that particular writing space. *Getting there*, the inner work that comes with the act of hanging around, is what counts. It's what serious poets work to cultivate all of their lives. It's backup, like the support needed for a singer's voice. It's this absence of source that invalidates poetry that doesn't come from there and makes it smack of not being the real thing. It lacks the chemical signature, the informative linguistic DNA.

Some people just have it and the mapping appears effortless. Reading a good poem is like biting into an apple for tangy zing. If I've pointed to the Elizabethan poets as exemplars of urgency, their work being written full on in the face of death, then the contemporary poet working today in the light of escalating global atrocities is faced with a not dissimilar set of values. How much time is there and does poetry count against nuclear weaponry?

The answer is, of course, yes. Creative imagination is all that counts. It's the ultimately irrepressible modality that ideologies can't suppress. It's our window on how inner events colour external reality. Imagination changes monochrome into marvellous 3D polychrome. It transforms the ordinary into lyric potential, the pouring London rain into streaming silver dazzle paint. It's our way of heightening reality to individual taste. Reading a poem is a quick way of stepping out of time into space. When I read poems like Lee Harwood's 'As Your Eyes are Blue', John Ashbery's 'Loving Mad Tom', Thom Gunn's 'The Fair in the Woods', James Schuyler's 'The Morning of the Poem,' or Andrew Marvell's 'The Garden', to name a few personal favourites, I do so to shift my level of consciousness. A good poem for me restores reality to the right liberating upbeat tempo.

In an ideal world, committed poets would be paid for heightening our awareness of reality, rather than downsized into the role of fugitive. This is again where hanging around can be an attractive option, for waiting out on time you sometimes meet people who are prepared to help you further your risk. Throughout much of the 1980s I went to an office off Bond Street once a month and collected a large bundle of banknotes from an admiring patron, wishing to free me from the financial anxiety that so often accompanies writing as an unpaid profession.

Today I still do what I did when I first came to London and that is use every available moment in the day in the interests of creativity. Certain obsessions feed into my writing, like the music of the pop and torch singer Marc Almond, whose work has deepened over a long, enriched creative trajectory into being the role of both inspirer and consoler to my listening hours, J.G. Ballard's extraordinary novels documenting the visionary present, the immersive shattering of Francis Bacon's paintings, the trait of obsessive people-spotting and picking up strangers in the West End, the practice of writing outside in Leicester Square, and over it all the big empty curve of the transitioning London sky that registers in me like a mood change.

I've never liked winners. I prefer losers or those who are born to win without honours, and whose care is for their work and not its reputation. A self-deprecating sense of humour is the necessary corrective to any artist taking himself too seriously. Beginning to scratch the surface of success, right at the end of his life, after a decade spent illegibly scribbling in exercise books, and paying for the intermittent publication of his novel, Marcel Proust received a sobering letter from a female reader, the irony of which he was willing to share with a friend. The woman wrote: 'And after three years of reading you non-stop, I've come to the conclusion that I understand nothing, but absolutely nothing. Dear Marcel Proust, don't be a poseur, come down from your ivory tower for once. Tell me in two lines what you're trying to say.'

It wasn't, of course, what Proust was trying to say, but arguably how he said it. Proust often threw the unnumbered pages of his work in progress on the floor, caring nothing for the scrambled chaos he was creating. The worth of the book to him was in the writing; the idea of readership was of secondary importance. He wrote without an advance or any conceivable commercial incentive and was free largely by default to construct the first anti-novel by deconstructing plot and linear time into a free-associated autonomy in which recollected time was situated in the parallel processing present.

I think it's a given that artists keep their influences secret, fearing that the role model might invasively chip away at their shine. Amongst my all time favourite poems, are two or three written by an unknown poet called John Carter, who lives in Reading. Written in 1984, when the teenage poet was living homeless in the Soho streets and working as a Piccadilly rent boy, they're the building blocks I carry around in my head on London days, as a reminder that the real thing turns up from time to time without the desire for recognition or any real place in literature. Sadly ill and flattened by the anti-psychotic drug Olanzapine, John is no longer writing, but his few poems continue to come up in me as of real importance at times of need.

Hanging around is work, not the evasion of it. It's a means not only of deepening one's awareness of the present, but also of connecting with others, the millions of anonymous strangers who are doing whatever is normal in their lives. In the streets we make eye contact as a reflex form of synchronicity with others who are alert to the same sympathies. Eye contact is like writing a poem, the surprise encounter with what you can never hope to recreate, but which for the moment is everything.

Somebody clearly disturbed and heavily medicated is watching me write these pages in a café. But that's all right. We're both dealing with altered geography on an inner level. The person, a woman of maybe 28, long black hair, snail grey eyes, black top, long black skirt, with a minder, stares through me, as though she wants to see language forming in image clusters in my head. I like the transfer of energies that constellate around us, like we're two strangers passing slowly through a space neither of us is ever likely to visit again. The experience is every bit as weird as writing a poem.

LIVING ON BORROWED TIME

On the afternoon of 7th June, 1935, the 20-years-old Denton Welch, then a student at the Goldsmith School of Art in New Cross, lay critically injured on the Brighton road near Hooley, the blood congealing in his naturally curly and tousled auburn hair. Hit from behind on his bicycle by a female motorist, he was thrown by the impact into the air before the unchecked car rolled over his crumpled body in the delayed attempt to brake. Denton was never to properly recover from the life-changing injuries inflicted by negligence on the driver's part.

Retaining consciousness sufficient to tell the police his identity, Denton, who had suffered a fractured spine, a broken ankle and alarming facial cuts and bruising, was to find he was for some months completely paralysed from the chest down. With extraordinary courage he taught himself to walk again, but the long-term effects of the spinal fracture were amongst other complications to cause both paralysis of the bladder, and partial impotence. The subsequent need to wear a catheter made Denton susceptible to frequent infections of the bladder and kidneys with the attendant symptoms of fever and dangerously high blood pressure. For the remaining eleven years of his extraordinarily creative life he was a semi-invalid, largely living on a small family allowance in the Kent countryside.

Given the catastrophe that so radically disrupted Denton Welch's youth, it's important to realise that he wrote and painted as someone intensely aware that he was living on borrowed time. Rather like Derek Jarman, whose urgent survivor's creativity kept on outliving the HIV virus copying itself in his cells, Denton Welch was acutely aware of his mortality in everything he experienced. It was there always as a fingerprint on the moment, a cautionary reminder that no matter how strongly he situated himself in imagination and the sensual pleasures in which he so delighted, the reality of his life in biological terms was almost perceptibly slipping away.

Granted compensation of £8,000 for his accident and additionally maintained by a yearly allowance of £300 from his father, Denton, on the advice of his sympathetic mentor Dr Easton, set about focusing his artistic talents into disciplined creative work. Initially renting a flat in Tonbridge before moving to the greater quiet first of the Hop Garden in the village of St Mary's Platt, and, after it was bombed, to Pitt's Folly Cottage, where he wrote *In Youth is Pleasure*, Denton lived and worked in a rural Kent billeted by wartime troops, but still relatively unspoilt as countryside. With his unreliable live-in acquisitive lover, Eric Oliver, in attendance, despite Eric's tendency to disappear for days or weeks on solitary drunken binges, Denton, who also employed a housekeeper, not only wrote and painted compulsively, but was able at times to bike around the neighbouring villages with Eric, or, in times of ill health, to get out in the Austin Seven car his father had bought him as a birthday present in 1937. His life was one of small significant journeys given detailed colouring by his imagination, so becoming events of magnitude that invariably found inclusion either in his largely autobiographical fiction or the Journals in which he kept an assiduous and remedially introspective account of his daily life.

If the patronage of Edith Sitwell had sanctioned the publication of his first novel *Maiden Voyage* (1943), then it was on her suggestion that he write 'something rather more violent and vulgar' that Denton set to work in April 1943 on an abandoned draft of *In Youth is Pleasure*, the title lifted from the refrain of an Elizabethan masque by Robert Wever.

Maiden Voyage had created something of a storm on publication, casting Denton as a precocious, but natural talent, as well as a writer inheriting a distinctly Proustian aesthetic, who seemed refreshingly uninhibited about his homosexuality.

Denton began *In Youth is Pleasure* soon after the heady rush of meeting Eric Oliver, and portrays himself in the book as the exceedingly sensitive adolescent Orvil invited by his affluent father Mr Pym to spend his summer holidays together with his two brothers in a suitably comfortable hotel that Denton in his Journals identifies as Oatlands, near Weighbridge in Surrey, a redbrick house famous for an elaborate grotto that had by this time fallen into disrepair.

Denton wrote without apology for making his deviance and sexuality so open: all of his obsessions with voyeurism, theft, transvestism and the celebration of the male nude are confessed as an illicit subtext to a novel that resists convention by its protagonist's defiance. Orvil, as the small vulnerable person used to being bullied by his brothers and branded a 'sissy' because he looked and acted femininely, is nonetheless inwardly and resiliently strong. In real life Denton's books were a way of standing up for himself and of being absolutely individual. Something of his obdurate resistance is apparent in the letter he wrote one of his more disparaging critics, Henry Treece, on 8th January 1944. 'It really has been horribly difficult, all through childhood and adolescence, resisting the jokes and prods of parents, guardians, brothers and even friends: and now that I am independent I absolutely refuse to cloak what honesty and transparency remain to me in the conventional cloaks of heartiness, sophistication, irony and satire, which most people seem to find so very useful.'

In Youth is Pleasure is Denton's summer book, a novel of characteristically detailed observations, in which everything that happens to the narrator is recorded on the senses. It's a work of arresting visual description in which the frightened, deeply introverted Orvil, aware of the need to defend his vulnerability and, even harder, to keep his homosexuality secret, compensates in part for his mother's death by gratifying his perversity. 'I don't understand how to live, what to do,' Orvil says of his confusion, manifesting a characteristic teenage death-wish so powerful that he thinks he would rather die than face the prospect of returning to his disciplinarian school.

At the age of sixteen Denton Welch ran away from his boarding school Repton, and something of the emotional insecurity of his youth – his mother Rosalind died in 1927, when he was 11, and his father worked in Shanghai as a partner in the trading firm Wattie & Co – contributed greatly to Denton's disaffection with normal society and his gravitation to those who lived on the edge of society. Denton was largely attracted to soldiers, casual encounters with farm workers, eccentrics, and apart from his correspondence with Edith Sitwell seems to have avoided literary friendships. It was the liking for rough boys who were his opposite that has one of the most memorable scenes in *In Youth is Pleasure* immerse the naturally voyeuristic Orvil in admiring the worked-out physiques of three muscular young men rowing an older one downriver. The scene is unforgettable, not only for its visual imagery, but for the way in which Denton links the boys' lean physicality to the river's curve, as though muscle and sinew are an extension of the current, as their paddles force forward.

'The sun filtered through in round spots that trembled like jelly-fish. Orvil lay back in the grass content to do nothing but watch the sight before him.

'After some time he heard the sound of distant singing. Gradually, it grew nearer and he recognized it as the sea-shanty "Rio Grande." He waited expectantly, ready to back through the hedge if he did not like the look of the singers.

'Suddenly a scarlet canoe appeared round the bend of the river. It was paddled by a young man and two boys of about Orvil's own age. They wore khaki shorts, and their chests and arms were brown as burnt sugar. Orvil saw the Adam's-apples rippling up and down in their throats as they sang lustily. They were grinning and laughing and swearing at each other under cover of the song. One of the boys splashed the man wickedly, and the man called him to order by beating him with his wet paddle...When he stood up, Orvil saw that he wore a stout leather Scout's belt from which dangled a clumsy knife with a handle of rough horn. Orvil now noticed that the others also wore these heavy belts to keep up their flimsy khaki shorts. The man's legs suddenly glinted like silk; the sun had caught the golden hairs, making the ordinary human legs look glossy and vigorous like those of a wild animal.'

Denton doesn't, as other gay writers of the time, omit his attraction to what he sees, but on the contrary accentuates the fetish of a heavy leather belt holding up flimsy khaki shorts.

There are writers conditioned by restraint to avoid all mention of their personal fetishes and there are others, like Denton Welch, who delight in making them public. That Denton was intent on shocking his contemporaries was all part of a sensibility that, repressed by convention, avenged itself by real or imaginary transgression. Orvil steals a lipstick from a chemist's and later makes up in it, he is a voyeur to his eldest brother having sex with Aphra, he admits to getting erect in red bathing trunks because of their association with the boys in the canoe, and to being mistaken for a girl by his friend Guy's grandmother, he finds pleasure in two brutally sadomasochistic encounters with the schoolmaster who is summering in a hut by the river and generally gets a kick from his more compromising actions.

It was doubtless Denton's attachment to the perverse that first attracted William Burroughs to his books and had him cite *In Youth is Pleasure* as a major influence on his own work. What

Denton does, and which Burroughs generously acknowledges, is to write well about everything, not just subject matter acceptable to literature, but its reverse, the underworld to our lives about which we usually remain silent. While complimentary about the quality of the prose, Denton's publisher Herbert Read, in accepting *In Youth is Pleasure* for Routledge, expressed not only disappointment at the book's similarities to its predecessor *Maiden Voyage*, but warned Denton that the sexual aspects of the novel would stick and work against his reputation. To my mind it's Denton's persistent courage in speaking up for the socially deviant, as well as making poetry out of the everyday events of his life, like a picnic, visiting a teashop, taking a drive across country with Eric Oliver, watching boys swim naked in the river, or his eye for purchasing bibelots, that makes him exceptional, and the writing unclassifiable. Denton, like Orvil in his novel who purchases an ornate scent bottle and a mended Chinese saucer with money given him by his father for the holidays, arranged his room to best display his serendipitous possessions. But if the purchase pleasure was temporarily rewarding then the fact of having things to which he was attached only increased Denton's unrelenting awareness of his mortality. In a Journal entry belonging to the time when he was working on *In Youth is Pleasure*, he wrote: 'As I lie in bed here, now, this morning, and watch the crystal glitters of the candlesticks, the white iron twisting table, the yellow satin chair, the grey morning light on the crusty bark of the trees; as I watch the patiently silent harpsichord and the scarlet lacquer screen behind it, and the four miniatures of people long since dead, I think of myself as dead. I think of the years and years to come, when the sun will rise and I shall be nothing but a burnt up cinder. I think of myself as two eyes looking down on my empty room, on my silent red velvet bed, on all my pretty things, and knowing that I shall never use them again.'

I suspect that, accident or not, Denton's neurotic obsession with death would have been total. It is probably true that those who live fully in the moment and concentrate their awareness into maximizing the use of its potential are correspondingly aware of its loss. And if the loss is gain in terms of creative endeavour, then any sense of personal fulfilment by way of immediate compensation is filtered by the recognition that death means an end to the individual's particular creativity.

Restricted by his disability, Denton notably has Orvil run everywhere. One of Orvil's escapist assets is his athletic agility. He runs rather than walks and uses his speed to his advantage. One assumes that the nervy, wired, teenage Denton also relied on his ability to run, not only exuberantly, but to get himself out of trouble if confronted by unwanted bovver boys. Some of the novel's great moments occur when Denton beams Orvil into flight, recreating through his fictional persona a faculty that he had irretrievably lost.

In a telling letter to Alex Comfort, Denton made real his thesis of traumatic youth by expressing something of the persistent fear he had experienced as a teenager. 'Early adolescence,' he wrote, 'was to me what I can only describe as a sordid and fearful time. I was frightened of everything and everything seemed sullied and slimed over with this fear. It is only just lately – I am now twenty-six – that I have come to realize what an unpleasant time it was.'

That Denton dedicated *In Youth is Pleasure* to his mother Rosalind Bassett is indicative not only of her continuing influence in his life, but of his identification of her as the powerful archetype by which he would come to measure all other women as failing the ideal. In his novel, women make a friend of Orvil – the promiscuous Aphra delights in showing him the contents of her makeup bag, her clothes and treasured possessions – because they recognize his fundamental lack of sexual interest in them. Aphra makes Orvil's two older brothers jealous by taking him as her confidant; but when Orvil, in a memorably voyeuristic scene in the night-time grotto, encounters her having sex with Charles, his eldest brother, he is both fascinated and shaken up by the realisation that Aphra is also an object of desire, something that immediately shatters his fantasy of her as sexually untouchable. For Orvil, as for Denton, women are seen as libidinously threatening if they step outside of the role of mother.

Perhaps the most powerful compulsion in *In Youth is Pleasure* takes the shape of the narrator's frustrated attempts to find, if not love, then at least some form of acceptance. When Orvil surreptitiously views the scene of the half-naked youths eating round a fire in the open created by the older man, who in turn reads to them, he does so 'in exasperation of their happiness.' The group's raw camaraderie and rough behaviour excites Orvil because they represent everything he imagines he would like to be, but can't because of his innate refinement. But in realising his disadvantage Orvil also recognizes his strength in submerging himself in a self-created world in which imaginary pleasures in part compensate for invigorating physical graft.

Orvil, it seems, is both attracted to and repelled by the older man, a schoolmaster working with a Bethnal Green mission that organizes holidays for deprived children and uses a wooden hut marked 'Buckingham Palace' as a holiday home; it's this friction of opposites that creates the book's unmitigated sexual tension. Caught out in a blinding rainstorm, Orvil is invited back to the hut by the sadistically authoritarian schoolmaster and told to strip off his wet clothes. After they have had tea together, the man orders the compliant Orvil to polish his brown boots. The man then, under the pretence of demonstrating how to tie knots, binds Orvil's wrists and suspends him from a metal strut by a long cord. The resultant bondage scenes offer Orvil a way of locating the violent primal core in himself that his conditioning attempts to suppress. He discovers not only that he has the capacity to enjoy humiliation, but also the power to inflict it in return with equal pleasure.

That Denton Welch was impossibly highly strung and naturally deeply angry over his disabilities made at times for the sort of hysterical behaviour that compels Orvil to periodically explode out of character. Orvil attempts to overdose on cascara sagrada tablets in his hotel room in the way that Denton, emotionally fixated on and rejected by his practitioner Dr Easton, attempted to kill himself by taking a large number of Prontosil tablets. Part of Denton Welch's greatness as a writer is his ability to conceive of and portray acts of liberating madness. In an unforgettable scene, Orvil ties himself up in a roller's heavy chain in a field and chants obsessively, 'You bet I'll lick your boots, Sir!', compulsively drinks a bottle of communion wine he discovers in a church, and irrationally risks drowning by diving into the river's brown ooze as a way of punishing his brothers for having betrayed him.

Denton Welch's fiction, always and unmistakably the real thing, oscillates between moments of lyrical serenity and outbreaks of psychological disorder. He argues a case for the best poetry often being expressed in the form of prose, his startlingly beautiful imagery shocking the reader into the awareness of how even the most simple things are invested with magic by a poet's eye. And that so much of his writing involves seeing either things or into other peoples' lives gives it the compelling visual quality of film. Denton is distinctly modern in that he made himself available to whatever was there at the moment of writing and gifted it with immediacy. It's this inexhaustible openness to experience that for me singles him out not as a curiosity, but as one of the great writers of his generation. Denton was a one-off and his individuality colours everything he wrote in prose sometimes as delicious as strawberries.

It was only in his last, unfinished novel, *A Voice Through a Cloud*, that he came to tell the story of his tragedy. Like *Maiden Voyage*, *In Youth is Pleasure* magnifies a time when Denton lived with the prospect of a future and when his ambition seemed to be without closure. The adjustments he found it necessary to make in his life are poignantly expressed in a Journal entry. 'In my heart are hung two extraordinary pictures. One is called "Accident and Illness" and the other, exactly opposite, tilted forward as if to meet it, is called "Love and Friendship."'

Not that matters were ever easier in Denton's private life than they were in those of his fictional persona Orvil. His relationship with Eric Oliver survived its intellectual inequalities, but left him feeling misunderstood in relation to the finer things that were his natural expression. He often felt put down and reduced, in the way that Orvil does, by his usually patronising family. Of Eric he wrote: 'He treats me with a mixture of thoughtfulness and solicitude for my precarious health and an almost cynical realism about my thoughts and feelings. All my actions are put down to very mundane motives.'

In spite of it all, Denton worked relentlessly and often in excruciating physical pain, but always connected to the creative source that sustained him. There's that feeling about his art that it lived independently of him and that it was there for him as a natural resource no matter the circumstances. He never once mentions by name Mrs Annie Hutley, the negligent driver of the car whose impact so altered his life, but he must have wondered why they had been so incongruously drawn together on that hot, dusty afternoon in June 1937. What was it that attracted the two into a collision course, and why should their lives have intersected in this catastrophic way? There's no answer to what appears in this case an instance of negative synchronicity, but the outcome – we don't know the effects on the driver – was most certainly to accelerate the intense creative momentum by which Denton subsequently lived. It wasn't the accident that made him into a writer, it was more that it speeded up the process of writing out his life. Both *Maiden Voyage* and *In Youth is Pleasure* are books that, had his life been different, he may have located in himself at a later stage in his development. As it was their transmission became urgent and it's the hot immediacy imparted to the writing of *In Youth is Pleasure* that gives it its flagrantly controversial tone and amazing lyrical drive.

As he remarked in his Journals, the book caused a sensation in the homosexual world and brought him considerable fan mail. By not being part of the literary scene he had the freedom of the outsider to express himself individually and at the same time force his contemporaries into a realisation of their restraint. This was the Denton who liked pushing it, the person who would wear unusual sweaters to cause gossip to flow in village pubs and who overcame class inhibitions by seeking out the company of soldiers and airmen in the countryside around the Medway Valley.

One of the outstanding scenes in *In Youth is Pleasure*, as it accentuates Denton's voyeuristic capacities, occurs when Orvil looks out of his hotel window across the courtyard at a casual holiday acquaintance dancing to blues music dressed only in a towel. Orvil's brother Ben assumes that it is a girl undressing whom he is watching only to be corrected by the knowledge it is a boy. The incident is the perfect example of Denton Welch's facility to make a small event big.

'Orvil went to the window and looked out across the courtyard. A lighted window, the curtains still undrawn, glowed in the other wing. In the lighted room Orvil could see the Clifton boy moving about with only a towel round his waist. His gramophone stood on the wide window-sill pouring out music. Negro voices were singing, "Were you there when they crucified my Lord?" . . .

'And while the music played, the Clifton boy walked about his room opening drawers, pulling out shirts, rubbing his arms and chest, sprinkling oil on his hair from a bottle. He picked up two stumpy brushes and started to scrub his hair back brutally. He looked at his face in the glass and felt along his upper lip.'

'The Clifton boy was dancing now to the music. Crooking his arm round an imaginary partner, he hunched his shoulders and moved in a more gorilla-like and vulgar way than he should have dared to do in public. He stuck out his stomach and revolved his hips.'

That Denton risks making a boy the object of his voyeurism is one thing, but to impart to him largely female characteristics is another. Denton's way of seeing pushes the novel forward, and although he wasn't to live to benefit from the changes made, his reaction to his times anticipated the altogether more liberal counterculture movement ushered in by the Beats, Kerouac, Ginsberg and Burroughs in the late 1950s, and in Britain by the novels of Colin MacInnes, like *City of Spades* and *Absolute Beginners* that give a subversive voice to youth culture.

'I think all I can do is to keep my work going on as long as I can,' Denton wrote in his Journals. 'And if I can no longer, then I will die.'

But Denton's legacy persists, and each new generation of readers picks up his work, in a small way ensuring his continuity as that best of all things, a cult. William Burroughs, in his insightful Foreword to a US reissue of *In Youth is Pleasure* in 1998, named Denton Welch as the formative influence on his own work when he began writing in the late forties, comparing Denton's method to that of the other enduring miniaturist, Jane Bowles, and how both focused on the sort of anomalous phrase that nobody else could have written.

Denton Welch wrote in a hurry and often in chronic pain attendant on symptoms associated with his fractured spine, completing three novels, *Maiden Voyage*, *In Youth is Pleasure* and *A Voice Through a Cloud*, as well as a book of short stories, *Brave and Cruel*, and the posthumously published *A Last Sheaf*, *The Journals* and *Dumb Instrument*, a comprehensive selection of his poetry. When he wasn't writing or painting, his recreation was the serendipitous purchase of junkshop collectables, old china, bric-a-brac, prints, paintings, vintage clothes and whatever caught his acquisitive eye. He wrote in bed wearing a red Aldermanic gown, and was attracted to his opposite in his loosely defined partner, Eric Oliver, writing to Eric, 'It is just because you are different that I like you. You wouldn't touch my imagination in the very least if you approximated more to my type.' Eric Oliver became, in turn, Denton's carer and nurse, and was alone with him when he died in his arms at 2 p.m. on 30th December 1948, appointing himself executor and without consultation selling the copyrights of Denton's works to an alcoholic bookseller, James Campbell, who promptly resold them to the University of Texas. Eric Oliver was virtually illiterate, hard drinking, rough and worked on the land, and characteristically exploited Denton's total dependency on him, while unexpectedly discovering within himself a facility to genuinely care for the incongruous invalid attempting in small ways to educate him in the finer things of life.

Nothing was easy for Denton Welch, but persistent courage to put his work before often intolerable mental and physical suffering got him somehow into the creative window in which he could write, pinching up corners of imaginative space in which writing shone for him as the closest thing to reality he knew. In a *Journal* entry for 28th January 1947, less than a year before he died, he described a hallucinatory episode in which both he and things changed shape in a sort of eerie interactive morph. 'In all the illness, I have the horrible sensation that the tables, chairs, lamps and confusion of books near me were writhing into life and becoming extensions of myself, like new limbs, utterly unwanted, but insisting on living and doing my bidding. And I even myself grew to a wretched largeness and was invaded too with the activity of nothingness. Sight, sound, touch were all distorted. I was living in a twisted stretched world, where I invaded everything and was the horror I could not escape.'

The asphyxiating existential crisis documented here, a collision between hallucinated perception and ontological alienation from the world, was a familiar biochemical state for Denton, who was sometimes medicated with morphine. At the end he'd accumulated fifteen manuscript notebooks by his bed of his still unfinished novel *A Voice Through a Cloud*, and that was what he died into, the realisation he was irretrievably leaving his work behind. The separation anxiety was acute, parting with work he would never see again or reclaim as his own property. He, more than anyone, was optimally aware of biological time as a phenomenon actively eroding him, and that you can't run time backwards, or oppose its arrow. Denton lived on the frontline for over a decade, each second big as a raindrop in its transitioning, and so fast it didn't seem to have happened. The condensed time between his accident and his death was a sustained moment, and he didn't wish either.

WILLIAM BLAKE'S *VALA* AND BOB DYLAN'S *DESIRE*

She's done her generic black bob the colour of manuka honey, just on the right side of blonde. Her bare brown arms cradle, as she tells me, a new techy iPhone that proactively offers contextual information and suggests apps. She's Lily, selecting, like most Chinese girls, a dead English names to substitute for her own. As part of her retrofit she tells me she's a Dylan fan, but doesn't know William Blake, he's too far back in time, like an evanescent runaway neutron star. Blake to her is like trying to remember a hazy scarlet sunset seen from a Beijing tower at ten, when she's now twenty-five, knee-holes in her skinny jeans, blue tortoiseshell frames to cool eyewear, and a consciousness visibly split between real time, VR and reality as a new species gene that is altering human perception. You can't live anywhere but in the present, and we're both sitting talking in the window of the large Café Costa on two floors on Shaftesbury Avenue facing out into Soho's Wardour Street, an ATM opposite and every face a stranger in the edgy momentous foot traffic. We're not so far from the site of William Blake's 18th and 19th century Soho radius, I tell her, and by visualising him there I can still feel the electromagnetics of his sites in Marshall Street and Poland Street where his unstoppable creative industry went largely unnoticed by his contemporaries. Lily chases Blake's exhaust plume on her phone and he starts to come realer. To me he's a body composed out of words and visuals compounded into a highly personalised image-bank, a language anatomy extending across the globe like a lyric virus. Blake dealt in giants, macrocosmic physiognomy, because part of his warring genes resented physical limitations, the algorithmic use of his visionary imagination totally superseding the inevitable breakdown of his physical body. His launch-line for *Vala, or The Four Zoas* capitalises on war. 'For we wrestle not against flesh and blood, but against principalities, against powers, against the rulers of darkness of this world, against spiritual wickedness in high places.' Today he would have taken issue against corrupt politicians, criminal Libor riggers, hedge funder warlords like Tony Blair, corporate muscle, deregulated NHS admin and ubiquitous arms dealers. His frustration in all his prophetic books, including *Vala*, is that his offensive is initialised from an imaginative platform and conducted so unilaterally that his efforts, outside the immense struggle of writing, go uncontested in combat.

I'm as much interested in lipstick and its variant colours as I am Blake and Dylan, and Lily's created the subtle power of the nude lip using, she shows me impulsively, an orange-ish MAC Persistence lipstick crafted with lip shine so that it looks like she has the sheen of an expensive stocking pressed onto each lip. We've only been speaking twenty minutes and we're into the intricate calligraphy of makeup. That's what my writing days in West End cafés invite: the collusion of strangers.

Scarlet Rivera, she was a stranger to Dylan, a gypsy with three foot of black hair collapsed down her back, walking along 13th Street with a violin case in her hand when Bob spotted her out of his ugly green car adopted for disguise. 'Can you play that thing?' he asked, and she assured him she could, and was with a New York salsa band. What did I call it, the collusion of strangers? On the back of his consummately achieved *Blood on the Tracks*, Dylan was anxious to get back into the studio with a complete set of new songs worked out of his chemistry with an electrifying silver twizzle. Chancing it, Dylan told Scarlet he was Danny from Hungary, but at a close look she knew it was Dylan, despite the shades and the black woollen hat compressing his tangled hair. According to Scarlet, 'I actually was going to cross the street and disappear into a basement apartment for a rehearsal within probably less than sixty seconds. So our time of encountering each other, visually even, on the street was infinitesimally small. And had I disappeared across the street before his car crossed, it wouldn't have happened.'

It's Scarlet's fiddle, of course, that drives a gypsified layer of romantic colour through *Desire*, and most notably on songs like 'Hurricane,' 'One More Cup of Coffee' and 'Isis,' where her stormy arpeggios laminate the band's energies with searing virtuoso brilliance. But working with Bob in the studio, Scarlet was initially relegated to a substrate operating only in the corners of Dylan's sound and not in its central cone. 'I will say in the recording studio he gave me a couple of takes, but literally only a couple. At one point he said "Play under," play more under him, meaning the lower end, and then at one point he was going to do his harmonica solo and I stopped and didn't play and he actually said, "No go ahead and play with me." And I was just stunned that he asked me to play with his harmonica, and you know, just went into complementary mode, and fortunately I didn't have too much time to think about it.'

Some intercultural girl-code involves Lily in phone immersion and I look out at a mile of bleached denim-blue sky that Blake must have thrown looks at in his specifically Soho years, although unlike me looking for pollutant additives of colour, the sky for Blake was an arena of apocalyptic meltdowns, rather than atmospheric air miles. Blake didn't see West End cinematic sky – mine is full of particulates, nitrogen dioxide 69 ppm – but the insertion of visionary action happening as reality.

> But Luvah and Vala standing in the bloody sky
> On high remaind alone forsaken in fierce jealousy,
> They stood above the heavens forsaken desolate suspended in blood.
> Descend they could not, nor from Each other avert their eyes.
> Eternity appeared above them as One Man infolded
> In Luvah's robes of blood & bearing all his afflictions;
> And the sun shines down on the misty earth Such was the Vision.

Vala, or The Four Zoas was conceived at 13 Hercules Buildings in Lambeth – there was a vine in the small strip of garden – and Blake originally called it 'The Bible of Hell in Nocturnal Visions Collected.' Blake's affirmation 'That the Poetic Genius is the true Man,' a composite he himself represented through unstoppable work, appeals to my belief in a specific poetry gene, a chromosome or specific neural network that fires up language into lyrical coordinates. There's no specific explanation for intuitive creativity, only neural links activated by the process, but not accountable for the contents. While the stimulus for a lot of poetry connects with how the brain interprets signals from the eyes – I make acute visual raids on everything I see that's unusual – there's another process, Blake's, of real imagination, when the brain can no longer rely on connections shaped by past experience and invents an alternative reality. The reason most mainstream poetry is so predictable is that the poet copies reality instead of hitching it to an altered state. In poetry that has you genuinely re-think the world, the heavy lifting is performed by only a subset of finely tuned neurons with chemicals such as dopamine shuttled between the cells. Blake's total immersion in a self-created mythology has him largely bypass statistical reality for its visionary equivalents. The problem for the reader is that Blake's total absorption often fails to communicate, and I couldn't begin to explain a coherent mapping of the Four Zoas. Blake's signposting is a bit like trying to read street names in Chinese without translation. What you get as a non-academic enthusiast is what I call the pop hooks in the epic, those visionary surges that shock by what is at best quite literally cosmological recreation as furiously inspired poetry.

> While far into the vast unknown the strong wing'd Eagles bend
> Their venturous flight, in Human forms distinct; thro darkness deep
> They bear the woven draperies; on golden hooks they hang abroad
> The universal curtains & spread out from Sun to Sun
> The vehicles of light, they separate the furious particles
> Into wild currents as the water mingles with the wine.

It's Blake's long line that is so impressive, like a highway built out of his metric and coextensive with his thought it constructs linear beat, like if you put your ear to the hard shoulder you'd get the bass line of the whole motorway. Blake's line drives bass like Jack Bruce hacked it with Cream. Writing *Vala* didn't lift him either, rather it flattened him into introspection. Writing to his friend George Cumberland he noted his disorder. 'I begin to Emerge from a Deep pit of melancholy, Melancholy without any real reason for it, a Disease which God keep you from and all good men …I have been too little amongst friends which I fear they will not Excuse & I know not how to apologise for.'

The problem with being human is we simply don't know who we are other than the documentation of consciousness that streams a real-time movie. After rehabilitating from being shot three times by Valerie Solanas, Andy Warhol claimed he thought his own reality was like watching television. Blake's was too, only his dysthymic or depressive position lurched him into lows that alternated with sustained surges of elated vision. He set himself the impossible task of trying to recreate the Big Bang, or for him, without 20th century physics, the Jewish story of the creation myth that so fixated and distressed him he spent a lifetime rewriting possible sequels to the original. And what really did Blake's wife Catherine think of so solipsistic and humourless a pursuit? To our knowledge she lacked girlfriends or anyone to confide in about life with a singular genius locked into an iconoclastic methodology of importing apocalypse. Today she would have most likely received counselling. Catherine Sophia Boucher, daughter of a market gardener from Battersea, no education; what was it in her mix of London genes that accidently attracted Blake? What sort of intuitive signal brought them together like different planet species to share a life in which Blake dealt with aliens, giants, extraterrestrial invaders, whatever was coming through on his dimension. To our times, Blake's deviated mythologies read like no-tech science fiction. To Catherine Boucher, and Blake walked four miles to visit her, tracking over the wooden bridge slung from Chelsea to Battersea, he must have appeared monomaniacally weird. Every time I take a cut through Soho's Bourchier Street, an alley connecting Dean Street to Wardour Street, her name comes up in me (and if you need a piss it's one of those concealed corridors where you can). How did Catherine Boucher, a dark brunette with chestnut eyes, get her mind round *Vala* as her husband's cosmic reality? She shopped for him in Soho and Lambeth, knowing there was probably no one like him anywhere. And that's what I find so moving, her acceptance of his difference as her responsibility and reality.

Where Dylan meets Blake in the context of *Desire* versus *Vala* is in the subversive thrust of championing social outlaws and walloping convention. Dylan's scorching opener 'Hurricane' contests the conviction of the former middleweight boxer Rubin 'Hurricane' Carter for triple murder, asserting he was framed and the criminals are the judiciary. 'Now all the criminals in their coats and their ties/Are free to drink martinis and watch the sun rise/While Rubin sits like Buddha in a ten foot cell/An innocent man in a living hell.' At a time when rock music counted politically, Dylan performed a concert in Clinton State Prison on December 5th, 1975, in which Rubin Carter took to the stage to address the press, and was directly instrumental through his intervention in having Carter unsuccessfully retried. As self-taught anti-intellectuals, both Blake and Dylan have attracted an abnormal degree of academic commentary attempting often gratuitously to account for natural untutored talent. The thing is, you can't explain creative imagination through neuronal functioning; you can either navigate it or you can't, and if you lack that particular facility you're going to cause yourself a lot of frustration trying to write, like looking at a bright source hundreds of light years away.

After a rather chaotic, unfocused start to *Desire*, Dylan assembled a small enthused band comprising Scarlet Rivera, Rob Stoner on bass, Howie Wyeth on drums, and Sheila Seidenberg and Emmylou Harris providing backing vocals, and with typical driving impetuosity tore into the material with famous disregard for production, completing the album in two days. The acute emotional focus of the *Desire* sessions was when Dylan's estranged wife Sara arrived unexpectedly on the night of the second session, July 31st, having disappeared to Mexico for six months, to hear him sing 'Sara' directly to her as she watched from the other side of the glass. Catherine Boucher, name of the alley where I piss, was infertile, and Blake attempted to introduce a third party into the marriage, as a polygamy advocated by the Moravian, Swedenborgian and Falkian literature he read advocating sexual gratification as trance and physical states of free love. It was Catherine who understandably objected, and was probably unaware of Blake visiting a brothel called the White House in Soho Square, there between 1778–1801 as an early walk-up. Whatever Blake did he did and I believe him, when he writes, 'I am not ashamed, or afraid or averse to tell you what ought to be told – that I am under the direction of messengers from heaven, daily and nightly ... Behind me, the sea of time and space roars and follows swiftly.' (To Thomas Butts, Jan 19th, 1802). That Blake navigated psychic pathways and was partly delusional is hinted at by his first biographer, Thomas Gilchrist, who recounts how Blake would adopt the persona of any character he chose, 'I am Socrates or I am Moses,' convinced he was that character's reality. Catherine was apparently unquestioning as to Blake's polymorphic adoptions of character, after all, he wrote it out in language she could only partially read or understand.

Forgetting *Vala*, because all of Blake's writing is essentially one disordered epic, we get a great pop hook in 'Jerusalem', when he synthesises his purpose of opening out inner spaces so that they are potentially navigable to whoever picks up on them. He tells us exactly of the mental effort involved in his state.

> Trembling, I sit day and night. My friends are astonisht at me:
> Yet they forgive my wand'rings. I rest not from my great task:
> To open the eternal worlds! To open the immortal eyes
> Of man inwards; into the world of thought: into eternity.

I take a break from writing this and go hang around – a poet's active occupation – Jen Café in Newport Court, because I'm obsessed by the exact colour green it's painted, jade, menthol, juniper, and find a similar green in the map of the Hong Kong Island subway at the entrance to Newport Court in the line connecting Kowloon and Tsing Yi. I'm meeting Lily there, and spend time writing on the pagoda steps, wondering what

Catherine would think of today's makeup, and Asian girls in boots and denim micro-shorts. Writing in peoples' faces like I do is a strange attractor and energises me with the dynamic of place. It also suggests the nomadic freedom of the socially disinherited, to which me and other committed poets belong, those few who believe poetry occupies every moment of your life, unlike careerists who use it as a media platform, rather than an explorative unresolved inner journey. Blake's courage was working with a largely unacknowledged prolific past and the ambiguity of an empty future. Catherine was conditioned to take it all on trust. Getting enough food to eat was a priority, and also the purchase of paints, indigo, cobalt, gamboge, vermilion, ultramarine and Frankfort black to be mixed with carpenter's glue on a marble block. Humiliation and demoralising condescension was a common experience for Blake, and there's a passage in a letter to Blake from R.N. Cromek, a minor engraver and printer, in relation to Blake's drawings to illustrate Robert Blair's *The Grave* that points not only to his assumed monomaniacal obsessions, but to the low social status he occupied as an artist. Cromek writes to hurt: 'I was determined to bring you food as well as reputation, though, from your late conduct I have some reason to embrace your wild opinion that to manage genius, and to cause it to produce good things, it is absolutely necessary to starve it; indeed this opinion is considerably heightened by the recollection that your best work, the illustrations of *The Grave* was produced when you and Mrs. Blake were reduced so low as to be obliged to live on half a guinea a week.' Blake's solitude and social disenfranchisement liberated him into the visionary without any least care for the reception given his writings, because he had no reading public. *Vala or the Four Zoas* remained unpublished in his lifetime, and it's doubtful that anyone but serious Blakeans can rewardingly access its turbulently apocalyptic geography. Radically opposed to empirical order, the chaos theory inherent in *Vala* finds

Blake choking in the punitive meltdown of his own apocalyptic creation. Again, I go for a brilliantly coloured pop hook in the description of the serpent Orc, imagined as it was inhabiting the wired electric impulses of Blake's visual cortex.

> In fury, a Serpent wondrous, among the constellations of Urizen.
> A crest of fire rose on his forehead, red as the carbuncle;
> Beneath, down to his eyelids, scales of pearl; then gold and silver,
> Immingled with the ruby overspread his visage; down
> His furious neck, writhing contorted in dire budding pains,
> The scaly amour shot out. Stubborn, down his back and bosom,
> The emerald, onyx, sapphire, jasper, beryl, amethyst,
> Strove in terrific emulation which should gain a place
> Upon the mighty fiend – the fruit of the Mysterious Tree . . .

This battle of livid jewel-colours is marvellous , a lapidary serpent squeezing Blake's brain furiously and malevolently from the constellation of Urizen. What do you do with such a vision other than commit it to words, drink porter and wonder if there's anything to eat? The serpent from the stars is a lurid sci-fi precursor and the hallucinated beauty of each stone named makes it into a psychedelic artefact. What did Catherine Boucher think? Gilchrist reports Blake as saying, 'Do you think if I came home and discovered my wife to be unfaithful, I should be so foolish as to take ill?' Reverse the question, and what would she have thought?

When I write, which is all of the time, there's a line of Lou Reed's that comes up on continuous repeat, 'And me I just don't care at all,' and maybe that's the only way to work – you're so committed you're dissociated. Literature is ubiquitously self-regarding, but freed-up writers don't give a fuck, because freedom is the biggest part of the doing.

Blake's alienation, in part the consequence of his revolutionary politics of consciousness, was essentially so unshareable at the time that he sent it into the future knowing he wouldn't be there if or when it was discovered or ever again know anything about it. The total sadness of this demanded a corresponding courage to persist because the work was so much bigger than him.

For Dylan, it was the opposite. Rock fame stripped him of every layer of privacy, so that he was arguably more alone on stage than in any other aspect of his private or public life. 'Isis', off *Desire*, typifies one of Dylan's Wild West folk songs in which he heads for the lawless 'wild unknown country' – the same terrain staked out contemporaneously by Ed Dorn in his epic cowboy poem *Gunslinger*, one of the most adventurous life-changing poems of its epoch. Dylan heads off west with a friend in search of Isis, or, metaphorically, his estranged wife Sara, his fascination with jewels not unlike Blake's *Vala* pop hook when he sights a venomous serpent trailing jewels through the stars. 'I was thinking about turquoise I was thinking about gold/I was thinking about diamonds and the world's biggest necklace/As we rode through the canyons through the devilish cold/I was thinking about Isis how she thought I was reckless.' What the two adventurers or fictitious cowboys in the song discover is an ice pyramid, a sort of cryonic storage chamber, and Dylan's hobo partner dies trying to drag a body out of glacial interment. In Egyptian mythology Isis married her brother Osiris and conceived Horus with him. As the friend to slaves, criminals, artisans and losers, her myth played directly into Dylan's own counterculture subversion. When her brother was murdered by Set, she was instrumental through her magical skills in restoring his body to life after having gathered his body parts dispersed about the Earth and reassembled them. The appeal of the myth to Dylan with his own nomadic randomly dispersed touring life and the disintegration and brief reintegration of his marriage is there for the finding. With the song beginning with a reference to a marriage to Isis on the 5th May, the last verse completes some sort of unified cycle. 'Isis, oh Isis, you mystical child/what drives me to you is what drives me insane/I still can remember the way that you smiled/on the fifth day of May in the drizzling rain.'

'Isis' is an example of communicative clarity of narrative, the right side of enigmatic, but never obscure. Blake had the same marvellous facility for lyricism in the *Songs of Innocence and Experience* that remain modern to the reader by their direct lyricisation of shared experience. But you'd have to go to H.P. Lovecraft to find a similar pile-up of paranormal horror as infects much of Blake's internal works and wars of fantasy in the prophetic books, including *Vala* with its pathological usurpation of reality, delusions of persecution and intense sexual conflict. You need to be a Blakean code-breaker like Geoffrey Keynes, Mona Wilson or Kathleen Raine to hack his fantastic systemised mythology, and I'm not. As in all poetry I'm attracted to sensation, those visionary rips like exhaust plumes that scorch Blake's optimal visionary moments, and not at all to the theological debate of his turbulent inner politics. Blake is best for me when he is collapsed into a state in which poetry intercedes between him and madness, was it paranoid schizophrenia or psychotic episodes, and pulls back from the edge by relating. Splitting everything into four, the four Zoas are arguably Urizen, reason; Urthona, spirit; Luvah, passion; and Tharmas, the body as a self-created spacetime system. But it's also the neurological architecture of a shattered or fragmented personality looking to reintegrate through creative enterprise, a fiction in which most external reality goes missing. Perhaps the downside of *Vala* is that Blake leaves London behind, and it's the physical basis of London as a real humanly explored city that makes his Jerusalem so great by contrast. *Vala* is removed from all identifiable geography and is arguably an extended death fantasy – a sci-fi apocalypse without tech. And rather like the mythic allusions to dismemberment in Dylan's 'Isis', Blake visualises clips of psychotic implosion made into poetry as his effort.

> Tharmas reared up his hands & stood on the affrighted ocean.
> The dead reared up his voice, & stood on the resounding shore,
> Crying: 'Fury in my limbs, destruction in my bones & marrow,
> My skull is riven into filaments, my eyes into sea jellies,
> Floating upon the tide, wander bubbling & bubbling,
> Uttering my lamentation & begetting little monsters,
> Who sit mocking upon the little pebbles of the tide
> In all my rivers, & on dried shells that the fish
> Have quite forsaken . . .

I try this on Lily at Jen café. Did Blake try it on Catherine? Jen Café is painted Starbucks green, or it could be Lloyds green – I still can't get the precise colour. Lily can't make anything of jellyfish morphed into marine homunculi, except its possible components for a phone game. But I'd rather have spoonfuls of this than a poetry that keeps on describing reality as reality with no imaginative differential. And according to Frederick Tatham, who had it directly from Catherine, she would have to have been witness to Blake's violently physicalised delusions, and Gilchrist quotes an unnamed friend of Blake's as follows: 'She would get up in the night, when he was under his very fierce inspirations, which were as if they would tear him asunder, while he was yielding himself to the Muse, or whatever else it could be called, sketching and writing. And so terrible a task did this seem to be, that she had to sit motionless and silent, only to stay him mentally, without moving hand or foot: this for hours, and night after night.'

Shifting the world around in your head through neural activities as I've described it don't come easy on the system and does your nerves in. Blake described the process in a letter to Thomas Butts: 'for I, so far from being bound down, take the world with me in my flights, and often it seems lighter than a ball of wool rolled by the wind.'

I'm obsessed by dietary metabolics, what people eat, and, as I am a vegan, also what they shouldn't. Catherine was, by all accounts, a good cook, and would have prepared coarse, inferior meat, degraded by slow, unhygienic transport from farms to London, bread containing alum, a bleaching agent that made it look bigger, cheddar cheese, pea soup simmered with stock, celery and onion, and white soup comprising veal stock, cream and almonds thickened with breadcrumbs, and puddings. In 1790, individuals on average consumed four kilograms of sugar each year. To avoid drinking excrementally toxic Thames water, Blake drank porter, a dark style of beer developed in London from well-hopped beers made from brown malt. You could buy single, double or triple strength to get you high, OG (original gravity) 1.071 and ABV 6.6%. Drink relaxed Blake down from intense, unsparing, unstoppable work that brought little or no reward. His Soho and Lambeth years were the equivalent of pushing a tank across the Sahara by a single mental beam. 'I say I shan't live five years, and if I live one it will be a wonder.' June 1793.

I'm writing this not too far from 28 Poland Street, Soho, in the Patisserie Valerie on Marshall Street on the exact site of Blake's birthplace. His Soho was all he knew, like mine is the one I'm actively engaged in because your place in time is all you ever know. I can imagine and research his time as it's profusely documented, but he knew nothing of 2016, the window in which I'm reinventing him as a frontline visionary throwing irrefutable g-forces of self-invested myth at a uninterested public. Like Francis Bacon, whose propulsive re-anatomisation of physique in painting left him physically and mentally exhausted from the high-octane energies of manual assault on the canvas – and Bacon's use of physique owes something to the worked-out musculature of Blake's figures – relentless hard work wore Blake out and turned his hands into a mini-studio of printer's ink and paints and abraded lesions. I tell Lily, as she scalpels a pink berry mousse cake and casually roams her phone, of the association of place, but we can't run time backwards to hitch up with Blake. Whatever he was or is inhabits another spacetime to ours and, anyhow, a berry mousse cake is as good as a poem and singularly commands the present.

We get to talking of Dylan's 'Joey', a song about the life and death of the celebrated New York gangster Joey Gallor or Crazy Joe affiliated to the Profaci crime family, in which Dylan, as in 'Hurricane' from the same album, comes out controversially on the side of the outlaw, in the way that Blake's social conscience inevitably sides with the London underclass, telling us, 'that what are called vices in the natural world are the highest sublimities in the spiritual world.'

Lily likes the hook in 'Joey': 'Joey, Joey/King of the streets child of clay/Joey Joey/What made them come and want to blow you away.' Part of Dylan's iconic counterculture status in the sixties and seventies was, of course, conditioned by his total immersion through his art in the social revolution of the times that backed the establishment up against the wall. *Desire*, as an album, embodies Dylan's intransigent message that the outlaw is hero in a world where authority is corrupt – a moral platform arrived at by Blake with his fierce antagonism towards materialism as the weapon employed by systems to destroy individual freedom. Governments designate individuals who are not institutionally collectivised dangerous and Dylan in the mid-seventies was most defiantly that. In real life, Joey Gallo was convicted in November 1961 for attempting with force to extract payments from a café owner, suspected of being involved in two murders and, on December 21st, 1961 was sentenced to seven to seventeen years in a state prison. Joe, who was released in 1971, was killed the following year on his birthday at Umberto's Clam House in Little Italy on April 7th, 1972. Dylan's support in the 11-minute song is for the socially vilified, the implication being that, like Hurricane, Joey was framed. Dylan's conspiracy theories on *Desire* are its culturally antagonistic shotgun thrust aimed to annihilate racial prejudice and the often morally corrupt preconceptions of a class-bound judiciary. 'He did ten years in Attica, reading Nietzsche and Wilhelm Reich/They threw him in the hole one time for trying to stop a strike/His closest friends were black men 'cause they seemed to understand/What it's like to be in society with a shackle on your hand.'

Dylan's artistic championing of the socially oppressed is not unlike the compassion expressed by Blake for the inner-city poor in his early poem 'London' in which he observes: 'I wander thro' each charter'd street/Near where the charter'd Thames does flow./And mark in every face I meet/Marks of weakness, marks of woe.' At the heart of Dylan's tequila-fuelled *Desire*, mostly recorded in one all-night session, with its pervading theme of social injustice, was the emotionally distressing breakup of his twelve-years marriage to Sara. One year after the recording of Dylan's album of beleaguered anti-heroes, Sara filed for divorce, under which terms Dylan was 'restrained and enjoined from harassing, annoying, molesting, or in any way interfering with the peace and quiet and personal privacy of the petitioner Sara Dylan.' What does that tell you?

Part of the marital friction seems to have been caused not only by Dylan's nomadic touring, but a growing sense of intellectual inequality, something he personally attributed to his absorption into art classes conducted by Norman Rueben at his studio in Carnegie Hall, New York, where the seventy-three-year-old painter taught Dylan not to copy, but to reinvent what he saw, as the first principle of imagination. According to Dylan in an interview, 'I went home after the first day and my wife never did understand me ever since that day. That's when our marriage starting breaking up. She never knew what I was talking about and I couldn't possibly explain it.' And whereas Blake personally educated Catherine Boucher into his immersively creative lifestyle, Dylan and Sara found no compatible meeting point in the intellectual expansion that ran parallel with his artistic development.

Today Chinatown's a blond window of delayed October sunlight. I sit out on the pagoda steps in what is my time, wondering if I'm singularly there or quantum, so that I'm also virtually present somewhere else I don't know, writing a parallel poem as a variant to the one I'm writing here. In my line of view, there's a mini-skirted Chinese hooker soliciting what I call a paramilitary professional, a finance- or tech-head wearing a charcoal suit he doesn't understand or give personality.

When Lily arrives with a ponytail and extracts her white plastic ear buds I tell her I'm going to introduce the theme of toe-sucking into my Blake talk and, specifically, the left big toe. I can see she's wearing a little bit of concealer with green undertones and nude foundation with a subtle green tint.

Richard Cosway was an instructor at Par's Drawing School when Blake studied there in 1767–72 and became a lifelong friend. Cosway was a student of Moravian, Swedenborgian and Falkian sexual experimentation through trance-induced visualisation of a desired body. Now, Cosway, as a student, lived with Dr Husband Messiter, Swedenborg's personal doctor. Messiter was a close Soho neighbour of Blake's family at 28 Broad Street, for he lived on nearby Great Pulteney Street. Through this source Cosway acquired rare volumes of Swedenborg's works, books he shared with Blake. Blake regularly attended the Freemasons'

Hall and Tavern opposite Basire's studio on Great Queen Street. In fact, his name appears frequently in the 1780s and 1790s in surviving lodge records. In Blake's 'Eve Tempted by the Serpent' he notes 'Embraces are Comminglings: from the Head even to the Feet,' promoting the cabalistic belief that focused performance of the meditative sexual act rebuilds the Temple or New Jerusalem in the initiate's libido. Blake's specifically sexual drawings for *Jerusalem* and *Vala*, particularly of the left big toe, suggests he knew that in cabalistic yoga the cock was called the great toe, and in his *Milton* he adapts the left foot to a vehicle of spiritual ascent. Swedenborg specifically writes, 'the great toe of the left foot communicates with the genitals, for the genitals correspond to the Word.' Tantric aspirants were also aware that a nerve terminating in the large left toe regulates all cyclic changes and rhythms in the entire body. And that sucking one's own left toe is a technique facilitating the control of seminal flow during prolonged erection. As Blake's writings mostly imply acute sexual dissatisfaction, it's unlikely that Catherine Boucher was a toe-sucker, but the notion lies open. Lily's big left toe twinkling through open-toe strappy sandals is varnished peacock blue.

The foot traffic picks up in Newport Place and she goes off to meet a friend at Seven Dials. I stay on writing this, watching raspberry cumulonimbus clouds build a dense architecture, a rainband that will doubtless explode later. Writing's a strange attractor like me. Francis Bacon used to say to me, 'if you don't look like what you do you aren't it.' And poetry's a sort of neuromarketing; my assets, after all, are my nerves. I don't get no money for it, but the optimised thrill of writing saturates my brain like a junky's with dopamine. I think I'm fast in neural connections, but the galaxy speeds at 300,000 mph.

I used to call her my familiar junky outside Foyles, but now I know she's Andrea. Andrea Catherine Boucher? Just Andrea. She comes on again at me for change, wasted, track-marked arms, lesioned, totally beautiful ruin. 'Gimme luv, gimme H.'

There's the Foyles café, fixtures bandaged in silver foil like Andy Warhol's Studio, so I say, 'Why don't we go there for the sugar you need, a sticky cake, and of course I'll buy you your habit.' I'm waiting for it, and she looks at me out of dead eyes and says, 'You're wearing makeup, luv,' and that's our unmistakable reprise, the way she gets to me by discerning the odd from the normal. 'It really suits you, luv,' she says, as the rain comes on predictably.

A PARTIAL LIST OF SNUGGLY BOOKS

G. ALBERT AURIER *Elsewhere and Other Stories*
S. HENRY BERTHOUD *Misanthropic Tales*
LÉON BLOY *The Desperate Man*
LÉON BLOY *The Tarantulas' Parlor and Other Unkind Tales*
ÉLÉMIR BOURGES *The Twilight of the Gods*
CYRIEL BUYSSE *The Aunts*
JAMES CHAMPAGNE *Harlem Smoke*
FÉLICIEN CHAMPSAUR *The Latin Orgy*
BRENDAN CONNELL *Clark*
BRENDAN CONNELL *Unofficial History of Pi Wei*
RAFAELA CONTRERAS *The Turquoise Ring and Other Stories*
ADOLFO COUVE *When I Think of My Missing Head*
QUENTIN S. CRISP *Aiaigasa*
LADY DILKE *The Outcast Spirit and Other Stories*
CATHERINE DOUSTEYSSIER-KHOZE
   The Beauty of the Death Cap
ÉDOUARD DUJARDIN *Hauntings*
BERIT ELLINGSEN *Now We Can See the Moon*
ERCKMANN-CHATRIAN *A Malediction*
ENRIQUE GÓMEZ CARRILLO *Sentimental Stories*
EDMOND AND JULES DE GONCOURT *Manette Salomon*
REMY DE GOURMONT *From a Faraway Land*
GUIDO GOZZANO *Alcina and Other Stories*
EDWARD HERON-ALLEN *The Complete Shorter Fiction*
RHYS HUGHES *Cloud Farming in Wales*
J.-K. HUYSMANS *The Crowds of Lourdes*
J.-K. HUYSMANS *Knapsacks*
COLIN INSOLE *Valerie and Other Stories*
JUSTIN ISIS *Pleasant Tales II*
JUSTIN ISIS AND DANIEL CORRICK (editors)
   Drowning in Beauty: The Neo-Decadent Anthology

VICTOR JOLY
   The Unknown Collaborator and Other Legendary Tales
MARIE KRYSINSKA *The Path of Amour*
BERNARD LAZARE *The Mirror of Legends*
BERNARD LAZARE *The Torch-Bearers*
MAURICE LEVEL *The Shadow*
JEAN LORRAIN *Errant Vice*
JEAN LORRAIN *Fards and Poisons*
JEAN LORRAIN *Masks in the Tapestry*
JEAN LORRAIN *Nightmares of an Ether-Drinker*
JEAN LORRAIN *The Soul-Drinker and Other Decadent Fantasies*
ARTHUR MACHEN *N*
ARTHUR MACHEN *Ornaments in Jade*
CAMILLE MAUCLAIR *The Frail Soul and Other Stories*
CATULLE MENDÈS *Bluebirds*
CATULLE MENDÈS *For Reading in the Bath*
CATULLE MENDÈS *Mephistophela*
ÉPHRAÏM MIKHAËL *Halyartes and Other Poems in Prose*
LUIS DE MIRANDA *Who Killed the Poet?*
OCTAVE MIRBEAU *The Death of Balzac*
CHARLES MORICE *Babels, Balloons and Innocent Eyes*
DAMIAN MURPHY *Daughters of Apostasy*
KRISTINE ONG MUSLIM *Butterfly Dream*
PHILOTHÉE O'NEDDY *The Enchanted Ring*
YARROW PAISLEY *Mendicant City*
URSULA PFLUG *Down From*
JEREMY REED *When a Girl Loves a Girl*
ADOLPHE RETTÉ *Misty Thule*
JEAN RICHEPIN *The Bull-Man and the Grasshopper*
DAVID RIX *A Blast of Hunters*
FREDERICK ROLFE (Baron Corvo) *Amico di Sandro*
FREDERICK ROLFE (Baron Corvo)
   An Ossuary of the North Lagoon and Other Stories

JASON ROLFE *An Archive of Human Nonsense*
MARCEL SCHWOB *The Assassins and Other Stories*
MARCEL SCHWOB *Double Heart*
CHRISTIAN HEINRICH SPIESS *The Dwarf of Westerbourg*
BRIAN STABLEFORD (editor)
 Decadence and Symbolism: A Showcase Anthology
BRIAN STABLEFORD (editor) *The Snuggly Satyricon*
BRIAN STABLEFORD *The Insubstantial Pageant*
BRIAN STABLEFORD *Spirits of the Vasty Deep*
BRIAN STABLEFORD *The Truths of Darkness*
COUNT ERIC STENBOCK *Love, Sleep & Dreams*
COUNT ERIC STENBOCK *Myrtle, Rue & Cypress*
COUNT ERIC STENBOCK *The Shadow of Death*
COUNT ERIC STENBOCK *Studies of Death*
MONTAGUE SUMMERS *The Bride of Christ and Other Fictions*
MONTAGUE SUMMERS *Six Ghost Stories*
GILBERT-AUGUSTIN THIERRY *The Blonde Tress and The Mask*
GILBERT-AUGUSTIN THIERRY *Reincarnation and Redemption*
DOUGLAS THOMPSON *The Fallen West*
TOADHOUSE *Gone Fishing with Samy Rosenstock*
TOADHOUSE *Living and Dying in a Mind Field*
RUGGERO VASARI *Raun*
JANE DE LA VAUDÈRE *The Demi-Sexes and The Androgynes*
JANE DE LA VAUDÈRE *The Priestesses of Mylitta*
JANE DE LA VAUDÈRE *Syta's Harem and Pharaoh's Lover*
AUGUSTE VILLIERS DE L'ISLE-ADAM *Isis*
RENÉE VIVIEN AND HÉLÈNE DE ZUYLEN DE NYEVELT
 Faustina and Other Stories
RENÉE VIVIEN *Lilith's Legacy*
RENÉE VIVIEN *A Woman Appeared to Me*
TERESA WILMS MONTT *In the Stillness of Marble*
TERESA WILMS MONTT *Sentimental Doubts*
KAREL VAN DE WOESTIJNE *The Dying Peasant*

www.ingramcontent.com/pod-product-compliance
Lightning Source LLC
La Vergne TN
LVHW041623060526
838200LV00040B/1413